5/02

Black Nationalism in American Politics and Thought

Black Nationalism in American Politics and Thought revisits the activism and arguments in support of separate black statehood from the mid nineteenth century to the present, detailing the ways in which black nationalism historically mirrors broader currents in U.S. politics and thought. This book challenges the idea that black nationalism is an essentially timeless, unchanging, and anti-assimilationist impulse with respect to the alternative goal of racial inclusion. It argues that black nationalism in the United States draws on homologous political strategy and thinking unique to specific historical eras – often inadvertently reproducing strategies and thinking responsible for racial inequality in the first place.

Dean E. Robinson is Assistant Professor of Political Science at the University of Massachusetts, Amherst.

D0209374

Black Nationalism in American Politics and Thought

DEAN E. ROBINSON

University of Massachusetts, Amherst

VILLA JULIE COLLEGE LIBRARY
STEVENSON, MD 21153

CAMBRIDGE
UNIVERSITY PRESS

PUBLISHED BY THE PRESS SYNDICATE OF THE UNIVERSITY OF CAMBRIDGE
The Pitt Building, Trumpington Street, Cambridge, United Kingdom

CAMBRIDGE UNIVERSITY PRESS
The Edinburgh Building, Cambridge CB2 2RU, UK
40 West 20th Street, New York, NY 10011-4211, USA
10 Stamford Road, Oakleigh, VIC 3166, Australia
Ruiz de Alarcón 13, 28014 Madrid, Spain
Dock House, The Waterfront, Cape Town 8001, South Africa

http://www.cambridge.org

© Dean E. Robinson 2001

This book is in copyright. Subject to statutory exception
and to the provisions of relevant collective licensing agreements,
no reproduction of any part may take place without
the written permission of Cambridge University Press.

First published 2001

Printed in the United States of America

Typeface Sabon 10/12 pt.   *System* QuarkXPress [BTS]

A catalog record for this book is available from the British Library.

Library of Congress Cataloging in Publication data
Robinson, Dean E.
Black nationalism in American politics and thought / Dean E. Robinson.
p.   cm.
Includes bibliographical references.
ISBN 0-521-62326-X (hardback) – ISBN 0-521-62627-7 (pbk.)
1. Black nationalism – United States – History – 19th century.   2. Black nationalism –
United States – History – 20th century.   3. Afro-Americans – Politics and government –
19th century.   4. Afro-Americans – Politics and government – 20th century.   5. United
States – Politics and government – 19th century.   6. United States – Politics and government – 20th century.   7. United States – Intellectual life.   I. Title.
E185.61.R679 2001
320.54′08996073 – dc21   00-031277

ISBN   0 521 62326 X   hardback
ISBN   0 521 62627 7   paperback

To my parents

Contents

Acknowledgments

I would like to extend my sincerest thanks to all who made the book possible. I would like to thank my family and friends for their support over the years. I would also like to thank my colleagues at the University of Massachusetts, Amherst, for their advice and encouragement. Special thanks to George Sulzner and Carlene Eddie. Criticism from a number of readers has made the book better. Thanks to Lida Lewis, John Stifler, Wilson Moses, Daryl Scott, David Mayhew, Brett Gadsden, Moise Tirado, Robert Venator Santiago, Richard Iton, Preston Smith, and Lisa Magged for their comments and suggestions at various stages of the project. Rogers Smith offered significant input throughout the process. Adolph Reed, Jr., provided careful readings, invaluable input, and much-needed inspiration.

Introduction

Over the course of political history in the United States, black nationalism has appeared in a number of guises. During the mid nineteenth century, under the looming shadow of the Fugitive Slave Act of 1850, Martin Delany, James T. Holly, and others argued that black people should relocate to the Caribbean, Central America, Canada, or Africa in order to establish an "African nationality." During the early 1920s, Marcus Garvey urged his followers to do the same. Dressed in military garb, topped with helmet and plume, he told black people to reject white propaganda, resettle to Africa, and redeem the race. Building partly on Garvey's legacy, in the 1960s Malcolm X also encouraged black people to separate, on the grounds that integration meant conforming to the roles and status demanded by whites in America. And Malcolm X's one-time rival and the current head of the Nation of Islam, Louis Farrakhan, offers the most visible example of an old posture. Self-determination. Reclaiming one's roots and identity. Manhood and esteem. These are the ideas that have been manifested in black nationalist movements, past and present.

But, in terms of politics, black nationalism's militant rejection of things American and European is not its most vital political feature. It hasn't always done that. As Wilson Moses has persuasively argued, nationalists before 1925 or so were assimilationists – they embraced Western culture.[1] Nor is patriarchy black nationalism's most vital feature.[2] This is a common, if not universal, characteristic of all kinds of nationalism. Nor is it, as Moses suggests, its messianic quality. All nationalism is, as Anderson notes, inherently quasi-religious.[3]

Rather, I will argue that the most politically consequential feature of black nationalism is its apparent inability to diverge from what could be considered the "normal" politics of its day. By accepting the notion that black people constitute an organic unit, and by focusing on the goal of nation building or separate political and economic development, black nationalism *inadvertently* helps to reproduce some of the thinking and practices that created black disadvantage in the first place. Most white Americans have long thought blacks to be essentially different; and they have used that idea to justify expelling blacks, restricting black movement, and limiting the range of rights, privileges, and opportunities available to black people. It stands to reason, then, that most attempts by black people to identify their differences from the majority population and pursue political and economic autonomy on that basis, conform to one of the oldest American political fantasies – what Ralph Ellison calls the desire to "get shut" of the Negro in America – to "banish [blacks] from the nation's bloodstream, from its social structure, and from its conscience and historical consciousness."[4]

First, some remarks about my characterization of black nationalism. For the "classical" period of black nationalism (roughly 1850–1925), I use a strict definition – activists must have worked for separate statehood. For the "modern" period, particularly the post–World War II era, I employ a broader definition to include both those who favored separate statehood, as well as self-identified "nationalists" who supported the more modest goal of black administration of vital private and public institutions. I do this for historiographical reasons. By understanding black nationalism as an affective state, or as any form of racial solidarity, scholars have often glossed over many significant distinctions and outright conflicts among historical agents. They have put forth the view that black nationalism reflects a timeless, recurring impulse that rejects integration and cultural assimilation.

For instance, numerous studies have labeled political leaders like Booker T. Washington, W. E. B. Du Bois, and Marcus Garvey as "nationalist." However, while each activist understood blacks to share a common destiny, and while each encouraged blacks to work together toward common political and economic goals, only one, Garvey, wanted a separate state. Similarly, during the Black Power era of the late 1960s a wide range of activity fell under the heading "nationalist." However, according to my formulation some of this was "purer" nationalism, while most, as I will argue in Chapter 5, is better described as a black version of ethnic pluralism.[5]

Indeed, black activists in the nineteenth and early twentieth centuries operated in profoundly different intellectual and political realms from those of the modern period. They unhesitatingly valued Christianity and "civilization," understood "race" as nearly synonymous with "nation," and often thought that "nations" possessed essential traits. While these nationalists sought to establish "a distinctive tradition in art, architecture, music and letters . . . classical black nationalists did not employ the term 'cultural nationalism,' which was not coined until the twentieth century."[6]

By contrast, modern black nationalists, especially those operating after World War II, outwardly rejected Western values, opposed "integration" as the central programmatic goal, and instead pursued projects ranging from separate statehood to black administration of key institutions of social, political, and economic life.

Characterizations of black nationalism that are broad and generally inattentive to historical context tend to encourage the view that black nationalism reflects timeless, recurring concerns in black politics, particularly its rejection of integration and acculturation into Euro-American institutions and ways of life. Following Moses, and against the view of most accounts of the historical phenomena, I set out the view that black nationalism reflects (and sometimes influences) the dominant trends concerning race and politics of specific historical periods. While black nationalists continually react to white racism across time, the sorts of ideas and the types of activism they advocate typically have homologues in the broader political and intellectual landscapes of specific historical periods. This explains why black nationalists often reproduce ideas about racial distinctiveness and calls for separate political and economic development that have often been linked to black disadvantage.

A number of anthologies published in the late 1960s and early 1970s that compile writings by black nationalist writers of the eighteenth, nineteenth, and twentieth centuries display the tendencies I have outlined here.[7] The most notable among these is Bracey, Meier, and Rudwick's *Black Nationalism in America* (1971). According to the editors, black nationalism – the basic sentiment of racial solidarity – can have a territorial, religious, bourgeois reformist, revolutionary, cultural, or religious orientation. These categories are not mutually exclusive. Under these headings, Bracey, Meier, and Rudwick place a wide range of thinkers and activists, including James T. Holly, Booker T. Washington, and Malcolm X; and they provide often-insightful historical and biographical background for the specific texts and authors they feature. However, their initial characterizations of black nationalism are so broad that they actually inhibit careful comparison across time. Indeed, as I will argue more fully in Chapter 3, their typology conceals as much as it reveals. Due to shifting political and intellectual landscapes, black nationalism of, say, 1859 shares more in common with politics and ideology of its historical context than with black nationalism of 1959. Thus, categories like "religious" and "cultural" capture the emphasis of an individual or group only after we know something about the time in which they operated.

Considering the fact that much of the secondary literature on black nationalism appeared at the height of the black liberation struggles of the 1960s and 1970s, we should not be surprised that scholars were not closely attentive to changes in black nationalism across time, or to the close relationship of black politics, thought, and culture to "mainstream" politics, thought, and culture. After all, these studies reflected the spirit of the times, and by the late 1960s black nationalism represented the vanguard of black radical activism and theory. By the early 1970s, the importance of the paradigm was evident in black studies programs across the country. It was also evident in black popular and scholarly journals, as well as in the fields of drama, poetry, and literature in the early 1970s.

But even more recent studies reproduce ideas of black nationalism as a tranhistorical, and hermetically sealed, phenomenon. One prominent example is Sterling Stuckey's important *Slave Culture: Nationalist Theory and the Foundations of Black America* (1987), in which he attempts to trace the roots of black nationalist theory to slave culture. After an initial chapter on slave culture, Stuckey's remaining chapters analyze various thinkers of the eighteenth and nineteenth centuries, including David Walker, Henry Highland Garnet, W. E. B. Du Bois, and Paul Robeson, to determine the extent to which these thinkers recognized the "Africanness" of blacks in America – their connection to forms of slave culture – and the extent to which this realization influenced their brands of nationalist ideology. Stuckey's otherwise provocative and richly researched study is bothered by the problem of loose characterization. His definition of nationalism is available only by inference; he uses the term to mean such things as belief in racial solidarity, self-help, and the idea that blacks share a common destiny. However, these basic ideas underlie the thinking of *most* black political activists, past and present; but, of course, most black political activists have not supported the goal of separate statehood, nor have they identified themselves specifically as nationalists. Nor does conscious or unconscious deference to African roots and culture determine "nationalist" consciousness. Before World War II, black nationalists did not embrace indigenous African cultures.

In an essay that seeks to characterize dominant trends in black political ideology in the post–civil rights era, Marable and Mullings also describe nationalism in terms too broad to capture historical nuance. In contrast to "inclusionists," who believe that "African-Americans are basically 'Americans who happen to be black'" and demand an end to all "sites of racial particularity and social isolation," "the orientation of black nationalism assumes that 'race' is a historically fixed category, which will not magically decline in significance over time; it suggests that blacks must define themselves within their own cultural context; and it is deeply pessimistic about the ability or willingness of white civil society to transform itself democratically to include the demands of people of color." Marable and Mullings add that "[c]ulturally, [black nationalism] suggests that African-Americans are African people who happen to speak English and live in America."[8] Yet while black nationalists demonstrate pessimism about the prospects for equality in the United States over time, they sometimes reject "inclusionism" or integration reluctantly. Further, their understandings of culture have varied considerably over time.

While more attentive to the political context that has defined "modern" black nationalism, William L. Van Deburg's introduction to his anthology *Modern Black Nationalism: From Marcus Garvey to Louis Farrakhan* (1997) also defines the term "black nationalism" broadly. For Van Deburg, black nationalists, like nationalists generally, place a high value "on self-definition and self-determination." They are "determined skeptics" about the prospects for interracial peace and equality, and seek to "strengthen in-group values while holding those promoted by the larger society at arm's length."[9] The editor notes that "[t]heir issue orientation may tend toward territorial, religious, economic, or cultural concerns," and he offers a "rule of thumb": "Since most people are known primarily by their deeds, if someone looks, speaks, writes, and acts like a nationalist, others may be justified in treating them as such until compelling evidence to the contrary is produced."[10] Van Deburg's criteria, particularly his rule of thumb, have limited application for historiographical purposes. Again, words do not always carry the same meaning over time. Van Deburg's formulations establish a standard of evidence that is far too broad for historical purposes. After all, many avowedly non-nationalist blacks have favored "self-determination," and many have been skeptical about the prospects for racial equality. In addition, black nationalists often share the values of the larger society even when they seek to do the opposite. Indeed, I will argue that, more often than not, nationalists share conventional assumptions common to their historical periods about "race," "culture," gender, class, and group mobility.

My argument builds on a number of insights and analyses of black nationalism which stand out with respect to the rest of the field. Wilson J. Moses's scholarship grounds the study of black nationalist thought in particular historical contexts, suggesting that "[b]lack nationalism assumes the shape of its container and undergoes transformations in accordance with changing intellectual fashions in the white world." Classical black nationalism, according to Moses, was "abolitionist, civilizationist, elitist, and based on Christian humanism. After the first world war, new tendencies arose that were relativist, culturalist, proletarian and secular."[11] Robert Hill's and Judith Stein's scholarship also challenges the notion of a "timeless" and recurring black nationalist tradition by emphasizing the historical particularity of the Garvey movement.[12]

These studies show that while black nationalism of different eras has had recurring characteristics, these are due to responses to similar problems, all stemming from white racism. Nevertheless, across time, political and intellectual activity among black nationalists has differed enormously. There is no "essential" black nationalist tradition, despite similarities; the positions of nationalists of different eras have diverged because their nationalisms have been products of partly similar but largely unique eras of politics, thought, and culture. Missing this point can result in an ahistorical, teleological interpretation of black nationalism as an historical phenomenon.

The previous point derives from a broader one: as Ralph Ellison and others have noted, Afro-American politics and thought and "mainstream" politics and thought are *mutually constitutive*. To conceive of Afro-American politics and thought as separate from the "mainstream" is to misrepresent both sets of phenomena.

In order to make my case about black nationalism in the United States, I will begin with proposals and ideas from the nineteenth century and, bringing the analysis to the present, will offer evidence that details the changes black nationalism undergoes as the historical, political, intellectual, and economic landscape changes. By situating black nationalism in specific historical contexts, I will evaluate the phenomenon with respect to competing strategies and with respect to broader currents of American politics and thought.

Chapter 1 analyzes black nationalist ideas and projects appearing from the antebellum period to the Great Depression, concurring with Moses's finding that classical black nationalism was a conservative rather than a radical tendency in black politics.[13] Chapter 2 reconsiders the significance of Elijah Muhammad's Nation of Islam and his one-time disciple Malcolm X to black nationalist theory and practice during the post–World War II era. I argue that Elijah Muhammad provides the template for black nationalism during the postwar period and show how Malcolm X takes on enormous significance to many subsequent groups and activists as they canonize the slain leader. Chapters 3 and 4 elaborate the forms black nationalism took during the 1960s and early 1970s, and the political and discursive developments that propelled the ideology. I argue that, despite frequent and significant efforts to characterize black nationalism in the United States as one of many Third World independence movements, black nationalism in the United States typically conformed to local political and intellectual terrain. By examining black nationalist politics in the context of model cities program and especially the War on Poverty, Chapter 5 shows how and why black nationalism mostly took the form of "ethnic pluralism" – pursuit of racially solidaristic efforts in a pluralistic political system subsumed by a capitalistic economic one. Chapter 6 shows that, like the classical varieties, modern nationalism shared deeper assumptions about "culture" and mobility that shaped thinking about race, acculturation, poverty, and empowerment for the better part of the twentieth century. These assumptions I call the "ethnic paradigm." Chapter 7 takes my thesis to the present, examining the two most prominent manifestations of black nationalism, the Nation of Islam under Farrakhan, and Afrocentrism as principally defined by Molefi Kete Asante.

I give special attention to the postwar period – the bulk of the study – for two reasons. First, while many studies explain black nationalism's resurgence in this period, they do not show how, nor explain why, black nationalism adapts to its local terrain, and why its radical potential is unrealized. Second, while a number of studies focus on individual groups like the Nation of Islam and the Black Panther Party, few studies systematically scrutinize the deeper, epistemological premises of black nationalist ideology during the postwar period.

Throughout my study I will invariably examine some phenomena that fail to meet my strict definition, like many forms of Black Power activism of the 1960s and early 1970s, but which have been discussed by activists and commentators as "nationalism." Similarly, in the final chapter I will discuss the mostly scholar-led Afrocentric perspective not because proponents favor separate statehood, but rather because Afrocentricity derives from "cultural" nationalist tendencies of the late 1960s and early 1970s.

Anglo-African Nationalism

Marcus Garvey thought that the solution to the problem of black inequality required a powerful black nation in Africa. And so, beginning in 1918, he faced off against the National Association for the Advancement of Colored People and rejected the goal of "social equality." He also rejected trade unionism as a vehicle for black advancement, as well as more radical alternatives. Instead, he offered an aggressive black-politics-as-business-enterprise, and he sold his entire scheme with a militantly pro-black rhetoric. By so doing, Garvey anticipated the style of much of the black nationalism that would follow – its principled rejection of American identity, and its notion that black enterprise could somehow lay the foundation for separate statehood. Yet, despite his own and his followers' militancy, and the U.S. intelligence agencies' assumption that his UNIA posed a threat to the political order, Garvey's theories and strategies hardly escaped the conventions of his era, particularly those concerning racial purity, gender, capitalism, social Darwinism, and, most importantly, the idea that the United States was the domain of Protestant Anglo-Saxons. Garvey's failure to articulate an alternative "African" culture proved to be an important paradox. He was militantly pro-African, in a pro-European or "Eurocentric" kind of way. Most significantly, his plan to build power through enterprise failed as a short-term and as a long-term strategy. Nevertheless, his flamboyance, militantly pro-black rhetoric, and ambitious business ventures attracted hundreds of thousands of members and several times more supporters.

Garvey's nationalism embodied the past and anticipated the future. Black nationalists who preceded him, men like James T. Holly and Martin Delany in the antebellum period and Bishop Henry Turner in the 1880s and 1890s, worked to relocate the black population outside the boundaries of the United States. They shared with Garvey a certain orientation toward Western culture and capitalism, operating out of what we today would call a "Eurocentric" framework. They focused on the ideals of "manhood," "African nationality," Christianity, and civilization. The notion of "manhood" referred to a nineteenth-century self-concept developed by the middle class to stress "its gentility and respectability." But manhood was not only a gendered term, it also applied exclusively to the white race.[1] Black nationalists of what Moses calls the classical period (roughly 1850–1925) assumed that the proper practice of Christianity and the establishment of civilization were both means and ends to manhood and African nationality. Neither Garvey nor the black nationalists who preceded him had any intention of reclaiming African culture, as some 1960s "modern" nationalists would. They wanted to be rid of it.

Classical black nationalism mirrored what we could loosely call "white American nationalism" of the time. White American nationalism reflected a sentiment that the United States was, or ought to be, the domain of the white man. This idea, in turn, rested upon a set of notions concerning innate traits that white people in the United States supposedly had, the different traits that blacks (and others) allegedly had, and the appropriate station or social status these traits demanded. In the face of white American nationalism, some black people considered Africa, Central America, Canada, Haiti and various parts of the United States as sites for relocation.

This is where the similarities end. The landscape of black politics during the antebellum, Reconstruction, and post-Reconstruction periods differed considerably from the political context in which Garvey would operate. Garvey moved in a political landscape shaped by World War I, black migration to northern cities, extreme xenophobia, racial riots, militant unionism, and the Red Scare. Moreover, earlier black nationalists did not reject the idea of citizenship in the United States in principle; rather, as their rights were increasingly restricted and as political and economic opportunities vanished, black nationalists, or perhaps more precisely "emigrationists" or "repatriationists," hoped that they could secure a better life elsewhere. This explains why emigration schemes vanished during the period of Reconstruction, when black Americans, with support from the Republican Party, began to participate in state and national politics. By the time Garvey built his Universal Negro Improvement Association, Jim Crow had been codified in law, and Anglo-conformity – the notion that all citizens of the American republic needed to follow the ways of the WASP – had been heightened by the United States' participation in World War I and the political impact of the Bolshevik revolution.

ANGLO-SAXON NATIONALISM

Black nationalism grew out of the context of white American nationalism – the desire for, and the practices that supported, white racial homogeneity within the United States. White American or Anglo-Saxon nationalism took a variety of forms, the most extreme being "Indian removal." Indeed, from the earliest times, American expansion meant removing native peoples, securing land and resources for Euro-American settlement. The Civil War slowed white migration westward, but through conquest and disease, by trickery and by treaty, whites slowly seized control of more territory and confined Native Americans to less.

Many Euro-Americans imagined a nation free of black people, but the viability of slavery consistently rendered that dream impossible. Nevertheless, the idea of a nation purged of its black inhabitants appeared throughout the nineteenth century. Thomas Jefferson was one of a number of significant white statesmen who figured that blacks and whites simply couldn't coexist:

Deep rooted prejudices entertained by the whites; ten thousand recollections, by the blacks, of the injuries they have sustained, new provocations; the real distinctions which nature has made . . . will divide us into parties and produce convulsions which will probably never end but in the extermination of one or the other race.[2]

Jefferson wasn't quite sure what created the difference in color – whether it derived from a membrane just below the skin, or whether the color of blood created the pigment. But he concluded that the differences between races were real, because they were "fixed in nature." He called for a government agency that would deport free "Africans" and replace them with European immigrants.[3]

Abraham Lincoln also considered a colonization scheme. His reasoning grew out of the crisis of the Civil War, and his thoughts about what to do about free blacks were based on an assumption that racial prejudice was a permanent feature of American politics. Lincoln presented his own argument for black colonization in an "Address on Colonization to a Committee of Colored Men" in 1862: "even when you cease to be slaves, you are yet far removed from being placed on equality with the white race . . . It is better for us both, therefore, to be separated."[4] Lincoln favored Central America, and an appointed select committee produced a bill that would compensate former owners of the emancipated slaves of the border states, and colonize these freedmen outside the United States.

Decades before Lincoln thought seriously about colonization, the American Colonization Society (ACS) pursued a similar idea until they established the colony of Liberia in 1822. The founders of this society had various motives. Some thought that free blacks in the United States were a dangerous population that displayed poor work habits and criminal tendencies. Some thought that free blacks might trigger a revolt among slaves. Most thought that blacks from the United States could serve in a missionary capacity to Africa – they would redeem and advance a barbaric continent – and all assumed that the future of the United States was not one of racial cohabitation. Rather, philanthropists, hard-line racists, and evangelists all thought that the future of the United States was an Anglo-Saxon one. Continuing its efforts and activities into the early twentieth century, the ACS was largely unsuccessful. The organization never had sufficient resources – political or monetary – to buttress the fledgling Liberia. As we will see, even when the organization experienced a brief resurgence during the early 1890s, it had insufficient funds to resettle very many blacks.

Less dramatic, but more important to the development of black nationalism, was the daunting array of nineteenth-century practices, formal and informal, that denied Afro-Americans the rights and privileges of full citizenship. Of course, during the antebellum period, the vast majority of blacks were defined by the institution of slavery. But even free blacks were generally excluded from civic rights. The South's free black population, which grew to about 260,000 by the 1860s, faced elaborate "black codes" that constrained their movement, limited their opportunities, and imposed rules of conduct targeted toward black people. For instance, some states punished black people for "insolence." Avoiding the problem of having to classify people with insurmountably arbitrary racial categories, southern states handled the matter by stripping of civic rights any individuals who had one drop of "black blood." Whites prohibited free blacks in the South from assembling for political and self-help purposes, they restricted black movement from state to state, and they denied blacks opportunities to work in particular trades or to buy or sell certain commodities. When whites couldn't rely on formal restrictions, they used informal ones.

On the eve of the Civil War, free blacks in the North, who comprised less than two percent of that population, also faced enormous obstacles to economic opportunity and were locked out of the democratic process. There too, blacks faced pervasive discrimination.[5] Over ninety percent of these blacks could not vote. In the North and the West, blacks faced less severe but still limiting restrictions. While blacks in the North could assemble for political and benevolent purposes, as Rogers Smith notes,

They faced worse conditions in the old Northwest Ordinance and the later western states, which all resisted free black immigration with varying degrees of success. Here, as in the slave states, free blacks generally could not testify against whites and were otherwise more legally disabled than in the east.[6]

For the purposes of understanding black nationalism during the antebellum period, the Fugitive Slave Act of 1850 is especially important.[7]

Part of the Compromise of 1850, the Fugitive Slave Act denied captured slaves the right to a trial and granted marshals the power to force citizens to assist in the recapture of runaway slaves. This bill attempted to counter the success of the Underground Railroad.

And, of course, the infamous *Dred Scott* (1857) decision captured the spirit of white American nationalism on the eve of the Civil War. Concerning the phrase "all men are created equal," Justice Taney explained that "it [was] too clear for dispute that the enslaved African race [was] not intended to be included and formed no part of the people who framed this declaration." The African race, Taney argued, had "no rights which the white man was bound to respect."[8]

The result of these formal and informal measures was what Frederickson refers to as "pseudo-homogeneity."[9] Short of removing the minority, the pseudo-homogenist secures political privilege and economic opportunity exclusively for the majority and limits the range and types of interaction between the majority and minority populations. Across the nineteenth century, this impulse took the form of prohibitions against intermarriage, rules that made black migration to different states impossible, and laws that denied suffrage and imposed formal segregation.

As Barbara Fields suggests, humans tend to view their social customs and hierarchies as ordained by nature. Hence, most white Americans of the North and South didn't need elaborate theories of black (or Native American, or Chinese) inferiority to justify their assumption of superiority. They most likely developed their ideas about black inferiority simply by rationalizing the obviously lower status of black people. It was blacks' degraded condition that demanded explanation, and when white people squared black inequality with their experience of freedom, they created "racial" explanations of human difference.[10]

A number of scholars offer similar "bottom-up" analyses of racial ideology. Alexander Saxton follows the process by which white working-class identity was forged in the nineteenth century through popular culture. He argues that trends in nineteenth-century theater – the dime novel folk heroes, blackface minstrelsy, and so forth – helped to articulate egalitarian tendencies among white males while simultaneously stressing themes of white supremacy.[11] David Roediger also tracks the making of "white" working-class identity in the context of slavery and Democratic party politics in the nineteenth century. These scholars suggest that in terms of American civic identity, "black" came to represent the antithesis of "white."[12]

The formation of racial consciousness among whites was nevertheless buttressed by thinkers of various sorts who provided alleged proof of black inferiority, and their explanations ranged from environmental and biological ones to biblical and paternalistic ones. The proponents of these views of black distinctiveness differed over political implications. Some thought slavery to be the appropriate condition for the African race. Others, as we will see, used the notion of essential black difference as an argument for white homogeneity and colonization of blacks to Africa. But all were part of a discourse that constructed a sense of white Protestant identity that thinkers referred to as "Anglo-Saxon," "Teutonic," and later "Nordic."[13]

A great surge of nineteenth-century writings – scholarly, popular, fictional, and scientific – legitimized the racial hierarchy by advancing the notion of separate "national" traits, an idea that traces back to the German philosopher Herder and his concept of *volk*. For instance, practitioners of romantic historiography, thinkers like William H. Prescott, Francis Parkman, and John Lothrop Motely, interpreted the history of a nation as a reflection of that nation's peculiar traits. Prescott generalized about the Spanish national character in his histories of the Spanish conquest of Mexico and Peru. Parkman described the struggle between the French and the English for control of America as a battle between the Anglo-Saxons and the "Celtic" French. Motely's *The Rise of the Dutch Republic* differentiated two stocks in the Dutch nation, the Germanic and the Celtic.[14]

Frederickson identifies a similar tendency among proslavery and antislavery "romantic racialists." Proslavery plantation romances written during the 1820s and 1830s depicted slaves in stereotypic ways: usually possessing a special capacity for kindness, loyalty, cooperation, affection, and piety.[15] The antislavery romantic racialist view was best articulated in Harriet Beecher Stowe's *Uncle Tom's Cabin*. Her characters were the physical embodiment of racial and national traits, from the pious and forgiving (and all black) Uncle Tom to the more rebellious mulattos, whose tendencies apparently reflected their freedom-loving Anglo-Saxon blood. Stowe wrote that when the black race developed a civilization it would

perhaps show forth some of the latest and most magnificent revelations of human life. Certainly they will, in their gentleness, their lowly docility of heart, their aptitude to repose on a superior mind and rest on a higher power, their childlike simplicity of affection, and facility of forgiveness.[16]

Better known for his transcendentalist thought, Ralph Waldo Emerson is also representative of the romantic racialist perspective. That races had essential traits was obvious. "Race is a controlling influence in the Jew, who, for two millenniums, under every climate, has preserved the same character and employments. Race in the negro is of appalling importance." The English, Emerson claimed, were "[m]ore intellectual than other races," and "assimilate other races themselves, and are not assimilated."[17] "The conservative, money-loving, lord-loving English," he wrote, "are yet liberty-loving; and so freedom is safe."[18]

These notions of innate racial/national traits were helped along by scientific studies, especially in the 1840s and 1850s – the first time, in fact, that "science" would play an important role in the justification of racial inequality. The "American school of ethnology" was launched by Dr. Samuel George Morton's flawed studies of skull capacity (as a measure of intellectual ability). *Crania Americana* (1839) and *Crania Aegyptica* (1844) placed Caucasians on top, followed by Mongols, Native Americans, and Africans.[19] Morton's work was immensely influential.

The Swiss naturalist Louis Agassiz was persuaded. He immigrated to the United States in the 1840s, served on the faculty of Harvard University, and concluded from his own observations that races existed as distinct "species." However, by his own admission Agassiz never formulated racial categories that were not arbitrary.

Agassiz wrote the introduction to the massive and popular *Types of Mankind* (1854), edited by Josiah Nott, a prominent physician from Mobile, Alabama, and Egyptologist George R. Gliddon. The book, dedicated to the memory of Samuel Morton, tackled the central questions that animated racial politics of its day: Is the human population one race or many? What is the capacity of different races or nations for progress as manifested through civilization? What is the appropriate place in the social, political, and economic system for each "type of man"? Not surprisingly, Nott and Gliddon first established, against the biblically based doctrine that all peoples descend from Adam (monogenesis), that by Agassiz's accounting the world consisted of eight racial or national types, each type connected to a particular geographic region.[20] They found that each type had innate traits that were generally impervious to change. Commenting on Native Americans, they wrote: "To one who has lived among American Indians, it is vain to talk of civilizing them. You might as well attempt to change the nature of the buffalo."[21] Mongols were described as "semi-civilized." The editors used Morton's conclusion that the ancient Egyptians were not black to argue that "[i]n the broad field and long duration of Negro life, not a single civilization, spontaneous or borrowed, has existed, to adorn its gloomy past."[22] Nott and Gliddon therefore reached the easy conclusion: "Nations and races, like individuals, have each an especial destiny: some are born to rule, and others to be ruled."[23]

Ethnology was very influential. Frederickson and Smith have both examined how elites used ethnology to justify policies of Indian removal, slavery, and limited civic rights for freed blacks. In *Types*, Nott and Gliddon indicated that Dr. Morton and John C. Calhoun had corresponded. Indeed, all types of periodicals spread these pseudoscientific ideas; and references to the American school of ethnology appeared frequently in the rhetoric of Jacksonian leaders.[24]

ANGLO-AFRICAN NATIONALISM

Building on the observations of Wilson Moses, I use the nineteenth-century term "Anglo-African" to capture the basic idea of political and cultural identity shared by black Americans of the time. Anglo-African nationalists of this period reacted to the growth of white American nationalism and to the corresponding legislative and political developments that affected Afro-American life. Yet, as Moses has amply demonstrated, they reacted in "Anglo-Saxonist" ways. Anglo-African nationalists rejected notions of innate inferiority, but not the idea of innate tendencies or traits. Black nationalists criticized the American Colonization Society, but offered an identical solution – resettlement – to the problem of black inequality.

McAddo argues that two tendencies of black nationalism actually dominated the antebellum period: one reactionary, one revolutionary.[25] The reactionary nationalists, or "black Zionists," accepted the permanence of slavery and wished to resettle the black population. Revolutionaries challenged slavery with action and calls to action. Of the two, McAddo argues that only the revolutionary nationalists truly advanced the cause of black equality.

By focusing on the aim of black abolitionists, McAddo draws a somewhat useful distinction between the two camps of black activists who operated on the eve of the Civil War. As I will attempt to show in Chapter 4, scholars have often blurred the differences among historical actors under a "nationalist" heading. However, McAddo doesn't explain why, precisely, all antislavery "revolutionaries" were "nationalists." For instance, McAddo describes David Walker as a revolutionary nationalist. Walker's *Appeal to the Coloured Citizens of the World* (1829) does in fact deliver a stinging and militant critique of the institution of slavery. Walker insists that "it is no more harm for you to kill a man, who is trying to kill you, than it is for you to take a drink of water when thirsty."[26] Nevertheless, Walker's *Appeal* is more accurately described as a black jeremiad – in its prediction of doom or apocalypse because of present-day sins – than a call for black nationalism. Although Walker understood black people to be a separate nation, he fiercely denounced colonization. For Walker, America's success and prosperity was as much the result of Afro-American effort as of anyone else's. The colonization idea, as one of his chapter titles suggested, contributed to the "wretchedness" of the black population by casting them as outsiders. As Walker wrote:

Let no man of us budge one step, and let slave-holders come to beat us from our country. America is more our country that it is the whites – we have enriched it with our *blood and tears*. The greatest riches in all America have arisen from our blood and tears: – and will they drive us from our property and homes, which we have earned with our *blood*?[27]

In light of this passage we can understand the extent to which Walker, a literate American, thought about social issues in a manner common to many literate Americans of this age. Walker's *Appeal*, in fact, responded directly to Thomas Jefferson's "racial theories and apocalyptic prophecies" as they appeared in his *Notes on the State of Virginia*.[28] But Walker's militant call for equal rights was hardly nationalistic in the stricter sense of the term.

Sterling Stuckey offers the challenging thesis that, rather than being a simple reaction to white nationalism, black nationalism had endogenous sources – specifically, slave culture. Stuckey suggests that the slave's retention of African culture fostered a nationalistic or proto-nationalist sensibility. An Africanized version of Christianity had in it the seeds of later political tendencies. Indeed, "the lack of concern for material possessions, and willingness to risk all in attempting to better the lot of one's people, through revolution or reform, was a powerful strain in nationalistic thought" and anticipated support for socialism among Afro-Americans of the twentieth century.[29] Stuckey offers richly textured analysis of a number of black activists of the nineteenth and twentieth centuries, including David Walker, Henry Garnet, W. E. B. Du Bois, and Paul Robeson, and explores the "African" roots of their nationalistic postures. Stuckey's analysis, however, fails either to identify the precise connection between slave culture and nationalism or, more importantly, to establish the political and philosophical connection his subjects share as nationalists. A shared concern for racial equality, even one rooted in "African" cultural values, does not explain the different political stances W. E. B. Du Bois and Paul Robeson would adopt over the course of their lives. Nor can conscious or unconscious acknowledgement of slave culture explain the disagreements between Henry Garnet and Frederick Douglass that I will take up later.

Indeed, Stuckey may place too much emphasis on slave culture as a sort of prophylactic against the influence of Euro-American beliefs and customs. After all, slave culture might have been the *conduit* by which Africans became Americanized. Further, even if slave culture was fundamentally different from Euro-American culture, and even if it provided a basis for a collective black consciousness, it still might not have fostered nationalism in the stricter sense of the word. In fact, as Hobsbawm notes, it is hard to assess the extent of nationalistic sentiment among illiterate populations.[30] Even among his literate subjects, though, Stuckey doesn't prove that activists like Walker and Garnet viewed African culture in a positive light and that this sentiment informed their political ideologies. The evidence more often suggests the opposite. As Moses demonstrates, Henry Garnet and other pre–Civil War nationalists flatly rejected indigenous African culture, as did Garvey, who nevertheless built an enormous nationalist organization. Indeed, the belief in collective political endeavor and common destiny among blacks need not have its roots in slave culture. More plausibly, its roots lie in the experience of racial subordination.

Rather than taking slave rebellions or slave culture as starting points, the evidence suggests that black nationalism as a political strategy traces back to a number of literate, mostly male, and mostly northern Afro-Americans of the nineteenth century – individuals who left a record of specific proposals to establish an "African nationality." Amid growing fear of the effects of the Fugitive Slave Act, and obvious signs that citizenship rights were reserved for white males, some free blacks pushed for emigration. Across the country, free blacks expressed interest in resettlement, and they put together a number of conventions to plan their exodus. These were the black nationalists of the mid nineteenth century. They differed from non-nationalists not in their stance against slavery, or in their belief in innate "national" traits, or in the indignation they expressed over their ill treatment. They differed over what to do about racial inequality. And they chose emigration.

Delegates to the first National Emigration Convention in 1854 offered pragmatic reasons for leaving the United States. In a document titled "Political Destiny of the Colored Race, on the American Continent," organizers mentioned the rights blacks were denied, and expressed doubt that conditions would change. "Whiteness" was a "mark of distinction and superiority," while "blackness" was "a badge of degradation, acknowledged by statute, organic law, and the common consent of the people."[31] For a people to know true freedom, they argued, they had to govern themselves. Only then could they reestablish their "original identity," which in turn would inform their social and political efforts. Indeed, when nations lost their "original" identities, they became extinct.[32] Just as the English, French, Irish, German, Italian, and Jewish people had "their native or inherent peculiarities," so too did the African. In fact, the colored races had the "highest traits of civilization": they were civil, peaceful, and religious. The white race excelled in mathematics and sciences, but "in ethics, metaphysics, theology and legal jurisprudence; in plain language – in the true principles of morals, correctness of thought, religion, and law or civil government, there is no doubt but the black race will yet instruct the world." Only by achieving self-rule could blacks as a nation create a civilization that reflected their unique qualities.[33] The convention assigned James T. Holly and James M. Whitfield to explore possible emigration sites in Africa and Central America.

The person most instrumental in staging this and subsequent emigration conventions was physician and writer Martin R. Delany. His interest in emigration as a strategy corresponded to the rise of "white American nationalism," most significantly the Compromise of 1850 and its attendant Fugitive Slave Act. In a letter to abolitionist William Lloyd Garrison – himself one of the most vocal opponents of colonization – Delany explained his interest in emigration: "I am not in favor of caste, nor a separation of the brotherhood of mankind, and would as willingly live among white as black, if I had an *equal possession and enjoyment* of privileges; but shall never be reconciled to live among them, subservient to their will – existing by mere *sufferances*, as we, the colored people, do, in this country."[34]

Delany enumerated his positions forcefully in his pamphlet *The Condition, Elevation, Emigration and Destiny of the Colored People of the United States Political Considered* (1852). In it, Delany reprinted significant portions of the Fugitive Slave Act, challenged the notion of black inferiority, and argued that black degradation did not reflect any innate lack of ability among black people, but rather their unequal condition. On the other hand, he did not deny the essentially different tendencies or traits that the black race possessed: "*We have native hearts and virtues, just as other nations; which in their pristine purity are noble, potent and worthy of example.* We are a nation within a nation; – as are the Poles in Russia, the Hungarians in Austria, the Welsh, Irish and Scotch in the British dominions."[35]

Anglo-African emigrationists organized two additional conferences, one in 1856 and one in 1858. Delany joined an exploration party, established to assess the "Valley of the River Niger" as a site for relocation, and he recorded his observations in his *Official Report* (1861). Here Delany coined the phrase "Africa for Africans," which Garvey subsequently appropriated. Delany observed that mission work had exposed the "natives" to Christianity but had failed to build the necessary supporting educational and industrial institutions. "Religion," Delany wrote,

has done its work, and now requires temporal and secular aid to give it another impulse. The improved arts of civilized life must be brought to bear, and go hand in hand in aid of the missionary efforts which are purely religious in character and teaching.[36]

James Holly agreed that establishing an African nationality was important, though he disagreed that Africa was the appropriate place.

Instead, Holly considered Haiti the ideal place for relocation, and eventually settled there. In support of his emigrationist plans, and in response to the widespread view among leading thinkers in the United States that Africans were incapable of civilization, Holly pointed to the example of Haiti. His review of its history suggested that the heroes and statesmen the island had produced compared favorably to any produced by "modern civilization."[37] For Holly, Afro-Americans had to buttress this symbol of Negro nationality so that Haiti could serve as "the lever that must be exerted, to regenerate and disenthrall the oppression and ignorance of the race, throughout the world." Afro-Americans could carry the knowledge of science and art that they had gained "from the hardy and enterprising Anglo-American" and thereby help to strengthen Haiti. This, for Holly, represented a better option than remaining in the United States "asking for political rights."[38]

Delany and Holly were joined by a few other noteworthy activists committed to the same cause. Henry Highland Garnet, Mary Ann Shad, Alexander Crummell, and Edward Blyden were all proponents of black nationalism-as-emigrationism during the second half of the nineteenth century. A former slave, Henry Highland Garnet in 1843 urged slaves to rebel, in one famous speech,[39] and in 1858 founded the African Civilization Society, a predominantly black organization similar in its aims to the American Colonization Society. Garnet's view regarding emigration was reflected in the constitution of the African Civilization Society, whose aims paralleled those of the American Colonization Society. Its goal was "the civilization and christianization of Africa" and "the destruction of the African Slave-Trade."[40] Despite its members' claims of independence from the American Colonization Society, membership in the two groups actually overlapped.[41] This organization had clear emigrationist sentiments, though none was made explicit in its constitution. In a "Supplement to the Constitution" the founders explained that the "Society" would not

encourage general emigration, but will aid only such persons as may be practically qualified and suited to promote the development of Christianity, morality, education, mechanical arts, agriculture, commerce, and general improvement; who must always be carefully selected and well recommended, that the progress of civilization may not be obstructed.[42]

While Delany, Holly, and Garnet struggled in the United States to garner support for emigration, other black nationalist leaders, like Alexander Crummell and the St. Thomas–born Edward Blyden, devoted their time to missionary activities in Liberia. Mary Ann Shadd emigrated to Canada, where she edited the *Provincial Freeman*.[43]

All of the aforementioned activists' efforts and writings conform to the tendencies I've described as Anglo-Africanist nationalism. All

supported resettlement. All assumed that people of African descent ben-
efited from exposure to Western civilization. All valued "manhood," and
figured that the race could achieve manly characteristics in another land.
Most assumed that Christianity would cleanse Africa of its barbarism.
Finally, Anglo-African nationalists assumed that the Afro-American and
Afro–West Indian elite had a special role to play in the redemption of
Africa, so they usually did not support the idea of mass exodus. They
expressed these ideas not as separate theses, but in "bundles."

For instance, from Crummell's perspective, Africans and Afro-
Americans were fortunate to have been exposed to Western culture, and
were inclined to absorb "Anglo-Saxon life and civilization." Crummell
even suggested that it was God's design that made the Anglo-Saxon race
responsible for "evangelizing" African people.[44] This was a matter of
"providence." The responsibility for contributing to African nationality
and civilization fell upon the backs of "black men themselves."[45]

But it was not the belief that black people needed to attain
"manhood" – a concept laden with assumptions about gender and moral
refinement – that set black nationalists apart from non-nationalists. Nor
was it the belief in the need for collective endeavor that set them apart.
The abolitionist Frederick Douglass – fiercely critical of almost all emigration schemes – favored group efforts that would combat the "lazy,
mean and cowardly spirit, that robs us of all manly self-reliance, and
teaches us to depend upon others for the accomplishment of that which
we should achieve with our own hands."[46] Nor did nationalists differ
from non-nationalists over the superiority of Anglo-Saxon civilization or
the importance of civilization. Douglass was an Anglophile; and his criticisms of U.S. society were not of Christianity itself – which would be
more true later among certain twentieth-century black nationalists – but
rather of the hypocrisy of Christians who defended slavery. Nor did they
differ in their opposition to reigning accounts of Negro inferiority, or in
their belief that blacks possessed peculiar traits. Douglass also forcefully
challenged the findings of the American school of ethnology. "Common
sense," he stated, "itself is scarcely needed to detect the absence of
manhood in a monkey, or to recognize its presence in a Negro."[47] The
naturalists were predisposed to "separate the Negro race from every
intelligent nation and tribe in Africa," and Douglass argued that Egyptians were clearly African. At the same time, Douglass held romantic
racialist views, pointing out that the "black man – *un*like the Indian –
loves civilization. He does not make very great progress in civilization
himself but likes to be in the midst of it."[48]

An exchange between Garnet and Douglass in the pages of the *Douglass Monthly* highlights the *essential* disagreement. Garnet asked Douglass to explain his opposition to the civilization and Christianization of

Africa. Douglass responded that he had no such objection, but thought that commerce and Christian missions would promote these general goals. He and most other black Americans simply preferred to remain in the United States. Regarding his objection to the African Civilization Society, Douglass faulted them for the same reason he did the American Colonization Society – for promoting the idea that blacks should not seek full equality in the United States. Douglass is worth quoting at length:

No one idea has given rise to more oppression and persecution toward the colored people of this country, than that which makes Africa, not America, their home. It is that wolfish idea that elbows us off the side walk, and denies us the rights of citizenship. The life and soul of this abominable idea would have been thrashed out of it long ago, but for the jesuitical and persistent teaching of the American Colonization Society.

Further, the African Civilization Society planted "its guns too far from the battlements of slavery for us."[49]

The relatively few blacks who supported emigration abandoned such plans with the onset of the Civil War. Suddenly the question of American political identity was again unresolved, and black Americans were increasingly optimistic about their chances, especially after the Confederacy was defeated. During the war, Delany and Garnet organized Negro troops. Delany was eventually granted the rank of major. Garnet became the first black to preach in the House of Representatives.

But the dream of purging blacks from the national mainstream did not die with the Civil War. Lincoln's aforementioned committee used Delany's report to the 1854 Cleveland convention to support their agenda. The committee reasoned that blacks and whites could never live together, and concluded that "the highest interests of the white race, whether Anglo-Saxon, Celt, or Scandinavian, require that the whole country should be held and occupied by those races alone."[50]

LATE NINETEENTH-CENTURY BLACK NATIONALISM

Black nationalistic schemes reappeared following the deconstruction of Reconstruction. Reconstruction efforts had been resisted from the beginning, and even before the Compromise of 1877, southern white leaders purged blacks – and many poor whites – from the political arena. Their efforts were aided by marauding groups like the Ku Klux Klan, who relied on intimidation and violence. The Supreme Court rendered a number of decisions that slowly chipped away at the gains blacks had achieved under the protection of civil rights laws. Of course, the *Plessy* (1896) decision gave legal sanction to the practice of Jim Crow.

The official retreat from Reconstruction was helped by revived and expanded theories of racial hierarchy that appeared even before slavery had been totally abolished. These new theories often made use of an application of Darwinian theory. Social Darwinist Herbert Spencer crafted his theory in the light of French zoologist Jean-Baptiste Lamarck's work, which argued that acquired characteristics could be inherited. Spencer supported claims that Anglo-Saxons were especially endowed with a desire for independence and freedom – a heritage coming from ancient Teutonic tribes.[51] As was the case before the Civil War, proponents of an Anglo-Saxon American nationalism had "harder" and "softer" varieties. The Rev. Hollis Read, longtime supporter of colonization, represented the latter. His *The Negro Problem Solved* (1864) offered the same solution – resettlement – on the same grounds – the impossibility of peaceful cohabitation of the races. He thought that resettlement of blacks to Africa would redeem the continent.

Our hope for Africa lies in the prospect of a Christian negro nationality; such as an enlightened commerce and an extensive scheme of colonization, and Christian government, laws, and institutions, all baptized in the spirit of Christianity, shall produce.[52]

Blacks themselves must further the work of civilization.[53]

John H. Van Evrie took the "harder" view. For instance, his *White Supremacy and Negro Subordination* (1868) sought to demonstrate the difference in racial types, and to show why black subordination was essential to white prosperity. Unlike Negroes, European immigrants come to the United States, "settle down, become citizens, and their offspring born and raised on American soil differ in no appreciable or perceptible manner from other Americans." Negroes, by contrast, were "absolutely and specifically unlike the American as when the race first touched the soil and first breathed the air of the New World."[54] Unlike Read, who saw a future for blacks as the redeemers of Africa, Van Evrie saw extinction.[55] Further, a population of free blacks would be a "considerable burden upon the laboring and producing citizens" because of their nonproductivity and "tendencies to petty immoralities."[56]

H. C. Kinne combined these perspectives, arguing for colonization on the ground that "no country inhabited by a mongrel population can ever come to the front rank in prosperity and power."[57] H. S. Fulkerson, in his *The Negro: As He Was; As He Is; As He Will Be* (1887), recycled the view that civilization reflected racial groups' innate tendencies. Blacks could not openly compete and should be given a country to themselves. Fulkerson, like Lincoln, thought that Central America offered a promising site for emigration.

Following the failure of Reconstruction, Delany again worked toward the goal of emigration. But the most noteworthy proponent of black nationalism in the post-Reconstruction period was Bishop Henry Turner, who, like Delany, had organized Negro troops during the Civil War, and had expected the prospects of black Americans to improve following the war. Although the African Methodist Episcopal Church membership generally opposed emigration, and despite Turner's explicit support for emigration, he was elected bishop in 1880. From his new position he constantly urged blacks to return "home to Africa." Bishop Turner used the influential newspaper of the A.M.E. Church, the *Christian Recorder*, to disseminate this position. Turner became associated with the provocative thesis that "God is black," thus foreshadowing arguments heard with more frequency during the twentieth century.

Among black elites in this period Turner was alone in his support for emigration. Although precise figures are impossible to gather, the bulk of his support came from peasant farmers who struggled under mounting economic pressure and, in Smith's words, a "militant WASP" assertiveness.[58] Redkey shows how hard times triggered the new interest in emigration, especially after 1890.[59] The economic depression was bad enough. The fact that many black farmers worked as sharecroppers, renting land for shares of the crop they raised, made things worse still. Under this system, and the "crop lien" system – where farmers mortgaged their crops against the supplies needed for the year – landowners and merchants took frequent advantage of black farmers. When the cost of cotton fell, many farmers could no longer make a living. As the economy fell during the 1890s, the American Colonization Society enjoyed a brief resurgence.

During the late decades of the nineteenth century, Turner was the only prominent black leader to offer support for a bill introduced by Senator Matthew Butler of South Carolina crafted to support Afro-Americans who wanted to leave the South and become citizens of some other country. Turner did not care "what animus prompted Senator Butler." If the bill passed it would "enable at least a hundred thousand self-reliant black men to go where they can work at their own destiny." The bill didn't make it out of the Senate.

In 1891 Turner visited Sierra Leone and Liberia as possible sites for emigration. When he returned, the A.M.E. leadership placed him in charge of overseas missionary activities. The church's *Voice of Missions* served as the organ through which he expressed his emigrationist position:

... the fool Negro who has no more sense than a jackass, yet he wants to be a leader, ridicules the idea of asking for a hundred million of dollars to go home, for Africa is our home, and is the one place that offers us manhood and freedom.[60]

MARCUS GARVEY AND THE UNIVERSAL NEGRO IMPROVEMENT ASSOCIATION

Anglo-African nationalism before the turn of the twentieth century did not produce any broad-based movement. Before the Civil War, the vast majority of free Afro-Americans opposed emigration. After the war, the vast majority of Afro-Americans still opposed emigration. Indeed, even proponents of emigration before the Civil War, like Delany, changed strategy in response to real and potential political and economic opportunities. Thus, prior to Marcus Garvey's appearance, black nationalism-as-emigration had little more than tepid support.

This changed when the Jamaican activist Marcus Mosiah Garvey established his Universal Negro Improvement Association and African Communities League in Harlem in 1918, and, by 1921, led "the major political force among blacks in the postwar world."[61] Under Garvey, support for black nationalism arguably reached an all-time high in the United States, until the expansion of the Nation of Islam in the late 1950s.[62] For the first time in U.S. history, black nationalism had significant *popular* support; and arguably, at least until the late 1920s, Garvey's "race first" style of politics trumped all other efforts to draw mass support. Drawing on radical, nationalist currents of the postwar period, as well as the assertive spirit of the "New Negro," Garvey denounced racism in American society, and colonialism in Africa and the West Indies. But Garvey's movement differed from place to place. In the United States during the early 1920s, Garvey's ideas would reflect mostly conservative, if not reactionary, tendencies of his day.

Garveyism as a political movement stood apart from the socialism of the short-lived African Blood Brotherhood (ABB) and the trade unionism associated with A. Philip Randolph and Chandler Owen. The founder of the ABB was Cyril Briggs, a native of St. Kitts, who argued that black people constituted a separate nation but who, unlike Garvey, sought to establish the nation by revolutionary means.[63] The Fenian Irish Republican Brotherhood, and its role in the Easter Rebellion of 1916, was the likely model for the ABB.[64] At its height the clandestine organization claimed several thousand members; and initially the organization attempted to ally itself with the UNIA. The ABB was eventually absorbed by the Communist Party.

Equally earnest competition for the support of the black working class came from A. Phillip Randolph and Chandler Owen, socialists who produced the *Messenger* and pinned their hopes on trade unionism.

Randolph's organizing efforts were, however, more successful in the 1930s than in the early 1920s.

These organizations appealed directly for mass support. Other organizations, like the National Association for the Advancement of Colored People and the Urban League, did not. Middle-class in orientation, and founded in 1909, the interracial NAACP settled on lobbying and litigation as its preferred strategy, and its target was racial apartheid. The Urban League, founded in 1910, attempted to link blacks, especially newly arrived migrants from the South, to housing, jobs, and social services.

During his tenure in the United States – from 1916 to 1927 – Garvey eschewed the strategies of the aforementioned political organizations, hoping to redeem the black race through economic power. In the United States, "the association did not officially engage in or engineer popular actions" against racial discrimination, lynching, or other practices that UNIA members denounced.[65] Rather, as Stein observes, the balance of Garvey and the UNIA's activities concerned a number of business enterprises, chiefly the unsuccessful Black Star Line, and, after that venture failed, the Black Cross Navigation and Trading Company. In addition, UNIA divisions in major cities in the United States opened a variety of businesses. The New York chapter promoted its Universal Restaurants and Universal Chain Store groceries. The Chicago division established a laundry, a hat factory, and a moving firm. Pittsburgh had "a short-lived publishing company."[66] In terms of electoral politics, Garveyism in the United States meant supporting political candidates who favored the goals of the UNIA.

UNIA activism has been misunderstood as primarily a back-to-Africa movement, as Garvey and his supporters struggled to explain at the time. Garvey did call for a strong African state, but his plans to establish such an entity did not involve mass exodus. Rather, like nationalists before him, Garvey favored selective emigration. Reflecting a spirit of "black Zionism,"[67] Garvey hoped to help Liberia by working to build the country's infrastructure, and by sending thousands of blacks from the Western hemisphere to settle there.

Garvey's movement was initially carried by the radicalizing winds of the Bolshevik revolution in 1917, the strength of the labor movement following World War I, and militant WASP assertiveness. Four million workers – longshoremen, carpenters, railroad workers, steel workers, and others – struck for higher wages in 1919.[68] Twenty-five race riots occurred in the United States in the last half of 1919, during which blacks were flogged, shot, burned, and tortured with impunity. At this same time, a rejuvenated Ku Klux Klan attained a larger following outside the South.[69] The Klan served as "part of the government affiliated network of voluntary groups that promoted patriotism and combated dissent," and its mission was "the preservation of Protestantism, motherhood, morality, patriotism, and education."[70]

The matter of white racial identity was in flux, and theorists and policy makers wondered about the long-term effects of immigration on the American gene pool. After all, many immigrant groups – Jews, Armenians, Greeks, and others – were not then regarded as white. This category tended to be reserved for Europeans of northern extraction. Prominent thinkers like E. A. Ross and Madison Grant[71] were among those who worried about the weakening of America's genetic stock by southern and eastern European immigrants.[72] The year 1916 saw the introduction of intelligence testing, which would be wedded to the eugenics movement and to arguments for restricting immigration.[73]

Other commentators discussed racial politics, and anticolonial stirrings, in almost apocalyptic terms. Lothrop Stoddard's *The Rising Tide of Color against White World-Supremacy* (1920) – introduced by Madison Grant – credited the internecine warfare of World War I to growth among nonwhites of a critical eye toward the West.[74] According to Stoddard, a new radical spirit was emerging out of Africa and Asia, and he worried about external and internal threats to white supremacy, suggesting that "migrations of lower human types like those which have worked such havoc in the United States must be rigorously curtailed."[75] In his introduction to Stoddard's book, Grant urged statesmen to look to those of "American blood" to stand up to the challenge:

The great hope of the future here in America lies in the realization of the working class that competition of the Nordic with the alien is fatal, whether the latter be the lowly immigrant from southern or eastern Europe or whether he be the more obviously dangerous Oriental against whose standards of living the white man cannot compete. In this country we must look to such of our people – our farmers and artisans – as are still of American blood to recognize and meet this danger.[76]

It was in this context that the UNIA held the first of several annual conventions in Harlem, New York City, in August 1920. A parade marked the beginning of the month-long event. People looked on as thousands of "black delegates strutted along sun-drenched Lenox Avenue to the syncopated rhythms of twelve bands."[77] The Universal African Legion – the military auxiliary of the UNIA – came next, followed by the Universal Black Cross Nurses, the youth contingent, and the general delegates.[78]

Twenty-five thousand delegates attended the opening session at Madison Square Garden. In gatherings that followed in the UNIA's Liberty Hall in Harlem, delegates adopted the "Declaration of Rights of the Negro Peoples of the World." They decried racial injustice of various forms, including "segregated districts, separate public conveyances, industrial discrimination, lynchings and limitations of political privileges." They also recognized the principle of racial political sovereignty: "Europe for the Europeans . . . Asia for the Asiatics . . . Africa for the Africans at home and abroad."[79] Convention delegates did not, however, formulate a method to secure these ends. Freedom and independence would depend on black enterprise.

For a time anyway, Garvey's UNIA worked in enlisting mostly working-class black men and women "to an elite model of progress."[80] This elite model, shared by black leaders of the NAACP, the Urban League, and the UNIA held that the interests of the race were one. The elite was obligated to pursue a politics of racial uplift, literally a mission to "improve" those beneath them.[81] Garvey shared the elite admiration of Western civilization and "expressed strenuous opposition to black folk culture, which he viewed as inimical to racial progress and as evidence of the retardation that for generations had made for racial weakness."[82] Garvey agreed with other black leaders of his era that blacks of the Western hemisphere had a role to play in the direction and development of the African continent. As Mitchell observes, Garvey agreed as well that gender roles and sexual behavior had to be controlled and monitored to promote the health of the race.[83]

To Garvey, however, his movement was not one of, or for, the elite. His movement was for the interests of the common laborer, the peasant, the migrant, and the immigrant in search of full equality and a better life. By contrast, activists with the NAACP, like W. E. B. Du Bois, might regard themselves as leaders of the black race but concerned themselves only with the black aristocracy. "The NAACP appeals to the Beau Brummel, Lord Chesterfield, kid gloved, silk stocking, creased trousers, patent leather shoe, Bird of Paradise hat and Hudson seal coat with beaver or skunk collar element," Garvey argued. "[T]he UNIA appeals to the sober, sane, serious, earnest, hard-working man, who earns his living by the sweat of his brow." The "UNIA appeals to the self reliant yeomanry."[84]

But while he acknowledged class differences among blacks, Garvey rejected class-based models of political organizing. Especially after an alliance with the ABB dissolved, and mindful of the criticism of rivals Randolph and Owen, he warned his followers to keep "far away from those Socialistic parasites who are receiving money from the Soviets and Communists to destroy governments everywhere and bring about universal chaos and destruction."[85] But in the United States, he also opposed labor organizing as a strategy for black empowerment. While Garvey urged blacks to "be as solidly organized as labor is today," he rejected trade unionism because of its record of racial exclusion. Further, it was the white working class that formed the lynch mob.[86]

In meeting halls, and in print, Garvey's appeals combined economic boosterism, Pan-Africanism, and social Darwinism. According to Garvey, powerful nations of the world were "preparing for a great commercial warfare," and he felt obligated to "prepare the mind of the race for this titanic struggle."[87] "Africa . . . is bleeding," he insisted in 1919, "and she is now stretching forth her hands to her children in America, the West Indies and Central America and Canada to help her."[88] It was time for "the sons and daughters of Ethiopia everywhere to buckle on [their] armor and . . . march 400,000,000 strong toward the destiny of a free and redeemed Africa."[89] Garvey reminded his followers that they were "living in an age of keen competition. Nation rivaling nation, race rivaling race, individual rivaling individual."[90] Black people would gain respect only by demonstrating their worthiness to other nations:

Being satisfied to drink of the dregs from the cup of human progress will not demonstrate our fitness as a people to exist alongside others, but when of our own initiative we strike out to build up industries, governments, and ultimately empires, then, and then only, will we prove to our Creator and to man in general that we are fit to survive and capable of ruling our own destiny.[91]

Garvey's UNIA prepared the mind of the race through propaganda and ritual. The weekly *Negro World* served as the UNIA's propaganda organ beginning in 1918 and reached a circulation of seventy-five thousand by the middle of 1921. By the middle of 1921 "it also contributed over $1,000 every month to the UNIA's general treasury."[92] In it, members and supporters saw the full articulation of Garvey's "race first" strategy – "Negroes should give their own racial concern precedence over all other matters"[93] – as well as Garvey's efforts to encourage racial pride. As Hill notes, Garvey worked to inoculate the black mind against "white propaganda" by offering a quasi-religious theory of racial pride and advancement – what Garvey would call "African fundamentalism." "The time has come for the Negro to forget and cast behind him hero worship and adoration of other races," he wrote, "and start out immediately, to create and emulate heroes of his own."

Foreshadowing arguments Malcolm X would effectively articulate as a minister of the Nation of Islam, and ones expounded by Afrocentric scholars in the 1990s, Garvey also argued that Negroes had been robbed of their history and that, in fact, the world was indebted to the black race "for the benefits of civilization." "The MODERN IMPROVE-MENTS are but DUPLICATES of a grander civilization that we reflected thousands of years ago."[94] Such historical revisionism did not set him apart from most of his black contemporaries, no matter what their political affiliations. Scholars, activists, and lay persons affiliated with fraternities and lodges, with varying degrees of precision and sentimentality, recovered an African past that vindicated the race. Nor did Garvey or his peers confront the open question of whether a positive historical sense actually enabled group progress.[95]

The *Negro World* published reports from hundreds of UNIA divisions, from California to Cuba, from Dominica to Detroit. These divisions reproduced the structure of the parent body. They opened meetings with prayer and song. They had local divisions of African Legions, Black Cross Nurses, and other auxiliary groups. They held parades, dances, receptions, and oratory contests. The locals also provided services – like death benefits – typically offered by fraternal societies.

Although improving the race and establishing a government in Africa were the UNIA's chief aims, members engaged in a wide variety of actions, all tied to the local political, economic, and social contexts in which they operated. In the United States, members participated in local politics, but their involvement varied from locality to locality and depended on a number of factors, including the size and distribution of the black population, the dominant industries and patterns of employment, and the prior history and relationship of blacks to local power brokers. The New York chapter favored the Tammany machine. Because the auto industry dominated local politics, "[t]he UNIA's public profile was low" in Detroit."[96] This was true as well in Gary, which despite having a substantial black population throughout the twenties, "rarely exceeded 185 dues-paying members."[97] The UNIA was never able to effectively mount a challenge to the black machine of Cleveland.[98] And in Cincinnati, the UNIA became involved in some third party politics, throwing its support behind the Charter Party in 1925 and 1927.[99] Chapters in the South were significantly more constrained, and UNIA activists faced frequent harassment and intimidation. In all cases, Garveyites in the South had to conform to Jim Crow standards of social and political behavior.[100]

From our contemporary vantage point, it is difficult to capture the salient features of Garveyism as an international movement. Garveyites attempted to build movements for independence in colonies of Africa, and to promote the rights of black workers in the Caribbean. While governments in all these colonies worried about Garvey's ability to promote unrest, the fact remains that movements for independence, worker solidarity, and economic justice were propelled by many forces, not the least of which was racial and economic oppression. Secondary literature on the UNIA suggests that Garvey's message certainly had wide appeal.[101]

As Garvey faced greater scrutiny from the United States government, he explained his objectives in a way that accommodated his movement even more to the dominant views of race and politics of his era. Hill identifies this shift following Garvey's tour of the Caribbean in 1921, after which the State Department was slow to allow Garvey's return. From this point forward, Garvey was anxious "to disavow his association with radicalism."[102] Where Garvey had once situated the UNIA's objectives in the context of a broader struggle of subordinate classes against European power, and laced his speeches with militaristic bombast, he now emphasized the "the dogma of racial purity . . . as the basis for the UNIA's search for legitimacy."[103] In his speeches and elsewhere, Garvey stressed that the UNIA opposed "social equality" – by this he meant "integration" in the more contemporary sense – as well as "miscegenation and race suicide."[104]

Where once Garvey had dared the Klan to come to Harlem, by June 1922 he had met with the Ku Klux Klan's Imperial Wizard, Edward Clarke, and found himself in agreement with the Klan's vision of the United States as the domain of the Anglo-Saxon. Martin speculates that Garvey received "assurance from Clarke that the Klan would refrain from harassing the UNIA, especially since the UNIA did not represent a threat to their phobias concerning intermarriage." According to Martin, "Garvey concluded that it would henceforth be more worthwhile to push forward with the UNIA program to build a strong government in Africa which would redound to the benefit of black people everywhere, rather than waste time attacking the Klan."[105] Two days later, after the meeting with Clarke, the New Orleans *Times-Picayune* quoted Garvey as saying:

This is white man's country. He found it, he conquered it and we can't blame him because he wants to keep it. I'm not vexed with the white man of the South for Jim Crowing me because I'm black. I never built any street cars or railroads. The white man built them for your own convenience. And if I don't want to ride where he's willing to let me then I'd better walk.[106]

Whatever Garvey's motives for meeting the Imperial Wizard, this act invited great criticism. The cover of Randolph and Owen's July 1922 *Messenger* read: "Garvey, Black Eagle, Becomes Messenger Boy of Clarke, Ku Klux White Kleagle," and Owen urged "all ministers, editors and lecturers who have the interests of the race at heart to gird up their courage, put on a new force, and proceed with might and main to drive the menace of Garveysim out of this country."[107] William Pickens of the NAACP rejected an invitation to the UNIA's August 1922 convention because of Garvey's "Ku Klux attitude." Pickens quipped: "If you are trying to fool the Klan, you have employed a losing stratagem. If you are sincere, then you are more unfortunate to the American Negro than the whole Klan."[108] W. E. B. Du Bois declared Garvey to be a "lunatic or a traitor . . . this open ally of the Ku Klux Klan should be locked up or sent home."[109]

Garvey consistently defended his action as a mission of surveillance. Garvey believed that the Klan represented the "spirit" of "white America."[110] "They are better friends to my race," Garvey insisted, "for telling us what they are, and what they mean, than all the hypocrites put together with their false gods and religions, notwithstanding . . . I like honesty and fair play. You may call me a Klansman if you will, but, potentially, every whiteman is a Klansman . . . and there is no use lying about it."[111]

Yet, even before Garvey's entente with the Ku Klux Klan, and the corresponding criticism that meeting triggered, the UNIA had passed its zenith. The failure of the Black Star Line was chief among the causes of its decline. The flagship *Yarmouth* (rechristened the *Frederick Douglass*) operated for less than two years, and at a loss. The same was true of the excursion ship the *Shadyside*, which was docked after five months, and the *Kanawha*, which was abandoned in Cuba in the fall of 1921. Garvey's financial struggles undermined his movement, as his business ventures were key to his plans for racial redemption.

At the 1922 convention there was dissension in the ranks, and the enthusiasm of earlier years had waned. Garvey's clash with the "leader of American Negroes," the Reverend James W. H. Eason, over the handling and direction of UNIA business led to the latter's impeachment. Tension between black Americans and West Indians was pronounced at this convention. And a number of female delegates complained about the subordinate status of women in the movement.[112] Garvey "gained virtually complete control of the UNIA by silencing his opposition," but this control came at "a cost to increasing disaffection inside, and outside, the movement."[113] Eason continued to challenge Garvey's leadership by organizing his own Negro Improvement Alliance. He was shot and killed in New Orleans by a Garvey supporter on June 1, 1923.

The United States government did its part to undermine Garvey's movement by arresting the activist on mail fraud charges on January 12, 1922, convicting him on the basis of questionable evidence, and sentencing him to five years in prison on June 21, 1923.[114]

After posting bail, and while awaiting an appeal, Garvey pushed forward his plans for Liberian colonization, launched a new shipping company, and created a new political entity, the Universal Negro Political Union. Although his Liberian colonization plans ultimately failed, until June of 1924 it appeared that the repatriation of several thousand families would happen as Garvey had hoped. By then, however, and for reasons not entirely clear, the Liberian government had renounced its earlier agreement.[115]

Garvey launched his second shipping venture in 1924, the Black Cross Navigation and Trading Company. Although Garvey was determined not to repeat the mistakes of the past, the new ship, the *S.S. Goethals* (rechristened the *Booker T. Washington*), quickly ran into financial troubles on its maiden voyage, which began on January 18, 1925. The ship was sold at auction in March 1926, for a fraction of its original cost.[116]

The UNIA also created an electoral arm, the Universal Negro Political Union, in 1924. In an October 26 speech, Garvey declared that it was time "for the Negro to stop allowing himself to be bamboozled and tricked and fooled by Tom, Dick and Harry." "Our duty," he explained, "was to put in office men who we believe will serve the interests of the Negro race."[117] The UNIA endorsed a number of candidates in that year's election.[118]

The United States Circuit Court of Appeals upheld Garvey's conviction, and he was imprisoned in an Atlanta penitentiary on February 8, 1925. After a lobbying campaign that combined the efforts of numerous UNIA members (principally his wife, Amy Jacques Garvey), former rivals like William Pickens, and new allies like Ernest S. Cox of the white supremacist White American Society, President Coolidge commuted Garvey's sentence after two years. Garvey was deported on December 10, 1927, and returned to Jamaica, where he tried in vain to rebuild the UNIA into the international presence it had once been.

That effort had essentially failed by 1929, the year of the sixth annual UNIA convention, held in Jamaica. Garvey insisted on controlling the organization from a new headquarters based in Jamaica, and this split the movement. Many of his former supporters directed the "UNIA, Inc." in the United States as a rival to his newly constituted "UNIA, August 1929, of the World." The rival factions clashed in "various parts of the United States in 1928–1929."[119] The animosity between Garvey and the American UNIA leaders would grow over the course of the 1930s, as would the challenges both faced from other black nationalist sects like the Moorish Science Temple of America and the Nation of Islam, as well as a stronger and more popular Communist Party. Nor was Garvey able to resurrect his movement when he left Jamaica for England in 1935; he died there in 1940.

CONCLUSION

Rather than adopting a style of nationalism that could be viewed as a mature manifestation of an earlier embryonic form, the evidence suggests that Garvey took his cues from his political environment, which was different from the one confronted by earlier proponents of black nationalism. Garvey's oratorical genius and propaganda fuelled the growth of the UNIA. It convinced black men and women of extremely modest means to offer financial support for his effort. But Garvey's mass appeal should not disguise the elitist, organic framework that drove his political vision, nor his acquiescence to white nationalist ideals of his period.

As Stein suggests, the fact that UNIA structure was modeled along the lines of a fraternal organization, that it had no coherent approach to electoral politics, and that it eschewed trade unionism arguably undermined its long-term vibrancy, because it never effectively engaged in "collective political action."[120] When the ambitious business schemes failed, divisions engaged in politics on the local level. But again, without some coherent plan and set of goals, the difficult challenge of winning gains for the black population proved to be even more difficult.

By the 1930s the terms of black political discourse had shifted in response to renewed labor militancy and a refashioned Democratic Party, and the UNIA lost much of its attractiveness. Garvey died in England in 1940, but the champion of black nationalism would become a powerful icon, as subsequent activists interpreted his politics in ways that matched their more immediate political concerns.

Malcolm X and the Nation of Islam

Mike Wallace's five-part television series "The Hate That Hate Produced" brought the Nation of Islam (NOI) to national attention in 1959. This broadcast came five years after the historic *Brown* decision, three years after the launching of the successful Montgomery bus boycott, and one year before black students would begin the "lunch counter" phase of the civil rights movement. In 1959 segregation remained the dominant feature of southern life; and that meant that segregation remained the dominant feature for twelve million of the nineteen million black people in America. Not surprisingly, the struggle against apartheid defined the black agenda. But Mike Wallace uncovered a movement in the other direction. Wallace introduced his viewing audience to a black organization whose members had abandoned Christianity, *rejected* the goal of integration, and believed that white people were devils.

The organization had been around for a long time before Wallace featured it. The Nation of Islam's roots traced back to a number of religious movements that developed in Afro-American settlements in northern cities during the early decades of the twentieth century.[1] These varied fringe religious groups displayed a number of common characteristics. They were generally messianic. They were overwhelmingly working-class. They "rejected Christianity as the religion of the hypocritical slavemaster," and they often propagated racially chauvinistic ideas.[2] The Black Jews of Harlem, for instance, refused to be called Negroes, and compared their oppression to that faced by Hebrews in Egypt. Another example, the Moorish Science Temple of America, was more important to the development of the Nation of Islam. The founder, Noble Drew Ali, referred to blacks as "Asiatics" and taught that Islam was the true religion of black people. Just as the Nation of Islam would do later, Ali encouraged the development of black businesses, and enforced a strict code of behavior in order to root out the vices – such as drugs and alcohol – that affected black people so greatly. Many members of the Moorish Science Temple were Garveyites. And one former follower of Ali, W. D. Fard (pronounced "Fa-ROD"), founded the Temple of Islam in Detroit in 1930.

After Fard's mysterious disappearance, and tumultuous and violent tussling over succession, Elijah Muhammad took control of the organization, and worked to build it during the 1940s and 1950s.[3] He defined his movement against the foil of integration. For Muhammad, blacks would secure their doom by more fully integrating into American society. The so-called Negroes of the United States were lost – they knew nothing of their original identity, of their true religion, or of what they needed to build a Heaven on Earth. Further, they wasted their time on political struggles. Allah would solve the problem of white racism, with His vengeance. In the meantime Muhammad encouraged blacks – not "Negroes" – to separate from an immoral and racist polity, and to assert their proper religious identity. This they could do through his particular teachings, Biblical and Quranic exegesis.

Elijah Muhammad set the stage for black nationalism in the post–World War II era. His vision, amplified by Malcolm X in the late 1950s and early 1960s, presaged the Black Power era by capturing the themes that would be most central to black nationalism during that period – opposition to integration, self-defense, black capitalism, and racial pride. Yet, where some nationalists would actually pick up the gun, and where some nationalists would seek power through electoral politics, Muhammad's conceptual and political innovations betrayed a conventional, even reactionary conservative core: in terms of ideas and practice, Muhammad mixed Horatio Alger themes of uplift, racial determinism, and gender subordination, with an apolitical millenarianism.[4]

Malcolm X figures prominently in Muhammad's story, because without his efforts the Nation of Islam would never have achieved the status that it did, either in terms of membership or in terms of influence. Conversely, participation in Muhammad's Nation was Malcolm X's political baptism. Following his departure from the Nation and subsequent assassination, Malcolm X arguably had a still greater impact on radical politics and thought of the 1960s than he had in life, especially as it concerned Pan-Africanism. His search for a new strategy for political organizing in the United States, however, was cut short, leaving at most a secular, and limited, version of Muhammad's black nationalism – black self-help, black pride, and black control of vital institutions.

The Nation of Islam's politics and agenda resonated with ideological trends already present among a segment of black Americans.[5] Segregation was a central feature of Afro-American life. It differed North and South, of course; but across the country black people led a separate existence. The government policies that helped build the suburbs included home financing plans that made housing accessible to millions of Americans. Unfortunately, "racially discriminatory practices all but eliminated black access to the suburbs and to government mortgage money,"[6] and thus locked blacks into ghettoes. In terms of basic rights, blacks in the North enjoyed political and civil rights, and their exercise of the ballot ensured Kennedy's victory in 1960. And blacks who lived in the North generally had higher incomes.[7] Yet this political equality had not translated into economic equality. Until World War II blacks had been completely shut out of the vast manufacturing sector, except for unskilled jobs. The shortage of labor led to the uneven integration of Afro-Americans into more skilled positions; but, at war's end, most still held unskilled positions. The year 1945 marked the height of black labor force participation. Nationwide, the picture of economic inequality was clear. In 1959, fifty percent of black families were classified as poor. The median family income for black families was roughly 54 percent that of whites. In 1960, 17.9 percent of black eighteen-year-olds, 13.8 percent of twenty-four-year-olds, and 13.5 percent of thirty-five-year-olds were unemployed, out of the labor force, or in jail.[8]

The basis of the Nation of Islam's appeal had to do with its public demeanor and what it appeared to offer. Potential members saw individuals who had been drug dealers, robbers, and addicts of various sorts transformed into law-abiding and "righteous" people. To its targeted audience – the young, domestic and factory workers, common laborers, the unemployed and imprisoned – the NOI offered a path to a better, more dignified life. Lincoln notes that some women who joined did so because the organization protected and honored them.[9]

For its predominately male, working-class following, the Nation of Islam offered an explanation and a solution to racial oppression and the problems it created for black people – everything from joblessness to drug and alcohol abuse, inferior education, police brutality, and poverty. The explanations drew upon their lived experiences, interpreted through the lens of Muhammad's unusual brand of Islam. The solutions required individuals to pool resources, "to rid" themselves of "lust of wine and drink," and to stop "forcing" themselves into places where they were unwelcome. Malcolm X's conversion is illustrative.

Malcolm X was born Malcolm Little on May 19, 1925, in Omaha, Nebraska, to working-class parents. Both had worked as organizers for Marcus Garvey's UNIA. Following the tragic and mysterious death of his father, and the subsequent institutionalization of his mother, Malcolm Little ended up in Boston living with this half-sister, Ella. After living among Roxbury's black middle class, Malcolm Little slowly began to explore Boston's ghetto of the 1940s. This was followed by a slow immersion into a life of hustling, drug addiction, crime, and ultimately, jail. This was his period of self-degradation. Not only was his life given over to drugs and crime, but he also adopted a personal style common among black working-class men during the 1940s – that of the "hep cat" – that confirmed his self-loathing. Thus was he distracted by the latest fashions and dance moves. He even straightened his kinky hair into a style called the "conk," thereby joining "the multitude of Negro men and women in America who [were] brainwashed into believing that black people are 'inferior.' "[10]

It was during his seven-year prison term that Malcolm Little heard the message of Elijah Muhammad and was saved, replacing his slave name with an "X." Muhammad's message wasn't complex: blacks should live a disciplined and moral life, eschew drugs and alcohol, and establish a separate nation. They should build separate schools and businesses in the meantime. His call for a separate state partly reflected Muhammad's predictions of apocalypse. He argued that American society was inherently and unchangeably racist, morally bankrupt, and destined to fall. Why, then, should blacks seek integration? Drawing on the jeremiadic tradition common to many thinkers in U.S. history, Muhammad insisted that "America is falling; she is a habitation of devils and every uncleanness and hateful people of the righteous. Forsake her ... before it is too late."[11]

In accordance with his vision of apocalypse and divine redemption, Muhammad avoided any kind of political activism. This obvious political acquiescence could take on a different, even radical, tone in the context of segregation-era black politics. In the late 1950s, when the Nation of Islam began to build momentum, it was hardly clear that Jim Crow would end. However, it was obvious after *Brown* that the white Southerner's idea of deliberate speed was not what most black citizens had in mind.

It would have been different if black people had come to the United States voluntarily, like millions of white immigrant groups. It would then make sense to agitate for inclusion, for social and economic rights. European immigrants were drawn to the United States to provide labor for its expanding economy. For the immigrants from Ireland, southern Europe, and the Mediterranean, jobs in the manufacturing sector and access to the ballot provided an avenue to socioeconomic mobility and *whiteness*. But, as ministers of the NOI would note, black people arrived in bondage, and unlike the Irish, the Poles, and the Italians they had no hope of jumping into the melting pot. Nor would any black person with "knowledge of self" want to jump.

Indeed, knowledge of "self" would demonstrate, first, that "Negro" as a referent was a misnomer: a Negro "is a person who has no history."[12] Knowledge of history, according to Muhammad, revealed that the so-called Negroes of North America were a transplanted African population stripped of its culture, language, and religion. This lack of knowledge "of self" resulted in the pathological behavior black people displayed and at least partly accounted for their lack of upward mobility.

Of course, the history motif had antecedents, and one didn't have to agree with the entire historical revision to agree with some of these observations. For Drew Ali, history essentially revealed the true "Moorish" identity of black Americans. And for Garvey and nationalists before him, history revealed the greatness of early African civilization. But these lessons were lost to contemporary blacks. As Malcolm X explained: "The teachings of Mr. Muhammad stressed how history had been 'whitened' – when white men had written history books, the black man simply had been left out . . . the history of the Negro had been covered in one paragraph."[13]

Yet, as Malcolm X explained, Elijah Muhammad's history involved making a particular leap of faith that neither Ali nor Garvey had demanded. Muhammad explained the origins of the races with an elaborate creation mythology that taught of a "big-headed" scientist named "Yacub" who forged the white race out of the black. Yacub, Malcolm X tells us in his *Autobiography*, understood that the differences between white and black people resulted from two germs, a dark one and a light one. One germ was dominant, the other weaker and therefore recessive. By using a plan that spanned hundreds of years, Yacub first grafted a race of browns from the original black, and subsequently a race of whites. These white mutants were evil. As Malcolm X explained: "On the island of Patmos was nothing but these blond, pale-skinned, cold-blue-eyed devils – savages, nude and shameless; hairy, like animals, they walked on all fours and they lived in trees." This "devil" race sowed the seeds of dissension among the black group, turning the peaceful heaven of earth "into a hell torn by quarreling and fighting."[14]

Again, the target was clear: a younger, working-class population, rooted in southern Christian traditions, and therefore accustomed to certain scriptural themes. The story of Yacub may have lacked the artistry of other creation mythologies – Yacub was big-headed, after all. Still, it was no more absurd than any other creation mythology. The point was not so much Yacub as it was a racial Manicheanism that the story constructed: white is evil, black is good. This account offered an easy explanation of white racism: white people oppressed nonwhites because of genetic programming. Elijah Muhammad thus avoided any complex sociological or political theories about racial hierarchy. He also inverted

the paradigm of white supremacy, allowing blacks to reclaim their right-
ful spot.

The "white devil" rhetoric was jarring and, according to Malcolm X,
especially effective with convicts.[15] As one-time Black Panther Party
leader Eldridge Cleaver noted, "There was a time when . . . [e]very black
inmate's thoughts centered on the question of whether or not to convert
to the Nation of Islam."[16]

Even for those who couldn't accept the story of Yacub and the white
devil literally, the tale offered a useful metaphor. Blacks had firsthand
experience with the evil of racial discrimination. In the North, white
people locked blacks into ghettoes and denied them opportunities for
employment. In the South, white people imposed a biracial, segregated
caste system, codified in law and buttressed by violence.

The Nation saw Christianity as a tool of the white devil-race aimed
at subjecting Afro-Americans to perpetual positions of inferiority. In their
view, Christianity represented a profoundly important medium through
which black people adopted the norms and beliefs of white American
society. Christianity not only offered a problematic conception of the
afterlife, but also promoted ideas of a white supremacy wholly at odds
with the psychological needs of the black population. Christianity had
black people worshiping a "blond-haired blue-eyed deity," a profound
reinforcing of black inferiority. Further, the teaching and practice of
Christianity obscured the fact that Asiatic black people had been
Muslims from the beginning.

The critique of Christianity took on special significance in the context
of the black freedom struggle. For the Nation of Islam, Christianity was
the opiate. It kept black eyes "fixed on the pie in the sky and heaven in
the hereafter . . ." Meanwhile, the blue-eyed devils "*twisted* . . . Christianity, to step his *foot*" on black backs.[17] Further, as the moral basis of
nonviolent passive resistance, Christianity encouraged blacks to suffer
great indignities. The images of attack dogs, fire hoses, and billy clubs,
on the one hand, and nonviolent black men, women, and children who
absorbed such attacks on the other, had transformed public opinion
regarding Jim Crow. But for the NOI, such images demonstrated how
Christianity led to black suffering – it transformed blacks into self-
effacing, patient, pious, forgiving Uncle Toms. It was Christianity – not
pragmatism – that required blacks to turn the other cheek. The Nation,
by contrast, offered a rejection of both the method and the goal of the
struggle against segregation.

The Nation of Islam's criticism carried still greater weight when
coupled with the idea that the integration-seeking black person was
middle-class, and therefore not allied with the black *lumpen*. Again,
as many observers have noted, the NOI's natural constituency was

lower-income blacks. By contrast, the composition of the main civil rights organizations – the NAACP, CORE, and SCLC – had a more middle-class inflection.

Malcolm X used the powerful metaphor of the "house Negro and the field Negro" to emphasize these apparent class cleavages. Malcolm X explained in a speech in 1964 that during slavery there were two types of Negroes: the house Negro and the field Negro. The house Negro "lived right up next to his master – in the attic or in the basement. He ate the same food as his master and wore his same clothes. And he could talk just like his master – good diction." The house Negro was also extremely concerned about the master's health and the protection of his property. The field Negro, on the other hand, lived in a hut and had nothing to lose.[18] Field Negroes did not wish to protect the master's interest. They tried to subvert it. Bringing his metaphor to the present, Malcolm X concluded that the black population still consisted of house and field Negroes. Malcolm X identified himself as a field Negro.

A number of publications helped spread Elijah Muhammad's ideas. The most important was the Nation of Islam's own newspaper, *Muhammad Speaks*, which Malcolm X had founded. Readers had access not only to theological musings of Elijah Muhammad, but also to commentary concerning black politics both domestically and internationally. Many other black newspapers of that period published Elijah Muhammad's articles, including the Pittsburgh *Courier*, Los Angeles *Herald-Dispatch, Amsterdam News*, Milwaukee *Defender*, and the Chicago *New Crusader*.

Finally, no minister articulated Muhammad's vision like Malcolm X. In sermons, on street corners, and in lecture halls, Malcolm X effectively and eloquently explained his black Islamic nationalism. His appeal stemmed partly from his ability to present himself as an "authentic" voice of the black urban community, in contrast to a seemingly more detached middle-class leadership. Malcolm X had unprecedented success recruiting people into the NOI, transforming the group into a thriving national organization; and with his input in the late 1950s and early 1960s the NOI became the largest, and wealthiest, black nationalist organization of the postwar era.

Elijah Muhammad's message was not the sole reason for the organization's growth and success. Members and nonmembers saw ideas in action. They saw impressive economic ventures. Indeed, entrepreneurship played a large role in the development of the movement during the 1950s.[19] The NOI ran laundromats, opened restaurants and hair salons, and even purchased a bank. Moreover, its newspaper generated significant, and guaranteed, revenue. The guarantee was due to the fact that the peddler was required to purchase his newspapers in advance of sales. Elijah Muhammad and his family enjoyed the benefits of their lucrative businesses, their affluence being clearly evident to observers. So successful were these ventures, in fact, that by the mid-1970s the NOI's assets were estimated to be 80 to 100 million dollars.[20]

There was the disciplined, and intimidating, security force, the Fruit of Islam (FOI). The FOI drew media attention many times for altercations with the police. They maintained the Nation's code, sometimes using rough tactics to do so. They were the physical embodiment of the discipline so central to Muhammad's doctrine.

The Nation of Islam also established separate schools for its children – "Universities of Islam" – first in Detroit in 1932 and then in Chicago in 1934. They succeeded in getting the curriculum approved by various state governments; and by 1974 forty-six cities in the United States had NOI elementary schools. These schools taught fundamentals and doctrine. Boys and girls attended separate classes, if space permitted.

Despite its radical demeanor, the NOI propounded fundamentally conservative themes. In fact, Muhammad's orthodoxy looked a great deal like fascism, minus the power. The NOI tied "race" to "nation" and believed in the superiority of the black race. They celebrated a militaristic ethic, embodied in the FOI. They relied on an undemocratic, autocratic leadership style. Clegg argues that the NOI's practices actually fell short of fascism. "Unlike fascists," he writes, "Muhammad and his Muslims did not glorify the exercise of force and violence for its own sake." "Nor," Clegg adds, "did they rely upon politics and military power to accomplish their goals, but rather, religion and economics. They never advocated or resorted to the use of force to seize state power or to exterminate 'inferior' populations."[21] However, Clegg's definition of fascism might place too great an emphasis on the element of power. Hitler and Mussolini were surely fascists even before they wielded the power of the state.

The NOI's economic model was conservative. It offered neither strategy nor action geared toward challenging the discriminatory labor practices of its day. Like many Americans of his era, Muhammad rejected communism because communism rejected God. Clegg notes that "[e]ven among third-world revolutionaries, Muhammad opposed any Marxist leanings and was outraged by a chance meeting of Fidel Castro and Malcolm X during a visit of the Cuban leader to the United Nations in September 1960."[22] Instead, Muhammad, like Garvey, adopted a model of capitalistic self-help. His followers did not seek a greater slice of the pie of economic opportunity. They attempted to establish a separate economy. Further, their model of economic development depended upon a kind of super-exploitation of their own workers. Many members who worked "long hours in the restaurants and bakeries didn't get paid for all the time they worked."[23]

The Nation of Islam's gender politics reflected the problematic tendencies of its era. Claims about respect for women were predicated on a typical patriarchal nuclear family model, in which women were expected to serve men. S'Thembile West suggests that the notion of "submissiveness" mischaracterizes the level of power and influence women had in the organization. Interviews of women who belonged to the NOI in Newark in the 1960s show that, for instance, "[i]nstilling values was a major role of Black Muslim women in the home and community."[24] But evidence of this power looks strikingly like the old "separate spheres" practices, where women lack economic power and social status but wield moral influence over the home. Indeed, Muhammad understood the function of women to be reproductive: "The woman is man's field to produce his nation," he wrote. In Muhammad's view "[u]sing birth control for a social purpose is a sin."[25] In his *Autobiography*, Malcolm X showed how he, too, accepted assumptions about gender common to his era. He mentioned Islam's teaching that "a woman's true nature is to be weak" and that while a man should respect his woman, "he must control her if he expects to get her respect."[26] These statements were borne out in practice. Men and women were separated in places of worship. Men dominated the leadership of the organization. And although most NOI women worked outside of the home, Muhammad encouraged them to stay home. The NOI trained boys and young men in self-defense, and girls "learned not to use profanity and not to raise [their] voices," proper posture, and home economics.[27]

Strong on criticism of the civil rights movement, Elijah Muhammad was weak on activism himself. In fact, he prohibited his followers from participating in politics. Shortly before his death, Malcolm X made this very point:

See, the Black Muslim movement . . . was organized in such a way that it attracted the most militant, the most uncompromising, the most fearless, and the youngest of the Black People in the United States. That's who went into it. Those who didn't mind dying. They didn't mind making a sacrifice. All they were interested in was freedom and justice and equality, and they would do anything to see that it was brought about. These are people who have followed him for the past twelve years. And the government knows it. But all these upfront militants have been held in check by an organization that doesn't take an active part in anything.[28]

In fact, the NOI trajectory was less in line with nationalist efforts in Africa, Latin America, and Asia than it was with the accommodation-ism of Booker T. Washington. Like Washington, Muhammad directed black efforts into entrepreneurial activities and moral "rehabilitation," and away from the political action. The appearance of radical militancy depended upon the contrasting stance of nonviolent protesters, not on any real agenda that challenged the status quo.

Invariably, the organization's behavioral requirements thwarted its growth in numbers and influence. Despite the fact that the NOI's teachings resonated within segments of the black population, neither the group's goal nor its method of individual transformation ever enjoyed wide appeal. It was one thing to agree with an easy criticism of racism in the United States. But to join a strange religious organization was another matter altogether. The NOI's nationalism arguably had limited appeal to the common understandings and experiences of most Afro-Americans and Afro–West Indians.

Muhammad understood the thrust of civil rights activism to be aimed in the direction of integration, which he equated with assimilation and racial amalgamation. Ministers of the NOI, like Malcolm X, polemically conflated terms that, by the 1960s, had different meanings. Integration meant, or at least had meant, the dismantling of legally imposed racial segregation. Assimilation generally meant the end result of a process of acculturation and social mobility, as opposed to amalgamation or racial mixing. But Elijah Muhammad rhetorically linked the various meanings. In this way, when ministers in the NOI criticized the integrationist vision of various black activist leaders, they were able to direct a more striking and powerful critique. They rejected the idea of becoming part of white society by positing the idea that becoming part of American society meant losing one's cultural and racial identity.

In fact, civil rights activists never defined the goal of integration in this manner. As scholars have recently noted, Muhammad and Malcolm X – before and after his break with Muhammad – were wrong to assume that Afro-Americans lacked "black consciousness," that they wholly identified with "white culture." Robin Kelley takes Malcolm X to task on this point, arguing that Malcolm X's categories – "militancy versus self-degradation, consciousness versus unconsciousness" – left him unable to fully appreciate the significance of black popular culture of the World War II and postwar era. Malcolm X argued that the hair-straighteners and skin-bleachers were evidence of white-centered behavior, as was the style of the "hep cat." But the subculture of the "hep cat," Kelley contends, "was not a detour on the road to political consciousness but rather an *essential* element"[29] (emphasis supplied). The zoot suit, street talk, and even the dance styles were not simple "ghetto adornments," but part of a political subculture:

... once we contextualize the conk, considering the social practices of young hep cats, the totality of ethnic signifiers from the baggy pants to the coded language, their opposition to war, and emphasis on pleasure over waged labor, we cannot help but view the conk as part of the larger process by which black youth appropriated, transformed, and reinscribed coded oppositional meanings into styles derived from the dominant culture.[30]

Kelley overstates his case. It is true that both Elijah Muhammad's and Malcolm X's overly simplistic understandings of black consciousness reflected rigid, and ultimately indefensible, notions of "black" versus "white" culture. From this angle, "ghetto adornments" did not constitute "self-hatred" – black people did not necessarily want to be white. On the other hand, ghetto adornments and hep cat style did not necessarily reflect opposition to the dominant culture either. Working class black males could simply have been pursuing the latest fad. Any artifact of popular culture among Afro-Americans appropriates some elements of the wider "mainstream" style and rejects others. Trends in such things as dress, language, and dance derive from the clash, or interplay, between black and white (and other) styles, mediated in turn by the market economy.

More important is Kelley's causal claim regarding the postwar black subculture and Malcolm X's evolution as a political leader. It was not Malcolm X's experience as a "hep cat" that defined his political evolution, but rather his passage through the NOI that explains his development from a religious sectarian convert into, as we will see, a politically engaged Pan-Africanist. Further, Malcolm X's own movement towards radicalism corresponded to similar trends in the wider black freedom struggle.[31]

The Nation's understanding of culture and consciousness was thus limited, as was its understanding of the connections between consciousness and class. Malcolm X's famous house Negro / field Negro tale shows how this was so. In his effort to link radical consciousness to class, Malcolm X suggested that field Negroes – who have no vested interest in the welfare of the master – were more likely to be against the status quo. They were more likely to rebel against slavery. This is simply wrong as an historical point, and unhelpful to strategic analysis in his day. Nat Turner, Denmark Vesey, and Gabriel Prosser were house slaves. Historically, the "field Negroes" of slave plantations and urban America offered varying responses to racial inequity – from quiet acquiescence to direct confrontation.[32]

THE LEGACIES OF MALCOLM X

Muhammad had given his ministers strict orders not to comment about the Kennedy assassination; so when Malcolm X referred to the assassination as a case of "the chickens coming home to roost," Elijah Muhammad silenced Malcolm X for ninety days. Malcolm X hoped eventually to be reinstated, to gain again the status and import he had once enjoyed in the NOI. Instead, Malcolm X found himself increasingly marginal to the organization; and so, in March of 1964, Malcolm X declared his independence from Elijah Muhammad.

There are a number of plausible explanations for Malcolm X's split with Elijah Muhammad, none of them mutually exclusive.[33] Malcolm X attributed the split with Muhammad to his discovery of the latter's infidelity – Muhammad fathered nine children outside of wedlock with women in the movement – and to jealousy within the organization, particularly among the Chicago leadership. There is reason to doubt that Malcolm X had been ignorant of Muhammad's behavior, although Malcolm X was right to suspect others of jealousy. DeCaro offers another plausible explanation that sees the leader Muhammad worried about a potential rival, a concern typical of a cult leader.[34] Clegg speculates that "[a]fter some reflection, and coaxing from others, the Muslim leader concluded that Malcolm had been too powerful and knew too much to remain in his high office in the Nation."[35]

Or perhaps Malcolm X's inclinations toward political engagement troubled Muhammad. Malcolm X did admit in his *Autobiography* that, as time went on, he became more impatient with Muhammad's policy of noninvolvement. He was certain that the "Nation of Islam could be an even greater force in the American black man's overall struggle – if [it] engaged in more *action*." Compared to the activists involved in the freedom struggle – from the lunch counter protesters to the freedom riders and to those trying to register blacks to vote in the South – the Nation of Islam was passive. Comments like, "Those Muslims *talk* tough, but they never *do* anything, unless somebody bothers Muslims," had bothered him greatly.[36]

In a speech to an audience at the Northern Grass Roots Leadership Conference, weeks before Kennedy's assassination, Malcolm X offered the Bandung conference of 1954 "as a model for the same procedure you and I can use to get our problems solved."[37] There, Africans were able to transcend their differences and to agree that they had a common oppressor:

When they came to the Bandung they looked at the Portuguese, and at the Frenchman, and at the Englishman, and at the Dutchman, and learned or realized the one thing that all of them had in common – they were all from Europe, they were all Europeans, blond, blue-eyed and white skins.[38]

He also described revolution in a way that implicitly endorsed a militant strategy of empowerment. His remarks clearly strained against NOI orthodoxy. Muhammad had not demonstrated any willingness to work with other groups. Nor did Muhammad expect racism to end without divine intervention.

Whatever the ultimate cause, Malcolm X's departure from the NOI was significant to the development of black nationalism in the 1960s because it led to his assassination. His thoughts of a secular black nationalism as a political, economic, and social philosophy; his exploration of Sunni Islam; his efforts to establish a Pan-African politics; and his rethinking of capitalism, all were amplified by his martyrdom. As we will see, numerous activists claimed a piece of Malcolm X's legacy and, by so doing, constituted that legacy.

Malcolm X established his Muslim Mosque, Inc., in March of 1964. This organization represented his move toward Sunni Islam, so Yacub was definitely gone, and so too was his universal indictment of white people. He now adopted a "socio-political" definition of white deviltry: "Anyone . . . mind you, I am saying anyone . . . who overtly, intentionally, and knowingly deprives another of his human right[s] is a devil. I said anyone who does this is a devil. And, if he consciously, knowingly and intentionally deprives the man of knowledge that will enable him to correct his condition, he is a double devil."[39] Thus did Malcolm X sever the alleged relationship between race and Islam. As he explained: "Islam . . . as a religion . . . has nothing to do with color."[40] Establishing the Muslim Mosque Inc., also signaled the end of his "religious nationalist" phase. The Muslim Mosque, Inc., reflected a principle of separation between religion and political activism. "It's true we're Muslims and our religion is Islam," he stated, "but we don't mix our religion with our politics."[41] Malcolm X was now willing to work with Christians, atheists, or agnostics, anyone who shared his political goals.

In the last year of his life, Malcolm X broadened his thinking about black politics at home, the links to African politics abroad, the need for self-defense and even a favorable consideration of socialism. His motto, "by any means necessary," reflected the pragmatic approach of his new organization, the Organization of Afro-American Unity, modeled on the Organization of African Unity. Its goal was

to fight whoever gets in our way, to bring about the complete independence of people of African descent here in the Western Hemisphere, and first here in the United States, and bring about the freedom of these people by any means necessary.[42]

At the founding speech in June of 1964, Malcolm X outlined an ambitious agenda that included unification of people of African descent, promotion of self-defense, education so that black children could "rediscover their identity and thereby increase their self-respect,"[43] and black control of political, economic, and social decisions that affected their lives. He called his political philosophy "black nationalism," and he explained the significance of black nationalism in the following way:

Even when I was a follower of Elijah Muhammad, I had been strongly aware of how the Black Nationalist political, and economic and social philosophies had the ability to instill within black men the racial dignity, the incentive, and the confidence the black race needs today to get up off its knees, and to get on its feet, and get rid of its scars, and to take a stand for itself.[44]

But in terms of method and goal, Malcolm X's black nationalism was not "African" in the sense that it was not, say, Angolan, Algerian, Kenyan, or Ghanaian. Further, despite his fiery orations, and journalists' frequent mischaracterizations, Malcolm X did not advocate violence as a means to an end. He encouraged armed self-defense, not armed offense. As he explained in a speech to the Militant Labor Forum titled the "Black Revolution," blacks could "bring about a bloodless revolution" if they were granted the vote. This "would wipe out the Southern segregationism that now controls America's foreign policy, as well as America's domestic policy."[45]

Where Malcolm X's intellectual and activist journey would have taken him is impossible to know. He didn't live long enough to translate his rhetoric into a specific set of actions. Neither his Muslim Mosque, Inc., nor his Organization of Afro-American Unity existed long enough to do much of anything. Indeed, Malcolm X's legacy owes something to the fact that activists and commentators have attempted to fashion a coherent ideology out of speeches given and interviews conducted after his break with Muhammad. In both, the thought that emerges is as much exploratory as it is exact. His famous "by any means necessary" formulation covers all possible agendas and strategies, even contradictory ones. Given the sweep of Malcolm X's statements in his final days, it is easy to see how activists could tie his words to a variety of agendas – socialist, cultural nationalist, armed revolutionary, and so forth.

And that is precisely what happened. Activists began to transform Malcolm X into an icon immediately following the leader's tragic assassination in 1965. Seen from our contemporary vantage point, Ossie Davis's moving eulogy was quite prescient:

. . . secure in the knowledge that what we place in the ground is no more a man – but a seed – which, after the winter of our discontent – will come forth again to meet us. And we will know him then for what he was and is – a Prince – our own shining Prince![46]

Davis could not have known how right he would be. For in death, Malcolm X achieved a stature that he probably would not have achieved in life. William L. Van Deburg details the beginning of Malcolm X's "enshrining in popular culture." Malcolm X's message lived on through a number of sources, including his "mass-marketed *Autobiography* (1965), several volumes of collected speeches, and spoken word record albums such as *Message to the Grass Roots* (1965)."[47]

Malcolm X's legacy was propelled through a number of forums. In the pages of the nationalist *Liberator*, A. B. Spellman suggested that Malcolm X "emphasized that Nationalism was *not* an end in itself but that it had a unifying potential." Nationalism could create "a new set of terms for dealing with those forces in American society which are continuously perverting the world." Spellman also suggested that Malcolm X had started to create a "coherent and cohesive" nationalist movement.[48]

Separatist or integrationist? One could choose, as many did, to remember the pronouncements Malcolm X made while a member of the NOI: the scathing criticisms of the black middle class and the assertions of black pride and superiority. Conversely, one could understand the thrust of Malcolm X's philosophy to be toward integration. The *Autobiography* settles this matter. There he makes it clear that whites would not be allowed to participate in his organizations. But the book leaves other developments untouched.

One such development involved his new appraisal of socialism. George Breitman noted a change in Malcolm X's political philosophy regarding socialism following his break with Muhammad. He suggests that Malcolm X worked to synthesize black nationalism and socialism. In a number of speeches to the Militant Labor Forum, and on other occasions, Malcolm X suggested that the lesson he learned from observing African independence efforts was the relationship between "capitalism" and "racism."[49] You couldn't have one without the other. And on other occasions he mentioned the choice of many African countries to construct socialist economies. We should note, however, that like all effective speakers, Malcolm X chose his words to suit his audience. We should also note that this apparent reappraisal of socialism failed to appear in the founding statement of the OAAU.

Militants of various sorts claimed Malcolm X's legacy. Revolutionary nationalists – those wishing to topple the social order – took Malcolm X's admonition not to turn the other cheek as a call to arms. Malcolm X was indeed open to such an interpretation. His final speeches are littered with references to Molotov cocktails and guerrilla warfare. On the other hand, upon elaboration, his call to arms was a call for self-defense. It was not Fanonian.[50]

Cultural nationalists like Imamu Amiri Baraka and Larry Neal took Malcolm X's legacy to mean political and cultural separation. In an essay titled "November 1966: One Year Eight Months Later," Baraka asserted that Malcolm X's legacy "was the concept and will toward political power in the world for the black man." To Baraka, Malcolm X taught that blacks must "build their own society" reflecting their distinctive world view.[51] In his "On Malcolm X from 'New Space/The Growth of Black Consciousness in the Sixties,'" Larry Neal explained Malcolm X's significance in a literary sense. For Neal, Malcolm X's words, more than King's, "seemed to spring from the universe of black music." Stating that he did not have "ready access to the rhetorical strategies of Martin Luther King [Jr.]," Neal explained: "My ears were attuned to the music of urban black America – that blues idiom music called jazz. Malcolm was like that music. He reminded many of us of the music of Charlie Parker and John Coltrane – a music that was a central force in the emerging ethos of the black artistic consciousness."[52] Neal also attributed to Malcolm X two philosophical points that he felt black radicals came to understand: first, that the desire for self-determination had entered a more serious stage; and second, that nonviolence had become anachronistic.[53] Neal suggested that untold numbers of black students became "radically politicized" as a result of Malcolm X's assassination. Further, for both Baraka and Larry Neal, black artists followed Malcolm X's mandate by linking art and politics.

These belated reflections constituted the legacy of Malcolm X. Yet, lurking beneath easy pronouncements lay one important point: Malcolm X did not have sufficient time, nor perhaps a clear and sophisticated enough analysis, to formulate a more concrete agenda. "By any means necessary" could work as a provocative call to arms, but it did not convey anything, really, about what political strategy and organizing should entail. Not surprisingly, then, the specific aims of the OAAU spell out a strategy that amounts to an essentially secular variety of Elijah Muhammad's nationalism. When he spoke of cleansing the black community of drugs, or of black control of politics and economics, he offered a secular, though certainly more engaged, version of NOI strategy.

CONCLUSION

There is an ironic aspect of Elijah Muhammad's and Malcolm X's relationship to black nationalism of the 1960s. Elijah Muhammad established the template – the special character of postwar black nationalism. But as an icon of black nationalism, Malcolm X arguably broadened the applicability of Muhammad's strategy. Because Malcolm X left behind two unsuccessful organizations – the Muslim Mosque, Inc., and the Organization of Afro-American Unity – his legacy became a matter of invention and debate.

Elijah Muhammad's and Malcolm X's nationalisms shed great light on the development of the phenomenon, because they reveal the same important paradox: black nationalism achieved certain conceptual innovations, but many of the core assumptions – about race, class, gender – reflect conventional thinking about such themes. For instance, Malcolm X would stress the need for history, but he would not advance a complex historical analysis of race. Nor would Malcolm X – perhaps for lack of time – build an analysis from the perspective of advancing a politics that reflected women's position of disadvantage. This made him no less of a nationalist. It simply demonstrates, as we saw with early nationalist movements, that the texture of nationalistic politics reflects ideas and political developments common to specific eras.

3

Black Nationalist Organizations in the Civil Rights Era

In order to understand the rise and significance of black nationalist groups of the 1960s, we must first grasp three important features of the political context of that era of black politics. One development involved the struggle for racial equality, embodied in the efforts of such groups as the National Association for the Advancement of Colored People (NAACP), the Southern Christian Leadership Conference (SCLC), the Congress of Racial Equality (CORE), and the Student Nonviolent Coordinating Committee (SNCC). The "black mass protests and insurgencies of the 1950s and 1960s," however, "were grassroots movements that emerged with little guidance from national African-American organizations or their leaders."[1] These movements held center stage in a postwar drama holding a captive American audience who had recently faced the horror of Nazism and who, especially in the context of the cold war era, had slowly begun to reexamine the question of racial inequality in the United States. The moderate success of the civil rights movement initiated, in turn, an important shift in the course of black politics. The call for Black Power in 1966 indicated a change in strategic orientation, and in movement demands.

Second, this ideological reorientation took on even greater significance in the context of the unrest that shook urban areas large and small during the 1960s. Prior to the uprising surrounding the Rodney King incident in 1995, the Watts riot of 1965 stood as the most destructive in U.S. history. More than 300 riots took place between 1964 and 1968, more than 100 following the assassination of Martin Luther King, Jr., alone.[2]

Third, television coverage mediated each of these developments, arguably assisting the cause of anti-apartheid efforts in the South, sensationalizing the Black Power mantra after 1966, and suggesting a closer-than-warranted connection between the activists who championed Black Power and the unrest that marked the era.

The tide of activism lifted nationalist groups of all sorts during the 1960s, and debates about political strategy defined the politics of nationalist groups more than at any other time before or since. "Modern" black nationalist groups and activists agreed on a number of matters. They agreed, for instance, that integration as a goal was problematic, partly because the civil rights leadership had not formulated strategies that confronted the dire conditions of black life, especially in urban centers, and also because they linked integration to undesirable cultural assimilation. Even groups that did not identify themselves as principally opposed to cultural assimilation waged a symbolic battle against white cultural hegemony, using poetry, cartoons, songs, and ritual to emphasize black distinctiveness and assertiveness. As Jordan notes, "if only because of various rituals and artifacts which were used to decorate organizations and their activities, and the language which such organizations chose to express their view of the world," all groups were *culturally* nationalist.[3] Most nationalists criticized the strategy of nonviolence, arguing that a strategy of that sort relied too much on the sympathy of whites. Securing that sympathy would be considerably more difficult as the scope of black demands increased. As many feminists subsequently noted, black nationalistic agendas typically ignored issues dealing with black women's inequality and, in fact, often demanded female subordination. Reflecting rather conventional notions of gender roles and expectations common to American society, most organizations, and their leaderships, were male-dominated.

These organizations also shared the scrutiny of U.S. intelligence. Far-left organizations like the Black Panther Party and the Republic of New Africa, as well as decidedly conservative groups such as the Nation of Islam, were all subject to FBI scrutiny. The inability of far-left organizations to advance their agendas in significant ways was partly, if not largely, due to intimidation, imprisonment, murder, and subversion linked to the FBI's COINTELPRO operation.[4]

Secondary studies of black nationalism typically divide the phenomenon into a typology of the following sort. "Religious" nationalists are individuals and groups that combine Christian or Islamic beliefs with a desire for a separate state. And where "revolutionary" nationalists seek to topple capitalism, "cultural" nationalists hope to resist assimilation into Western modes of thought and practice. "Bourgeois" nationalists combine mild cultural pluralism with a politics that seeks expanded opportunities in American society, and "territorial" nationalists demand separate territory. Following this typology, the Nation of Islam stands as the most important religious nationalist organization of this century, while the Black Panther Party's self-described "revolutionary" nationalism represents the most significant organization of that variety. Especially during the Black Power era, bourgeois nationalists made a number of efforts to combine racially solidaristic efforts with electoral politics and capitalist schemes, and territorial nationalist organizations like the neo-Garveyite African Nationalist Pioneer Movement pushed for a black state.

In the context of the black freedom struggle of the 1960s, one in which nationalist groups often competed with one another, and one in which nationalists often used these sorts of designations themselves, this taxonomy makes sense. Nevertheless, this typology, as spelled out initially by Meier, Bracey, and Rudwick, conceals as much as it reveals. First, it obscures the fact that certain tendencies of black nationalism might be closer to certain tendencies of *white nationalism* than to other varieties of black nationalism. Garvey's UNIA stands out in this regard. So too does the NOI, as I will try to demonstrate in Chapter 7. Second, this typology is strained as an historiographical device: it obscures the time-bound character of black nationalist politics and thought.

Black nationalist activists and organizations operating in the 1960s and early 1970s can be more usefully divided into two general categories: those connected directly or indirectly to earlier organizations, and those that formed during or after the legal dismantling of Southern apartheid. Many black nationalist organizations in New York City fell into the former category.[5] Among these, the Nation of Islam stood as the largest. It led to a number of splinter groups, most significantly those started by the late Malcolm X. The Five Percenters was another splinter group, founded in 1963 by Father Allah, a one-time member of NOI Temple No. 7 in Harlem. "The name, Five Percenters, is derived from the NOI lesson that teaches that 85 percent of the African Americans are still asleep."[6] Five percent are the "poor righteous teachers," and another ten percent have been coopted by the white devils.[7]

Charles "Nwokeoji" Peaker led a Harlem-based neo-Garveyite organization, the African Nationalist Pioneer Movement (ANPM). Peaker succeeded the group's Dominican Republic–born founder, Carlos Cooks, as head of the organization following the latter's death in 1966. Cooks had served as an officer in Garvey's UNIA and continued to organize around the theme of "African nationalism" from the time of Garvey's deportation until his own death. After serving in World War II, Cooks for a time helped organize the Universal African Nationalist Movement, another group formed out of the old UNIA. This one was led by one Benjamin Gibbons for over twenty years. Other splinter groups included the Garvey Club, the United Sons and Daughters of Africa, and the First Africa Corps.[8]

The Harlem-based ANPM, like the UNIA of the early part of the twentieth century, wanted to relocate the black population of the entire

Western hemisphere to some site in Africa.[9] There, Americans of African descent could finish the business that Garvey had started: "The real leaders want a nation where black people would have opportunity to surpass the high standards of Europe and America." For the ANPM, repatriation offered the logical solution to the problem of race in the United States. Peaker reasoned that since black people's problems "began in Africa . . . [the problems] must ultimately end in Africa."[10] The group's motto, One Cause, One Goal, One Destiny, captured the essence of its difference from the UNIA: the organization carried a decidedly secular orientation, due to Cooks's atheism. This orientation, in fact, set it at odds with many other Garveyites of the period.[11]

Peaker, like Cooks, argued that the civil rights leadership worked for a goal – racial integration – that white Americans simply did not support, and in fact forcefully resisted. In Peaker's view, leaders who had promoted the goal of integration had inadvertently caused great suffering among black people across the country:

My brains are bulging with stories of rape, murder, stonings, lynchings, humiliation and frustration . . . [I]t is an established fact that the suffering they endure is caused directly by a small band of so-called leaders (integrationists) and a caste[12] group of parasitic merchants.

Rather than agitate for integration in the hope of sharing "in the blessings of the whiteman," black people in the United States needed to promote "self-determination" by controlling and extracting "the nectar of their segregated communities (as long as they sojourn in America) and above all, use their genius in acquiring permanent refuge in their motherland (Africa)."[13]

Peaker defined the group's nationalism as "African nationalism," modeled on those African nations that had demanded independence from their colonizers in Europe. Carlos A. Cooks, some years earlier, had defined African nationalism as:

The mobilization and unification of the masses of the black race on the continent of Africa and the stern introduction of self-government and self-determination to the black race for the attainment of firm nationhood . . . the advancement of African economic, social and political life . . . and thus the survival of the black race.[14]

Hence, their main goal was either to become part of one of these new nations, or to establish their own. Only by promoting self-determination of this sort could black people achieve true equality with respect to whites. Peaker further claimed that "African nationalism," the idea originally pursued by Marcus Garvey, had also influenced the rise of African nationalist movements on the continent. "The flames of GARVEYISM,"

Peaker wrote, "ignited the minds of blackmen AT HOME AND ABROAD."[15]

The long-term objectives of the organization included an ambitious eleven-point agenda:

1. To establish a world wide hegemony amongst the Black Race.
2. To reclaim the fallen, administer to and assist the needy.
3. To establish a cultural union with people of all Independent Black Nations and States.
4. To promote Pioneering in Africa by qualified Black Youths.
5. To promote the development of Independence of Black nations and communities.
6. To establish agencies in the principalities of the world where members of the race reside.
7. To promote a conscientious spiritual worship in keeping with the ethnological characteristics of the race.
8. To establish Universities, Colleges, Academies and schools for the racial education and culture of the people.
9. To conduct a world wide commercial and industrial intercourse for the good of the race.
10. To promote Economic self-sufficiency in Black communities.
11. To represent the race Locally, Nationally, and Internationally in all instances where the rights of the people of African descent are involved.[16]

The U.S. federal government would help realize this agenda by establishing the African Resettlement Bureau. After the president of the United States and the State Department had negotiated with various African countries and acquired land for the resettlement project, the bureau would fund the shipping of the black population back to Africa and also ensure that black crews manned these vessels. Finally, the resettlement bureau would build temporary housing and medical facilities.[17]

The ANPM's criticisms of integration as a goal echoed those of Garvey, and shadowed those of the NOI. Like the UNIA and the NOI, the ANPM opposed racial mixing and stood instead for racial purity. Like the Nation of Islam, Cooks and his followers argued that "house niggers" dominated the civil rights movement. "These scoundrels," Cooks maintained, "have no program to offer the masses of Black people . . . Ideologically, this band of parasites has a bastard complex which they dramatize whenever the opportunity presents itself."[18]

The Moorish American Science Temple (MAST) traced its roots to the organization originally founded by Noble Drew Ali in Newark. They considered themselves members of a separate nation and actual descendants of the Moors. Like the Nation of Islam, the followers of the Moorish American Science Temple practiced a variation of Islam. And, also like the Nation of Islam, they were opposed to racial mixing of any sort. As one spokesman explained:

We Moorish-Americans do not ask for social equality (Integration) with the European, because we, as a clean and pure nation descended from the inhabitants of Africa, do not desire to amalgamate or marry into the families of the pale skin nations of Europe. Neither do we serve the Gods of their religion, because our forefathers are the true and divine founders of the first religious creed for the redemption and salvation of mankind on earth.[19]

The Moorish American Science Temple's social and political agenda was also similar to the Nation of Islam's. They wished to construct an insulated community by building businesses, factories, hospitals, schools, recreational facilities and other institutions that could serve the needs of "Moorish-Americans."

According to John Henrik Clarke, the heirs to the earlier black nationalist groups were not the only interesting forms in which black nationalist organizations appeared during the late 1950s and early 1960s in New York City. A number of them, like the Yoruba Temple, turned away from Christianity and Islam and attempted to reclaim their African roots. The self-proclaimed priest of the Yoruba Temple of New Oyo (the new African name for Harlem) called for a "return not only to African religions, but to an African way of life in its entirety." For Priest Adenfunmi, it was essential to "Africanise everything!" Names, clothes, churches, "schools, home furnishings, businesses, holidays," and so forth. To not do so was "unnatural and degrading," since people of African descent continued "European customs and habits forced upon them during their enslavement."[20]

Priest Adenfunmi also founded the Alajo Party, which sought to "re-Africanize" black people in America. Unlike traditional African societies, where adolescents must learn the culture, history, and political aims of their nation, blacks in America grow old with "little or no knowledge of themselves or political aims to which they should aspire."[21] The Alajo Party began a school that sought to eradicate this problem. Members of this party were "adding new glory to the pageantry of West African civilization, as they sacrifice, not for barren integration or separation but to restore to Africans, born in America, the foundations of their cultural genius."

POST–APARTHEID ERA GROUPS

Adenfumni's organizational efforts foreshadowed those of Maulana Ron Karenga. Karenga, the son of a Baptist minister, organized US in Los Angeles in 1965. At the time Karenga held a master's degree in political science from UCLA. After becoming disillusioned with the integrationist project following the Watts riots of 1965, he created an organization that could facilitate nation building among black people. Karenga argued that blacks were "fighting a revolution to win the minds of black people ... Let me tell you, brothers and sisters, black people suffer because they have a lack of culture."[22] He thought that the struggle for integration was ultimately counter to the true political and psychological needs of the black American. As Karenga notes, his organization, US (as opposed to "them"), revolved "around the ideology and practice of *Kawaida*. The basic concepts of Kawaida centered around the contention that the key crisis in Black life is the crisis, i.e., a crisis in views and especially, values."[23]

Instead, Karenga offered black people a number of pseudo-African principles by which black people could reclaim and more deeply understand the culture and ways of life from which they had been estranged. Karenga's seven "Nguza Saba" principles included a number of codes which, when followed, furthered the cause of nation building. These principles formed the "value system" that the proto-nation badly needed. *Umoja* (unity) instructed Africans in America to "strive for and maintain unity in the family, community, nation and race." *Kujichagulia* (self-determination) encouraged black people to control the explanation of the meaning of black life and culture. *Ujima* (collective work and responsibility) required blacks to build communities that could solve problems collectively; and *Ujamaa* (cooperative economics) asked that black Americans "build and maintain ... shops and businesses and ... profit together from them." *Nia* (purpose) called on people of African descent to work together in order that the "traditional greatness" of African people could be restored. Finally, *Kuumba* (creativity) would capture the sense of artistic expression; and *Imani* (faith) instructed followers to have "[f]aith in your leaders, teachers, parents – but first faith in *Blackness* – that it will win."[24]

US members wanted to recapture African identity and tradition. The lack of identity and tradition explained both the misguided political goal of integration and a number of deep social problems – drugs, crime, poor self-image – that plagued the black population. Therefore, US frowned on alcohol consumption and drug use as "slave habits." US members could reflect their true selves by shaving their heads, wearing African clothing and wraps, and learning and speaking Swahili. Women could do their part in nation building by supporting the men and performing other duties that would help the black family and, by extension, the black nation: bearing and educating children, and taking care of the home. US frowned upon use of contraceptives.

Karenga's most significant convert and one-time supporter, Imamu Amiri Baraka (formerly LeRoi Jones), formed a number of organizations in Newark based on Karenga's teachings.[25] The Newark-born Baraka had been known prior to his conversion as the author of a number of literary works concerning black culture, including *Dutchman* (1964), *Tales* (1967), *The System of Dante's Hell* (1965), and *Home: Social Essays* (1966). Baraka became a follower of Karenga following a stay in California during the spring of 1967, at which time Baraka taught at San Francisco State College.[26] When Baraka returned to his native Newark he used the US organization as a model for a number of organizations.[27] Baraka's political efforts will be taken up in Chapter 5.

Black nationalism also came in socialist flavors, the most well-known being the Black Panther Party. Huey P. Newton and Bobby Seale founded the Black Panther Party in Oakland, California, in October 1966. The organization was initially named the Black Panther Party for Self-Defense, in recognition of the fact that they regularly patrolled the streets of Oakland in order to reduce incidents of police brutality. They subsequently dropped "for Self-Defense" after they broadened the range of their activities. Bobby Seale, the party chairman, presented a dramatic declaration of their position regarding self-defense at California's capitol building in Sacramento on May 2, 1967: "The Black Panther Party for Self-Defense believes that the time has come for Black people to arm themselves against this terror [fascist America] before it is too late."[28] The Panthers' statement came at a time when the California legislature was debating the Mulford Act, a bill designed to prohibit the carrying of firearms.

By 1968 the party moved toward Marxist Leninism; the ultimate goal of the organization was to topple capitalism in the United States, not to form an independent black nation within the United States. Hence, as they developed their agenda along Marxist-Leninist lines they became increasingly willing to form alliances with other nonblack political organizations. Their platform included items like full employment, decent housing, education that taught "true history," exemption from military service for black men, and an end to police brutality.

During the history of the organization, the central committee of the Black Panther Party included a constantly changing cast of activists. The national leaders included a longtime friend of Huey Newton, David Hilliard, as chief of staff, Don Cox as field marshal, and George Mason Murray and Raymond "Masai" Hewit as ministers of education. Kathleen Cleaver held the post of communications secretary, and Emory Douglas served as cartoonist and minister of culture. Eldridge Cleaver, whose writings about racism, Black Power, and the youth movement – *Soul on Ice* (1968) – had brought him notoriety, held the post of minister of information.[29] All directives originated in the central committee, largely from the mind of Huey Newton. In an essay titled "The Correct Handling of a Revolution," Newton explained that "[t]he primary job of the party" was "to provide leadership for the people."[30] Black people living in urban areas would eventually realize that unorganized rioting had limited utility. Instead, guerrilla activities could produce more immediate results. As a vanguard party, the Panthers would attempt to "raise the consciousness of the masses through educational programs and activities. The sleeping mass must be bombarded with the correct approach to struggle and the party must use all means available to get this information across to the masses."[31] David Hilliard explained that Marxist Leninism was applicable to any group that was moving to destroy capitalism.[32]

In retrospect, perhaps the most noteworthy program the Black Panther Party established was the Breakfast for Children program, which they operated in several cities. The liberation schools provided education for children who had attended notoriously inadequate public schools. The Panthers organized voter registration drives, ran for office, held community political education classes, and, of course, watched the "pigs" (the Panther's term for police). The Black Panther Party spread their ideas through a newspaper, *The Black Panther*, which they published weekly after April 1967.[33]

The Black Panther Party became a major target of police and FBI surveillance and even attack, and the success that the Panthers enjoyed in moderating police brutality in Oakland did not come as easily in other cities. The Los Angeles chapter, for instance, never had any success in curbing acts of police brutality. The Los Angeles Police Department regularly stopped and harassed members of the Black Panther Party. Police regularly beat Panthers, and the Panthers' central office in Los Angeles was attacked on a variety of occasions.[34] In Chicago, charismatic Panther leader Fred Hampton was assassinated, and numerous other Panthers were killed.

After several years of violent confrontation with police and with Eldridge Cleaver and Huey Newton in exile, the Black Panther Party underwent significant changes. The Panthers expelled Cleaver from the organization. While in exile, Cleaver claimed that he and his more militant faction represented the true revolutionary vanguard, whereas the central committee represented a reformist, "feed the children" thrust. In 1974, Elaine Browne took charge of the party, and under her leadership the Panthers expanded their Breakfast for Children programs, created a number of commercial ventures in order to generate money for the organization's programs, and improved the liberation schools, particularly the one in Oakland. Upon Newton's return from Cuba, Browne was eventually forced to leave the party, frustrated by the insubordination many male members showed to women in leadership roles. Browne's difficulties as a woman conform to general patterns of sexism and black nationalism during the 1960s.[35]

Despite the fact that the Panthers referred to themselves as "revolutionary nationalists," the Revolutionary Action Movement (RAM) is more accurately described as a "nationalistic" organization. Founded on a Garvey-like motto – One Purpose, One Aim, One Destiny – RAM originated in 1963 from the efforts of a number of college-educated and urban youth to form a black nationalist organization that would offer a "third force" – something between the Nation of Islam and the Student Nonviolent Coordinating Committee. Max Stanford explained the objectives:

1. To give black people a sense of racial pride, dignity, unity and solidarity in struggle.
2. To give black people a new image of manhood and womanhood.
3. To free black people from colonial and imperialist bondage everywhere and to take whatever steps necessary to achieve that goal.
4. To give black people a sense of purpose.[36]

Especially active in Philadelphia, RAM attempted a system of rotating chairmen in order to develop an experienced and politically confident leadership. Unlike other black nationalist organizations, RAM did not attempt to publicize its activities with the help of mainstream media.[37] Instead, in order to infuse "fresh, young and new ideas" into the black community, RAM published the bimonthly *Black America* and the weekly *RAM Speaks*. RAM also relied on a number of "street meetings" designed to introduce its program to as many people as possible – particularly to black youth. RAM directed its recruitment efforts at black youth of the inner cities, since to RAM this section of the population had the most revolutionary potential. Noting the ages of the soldiers of the Angolan liberation army, the Congolese guerrilla force called Youth, and the Mau Mau guerrillas, RAM felt that younger Afro-American males would be more open to the use of violence for political ends.

RAM defined these political ends as follows:

1. The African-American in the U.S. should demand independent Black nationhood and take the U.S. government to the world court, the United Nations, and bring international indictment against the U.S. for its violation of Human Rights and racial war crimes of Genocide. 2. Black people in the U.S. must demand independent Black Nationhood (Land) and Reparations (repayment for racial crimes committed by the U.S. government).

Max Stanford elaborated this plan in a press release dated April 17, 1968, just after King's assassination: "We must fight for independence and nationhood . . . [by] . . . demanding an independent Black nation from the land that is rightfully ours: Mississippi, Louisiana, Alabama, Georgia, Florida, Texas, Virginia, South Carolina and North Carolina."[38]

An essential component of RAM's strategy, evident in their recruitment ideas, involved guerrilla warfare. If the federal government would not meet their demands, this would be the tactic of last resort. This position derived in part from the organized self-defense ideas of Robert Williams and Malcolm X. We have already examined Malcolm X's ideas about self-defense.[39] Max Stanford built his guerrilla warfare plan on the basis of Williams's strategies.

Max Stanford and RAM were confident that such tactics, once carefully orchestrated, could debilitate and ultimately overthrow the government of the United States. Stanford looked to slave revolts of the eighteenth and nineteenth centuries for guidance and inspiration, and wanted to "follow in the spirit of black revolutionaries" like Denmark Vesey, Harriet Tubman, Marcus Garvey, W. E. B. Du Bois, and others.[40]

Richard and Milton Henry (Brother Imari Abubakari Obadele and Gaidi Obadele) founded another socialistic nationalist organization, the Republic of New Africa, in Detroit in March of 1968.[41] The Henrys in 1967 had helped to found the Malcolm X Society, which encouraged self-defense and Pan-African solidarity. The Republic of New Africa combined aggressive "revolutionary" strategies with demands for separate territory – the states of Alabama, Georgia, South Carolina, Louisiana, and Mississippi – and calls for African socialism and cultural forms. Milton Henry based his call for separate territory not only on the notion that integration was undesirable, but also on the grounds that allegedly "innate, deeply rooted part[s] of nature of all loving species" wished to secure land for survival. It was not, according to Henry, "normal" for a person to "not have some inner desire to control the land or the house in which he must live." Like the NOI, the neo-Garveyites, and US, Henry repeated the idea that blacks had been robbed of their historical sense of identity: "the enslaver intended these captured men and women . . . to forget and despise their languages and tribal identities." The "end-product" was the "Negro."[42]

When the Henrys founded the RNA, they designated Robert F. Williams as provisional president. Milton R. Henry would serve as vice president, and Richard would serve as minister of information. After a convention of several hundred nationalists who supported their aims, the RNA claimed to function as the provisional government of Afro-Americans. They intended to purchase one hundred acres of land in Mississippi, which would serve as headquarters for the organization, and as a site for a number of cooperative and collective farms. Members of the RNA would operate the farms on the principles of *Ujamaa*, a variety of African socialism. Julius K. Nyerere, then president of Tanzania and architect of this doctrine of African socialism, explained *Ujamaa* thus:

The foundation, and objective of African socialism is one of extended family. The true African socialist does not look on one class of men as his brethren and another as his natural enemies. He rather regards *all* men as his brethren – as members of his ever-extending family. *Ujamaa,* then, or familyhood, describes our socialism.[43]

Further, according to Nyerere, the concept of *Ujamaa* was not learned from the West but reflected traditional African practices.

The Henrys believed that eventually the black population in the territories where the RNA existed would exceed the white population, leading to ultimate national autonomy. When black people outnumbered whites they could outvote them. But if this takeover did not occur peacefully and without resistance from the federal government, the RNA also had an elaborate guerrilla warfare strategy. They figured that separatist politics usually required bloodshed. This truth appeared to be borne out in the history of the United States. In both the Revolutionary War and the Civil War, rebels' demands for sovereignty were met with force.

The organization's only significant activities involved violent confrontations with the police. In fact, the repercussions from these confrontations helped drive the organization to extinction. One such confrontation occurred with Detroit police in March of 1969. In this conflict, one police officer died, and several RNA members were injured. Police subsequently arrested the Henry brothers. In September 1969, Robert Williams returned to the United States only to resign as president. According to Raymond Hall, Williams's resignation signaled a change in his ideology as a result of his stay in Cuba. There Williams had learned that socialism – at least Castro's variety – did not offer an appropriate analysis of racism and black nationalism in the United States. Williams returned believing that black people could work "within the system" in order to effect change.

Differences between the Henry brothers over tactics created further problems for the RNA. Where Brother Imari argued that the RNA must immediately purchase land in Mississippi, Brother Gaidi thought this plan asked for trouble: purchasing the amount of land that the RNA required would invite scrutiny and harassment from the authorities. Further, where Imari argued that the RNA needed a defensive force of 100,000, Gaidi believed that nationhood would come only when blacks used the ballot. The organization split in 1970 as a result of the brothers' differences. Brother Gaidi suspended Brother Imari, and each brother subsequently led a faction.

In 1971 the RNA was found guilty of attempting to take a Mississippi farmer's land. In August of that same year, Brother Imari was charged with "conspiracy to murder, an assault on a federal officer, and violation of a Mississippi 'treason' law which carried the death sentence."[44] Imari was convicted.

By the mid-1970s, the RNA's strategy moved along more Pan-Africanist lines. In 1979, for instance, the leader of the RNA urged the countries of OPEC to increase their oil prices and redirect the revenue into efforts to establish an "African Peoples Economic Congress," which would represent some 50,000 people of African descent. The RNA hoped that this congress would function as the supreme lawmaking, research, and military body "for the entire continent of Africa."[45]

SNCC AND CORE

For the simple reason that neither was founded as a nationalist organization, the Student Nonviolent Coordinating Committee (SNCC) and the Congress for Racial Equality (CORE) are two organizations that fit uneasily into my discussion of modern black nationalism. Nevertheless, I include these organizations because they became black nationalist with the emergence of Black Power.

Formed in 1960, SNCC became an all-black organization in 1966. Initially, SNCC's interracial membership used nonviolent tactics for political empowerment and integration of blacks in the South. Among numerous other efforts, SNCC had led the challenge against the Mississippi all-white delegation to the 1964 Democratic National Convention by helping to organize the Mississippi Freedom Democratic Party (MFDP). Their failure to move the Democratic Party, coupled with recurring physical and psychological assaults by whites determined to intimidate and obstruct black voters, forced many SNCC members to rethink their basic positions.[46] Further, a number of younger black SNCC activists questioned the roles – especially leadership ones – of white activists in SNCC.

The group that most projected the new nationalism of SNCC worked on the staff of the Atlanta Project. By the mid-1960s this group had begun to rethink SNCC's philosophy of nonviolent change and its goal of racial integration. Analyzing the previous failure of the civil rights movement, the Atlanta Project staff drew on ideas from Malcolm X and Frantz Fanon to formulate a separatist agenda that would increase SNCC's effectiveness. According to this faction, political efforts, even when militant, could not transform "the black community's racial consciousness," a prerequisite, in their view, to true empowerment. SNCC also needed to promote "racial values distinct from those of the surrounding society." They hoped to "encourage in blacks a sense of pride."[47] In the retooling of SNCC, the Atlanta Project staff argued that whites should not participate for two reasons. First, the presence of whites prohibited the fullest range of discussion and action because black members feared the relative power white members had with respect to black members. In the end, they reasoned, whites still had access to power that blacks did not. Second, many members believed that whites' presence during organizational drives only contributed to ideas of Western superiority.

Like SNCC, the Congress of Racial Equality (CORE) also began as an interracial, nonviolent protest organization aimed at achieving integration in urban ghettoes and the rural South.[48] However, in *Freedom – When?* (1966), CORE's leader, James Farmer, articulated the new politics CORE would pursue. Farmer articulated a number of changes, the first of which removed CORE's nonpartisan status. He also promoted the idea of developing cooperatives and suggested the need for "community development" as a means of promoting self-help among ghetto dwellers."[49] Still, it was Roy Innis's ascension as leader of CORE that signaled the moment of full ideological change to black nationalism.[50] In a paper delivered at a 1968 convention, Innis explained that Black Power was "the methodology for the implementation of the goals of black nationalism"[51] and suggested that black people pursue "liberation by any means necessary." In response to a number of critics who charged that Black Power amounted to segregation – that same evil so many had fought and died to abolish – Innis drew a distinction between racial separation and segregation. Segregation resulted from a system of governance where blacks were concentrated in specific areas but lacked control over public institutions – police, housing, schools, businesses, and so forth. Black nationalism as a form of voluntary racial separation required power to be decentralized, with black people controlling "separate but equal" parallel institutions.[52]

In this paper Innis delineated an "economic theory of nationhood" that explained CORE's subsequent efforts to link the takeover of blacks in economic, political, and social institutions for the purpose of fostering the economic development of black communities. For instance, Innis suggested that once black people controlled the schools in their communities, black companies could be established to provide school supplies. Driven by this basic idea, CORE unsuccessfully sought to create a Harlem school system that had no connection to New York City's Board of Education. CORE was successful, however, in convincing city officials to allow Harlem to run its own hospital. CORE also attempted to develop farm cooperatives. Each of these efforts, CORE hoped, would establish greater and greater autonomy for black inner-city residents across the country. This increasing autonomy would establish the basis for ultimate separation, independence, and a rewriting of the Constitution.

Aided by Senator Robert F. Kennedy, CORE helped to introduce two bills in Congress in 1968: the Community Self-Development Act and the Rural Development Incentive Act. The Community Self-Development Act would have established a National Community Corporation Certification Board intended to "encourage the development of the local community corporations, monitor their organization procedures, and issue charters." The Rural Development Incentive Act was meant to create incentives for the establishment of job-producing industrial and commercial firms in rural areas.[53] Unfortunately for CORE, these bills were not passed.

GENERAL SIMILARITIES

A number of points stand out with respect to the groups just considered, especially when we juxtapose these versions of black nationalism to earlier varieties. Like those of earlier times, modern nationalists' arguments grew more prominent in reaction to white nationalism. The often violent resistance to desegregation efforts, the complicity of the Democratic Party with conservative practices of the South, and the failure of the civil rights movement to open housing and labor markets in the North triggered black nationalism in the 1960s and early 1970s.

Differences from earlier black nationalism stemmed from a historical context that brought together a different tangle of forces – social, political, and intellectual – that informed the style of nationalist politics and thought of the 1960s and early 1970s. The general orientation toward African culture reflected the extent to which, beginning with Ghana in 1959, African nationalist movements served as models for Afro-American nationalists. Nationalists also formulated their positions with respect to governmental policies tied to civil rights, economic justice, and the Vietnam War. Of particular importance to nationalists' efforts in the 1960s were the riots that ripped the urban landscape. These "rebellions" of the late 1960s suggested that the era of nonviolence in black politics was over.

In nearly all of the organizations we have considered thus far, the ghost of Malcolm X loomed large. With the exception of groups like the NOI, the African Nationalist Pioneer Movement, and the Moorish American Science Temple – organizations whose nationalism had preceded the civil rights movement – the slain leader served as a symbol of militant black nationalist politics. Again, as we considered in the previous chapter, the meaning of Malcolm X's politics could be interpreted in support of a wide range of positions. The Republic of New Africa looked to Malcolm X as a source of inspiration despite the fact that Malcolm

X never seriously proposed any sort of guerrilla warfare strategy. He did speak of the need for self-defense; and he did refer to the efforts of Mau Mau forces in Kenya. However, much of his discourse about violence was rhetorical, as he had no intention of actually waging war. Nevertheless, a tenor of militancy characterized nearly all of the nationalist groups of this period. Most had defense groups like the Nation of Islam's Fruit of Islam. Many had arms.

The groups and activists shared with previous nationalists their tendency to rely on "race" as their principal category of analysis, with, of course, the exception of the Panthers. From this organic model, nationalist activists assumed that the race's interests were one, thus glossing over the very heterogeneous character of the black population in the United States, and the strategic and analytic implications that grow out of such a recognition.

Nation building thus generally took place without regard to how discrimination along gender lines might function to the disadvantage of women. Within the mostly male nationalist organizations, women did not typically have leadership roles, except when their roles involved traditional gender duties. The Nation of Islam and Karenga's organization are the most notable in this regard. Groups like US defined female "virtue" as "interdependence" and "femininity" as submissiveness. Both US and the Nation of Islam thought they would secure women's virtue in the context of patriarchal family structures. Reflecting on gender relations in US, Baraka notes that "Karenga's doctrine made male chauvinism a revolutionary legitimacy . . . When brothers (male members) went by, the women were supposed to 'salimu' or 'submit,' crossing their arms on their breasts and bowing slightly."[54] But these problems were also evident in revolutionary organizations like the Black Panther Party.

"Modern" black nationalists all responded to integration-as-assimilation, a notion that had certainly less meaning, perhaps none, for Garvey and nationalists who came before him. Unlike, say, Karenga, Garvey did not operate in a context where "integration" enjoyed legal sanction. And while Garvey worried about assimilation-as-race-mixing, he did not reject Western culture. Modern black nationalism all across the political spectrum rejected Western and Euro-American values, and had a more favorable appraisal of African culture as part of its "pro-black" sense of identity. Gone were the interests in civilizing or Christianizing a heathen African population. From the 1960s vantage point, African culture could provide guidelines for black conduct. Unlike nationalists of earlier times, modern black nationalists – again with the exception of the Panthers – saw indigenous African cultures not as something in need of Western revamping, but as folkways of a distinctly non-Western way of life worth emulating. To a large extent, these views were extensions of the organic model, wherein blacks were connected not only by color, but also by culture.

Most of these organizations also had in common intense scrutiny by J. Edgar Hoover's COINTELPRO, a government operation designed to infiltrate and undermine radical activity. It proved to be very effective. Agents did in fact infiltrate the organizations, stirring dissension and proposing ridiculous plans (like blowing up the Statue of Liberty). Leaders of the Black Panther Party and the Republic of New Africa were harassed, murdered, and convicted on a variety of counts. Indeed, the FBI, perhaps more than anything else, effectively undermined the various organizations.

These various groups shared one additional feature. It was not only FBI action that undermined their effectiveness. By fashioning nationalist theories in the manner that they did – highly abstract and elaborate – these organizations limited their own effectiveness in building a broader base of membership. Theories like *Kawaida*, and "revolutionary" paradigms like those offered by RNA were several steps removed from the more mundane issues of concern to the average black citizen. As aids to recruitment, these paradigms largely failed.

DIFFERENCES

At one point, SNCC and the Black Panther Party were interested in merging, and in fact they did enter into a short-lived "alliance." However, this alliance "ended a few months later in angry verbal exchanges and near-violence."[55] Before this moment, however, many of the two groups' views converged. Both advocated anticolonial struggle. Both thought that this struggle might require violence, and both expressed anticapitalist sentiments. According to Robert Allen, the memberships differed in age, with the SNCC members generally being older and better educated. With SNCC's demise a number of its former members – many of whom had been quite prominent – joined the Black Panther Party.

The Black Panther Party supported the efforts of the Republic of New Africa, but differed on the issues of separate territory and interracial alliances. The Panthers felt that the Republic of New Africa was "perfectly justified in demanding and declaring the right to secede from the union."[56] However, Newton argued that a black state proximate to the United States would still be at a major disadvantage. The Panthers therefore wished to overthrow the U.S. government.

The rivalry between Karenga's organization and the Black Panther Party proved deadly. In 1968 Newton explained what he thought was wrong with "cultural nationalism" or, in his view, "pork chop" nationalism:

It seems to be a reaction to, instead of an action against, political o[...]
The cultural nationalists are concerned with returning to the old African cultu[...]
and thereby regaining their identity and freedom. In other words they feel that
assuming the African culture is enough to bring political freedom. Many cultural
nationalists fall into line as reactionary nationalists.[57]

Linda Harrison of the East Oakland office of the Black Panthers also
summarized their position:

Cultural nationalism manifests itself in many ways but all of these manifestations are essentially grounded in one fact: a universal denial and ignoring of the
present political, social, and economic realities and the concentration on the past
as a frame of reference . . . And cultural nationalism is most always based on
racism. We hear 'Hate Whitey' and 'Kill the Honkey' . . . In all cases cultural
nationalism in the midst of struggle seeks to create a racist ideology.[58]

On the other hand, Ron Karenga and US rejected Marxist Leninism.
Karenga stated that "[a] lot of brothers play revolutionary; they read a
little Fanon, a little Mao, and a little Marx. Although this information
is necessary, it is not sufficient, for we must develop a new plan of revolution for Black people here in America." "There must be a cultural
revolution before the violent revolution. The cultural revolution gives
identity, purpose, and direction." Baraka added that the Panthers' tactics
were misguided. "When groups say 'Pick up the gun' that the devil will
wither up and die, or just by picking up that literal gun, without training, using the same sick value system of the degenerate slave master, the
same dope, the same liquor, the same dying hippie mentality, they will
liberate all the slave peoples of the world. NO."[59] Indeed, while
Karenga's later formulations would draw on socialistic ideas, his late
1960s pronouncements rejected the idea of class struggle.

  This rivalry turned deadly in Los Angeles. A member of US murdered
two Panthers, Aprentice "Bunchy" Carter and John Huggins, on UCLA's
campus. The Panthers were supporting the black students against
Karenga, who had assumed leadership of the new black studies program.
Bunchy was leader of the Los Angeles "underground" Panther forces.
This murder precipitated a number of shoot-outs between the Panthers
and US in the southern California area.

CONCLUSION

While the goals of the organizations differed in important ways, the
groups and spokespersons also agreed on a number of matters. The most
significant points of agreement were that integration as a goal was problematic, and that the civil rights leadership had not formulated strategies
that reflected the dire conditions of black life, especially in urban centers.
Nearly all of these groups criticized the method of nonviolence because

it depended too much upon the sympathy of white America. Fin
males predominated. They dominated the leadership; and, not
prisingly in retrospect, they did not formulate strategies for wom
empowerment.

All of the organizations we have considered had cultural components
Many of the groups incorporated ritual into their activities. While this
ritual was more evident in groups like US and Black Community Development, it was also evident in the Nation of Islam, the RNA, and the
Black Panther Party. As we will consider more fully in the following
chapter, most black nationalists assumed, like Mao, that artistic production should advance the cause of revolution.

Further, many of these organizations' strategies shifted across time.
The RNA eventually divided over the matter of appropriate tactics for
changing American society. Following the death or imprisonment of
many members of the Black Panther Party, the organization directed
more efforts toward their schools and their Breakfast for Children
program. The Panthers also became increasingly interested in forming
alliances with other revolutionary groups. Finally, with the exception of
the Nation of Islam, the African Nationalist Pioneer Movement, and the
Moorish American Science Temple, most groups developed critiques of
capitalism.

The following chapter will explore more deeply the character of
modern black nationalism by exploring a number of key themes – black
nationalism and Black Power, black nationalist traditions, and black
culture – that activists discussed in relation to the project of nation building. These themes and the premises that underlay them echoed in the
headquarters of black nationalist organizations, on the streets, and in the
academy. What's more, a dialectical relationship existed between these
ideas and black nationalist activism: the ideas worked to legitimize black
nationalism as an authentic, nationalistic politics; the existence of black
nationalist activism legitimized and generated further ideas.

4

Black Nationalist Discourse

Modern black nationalism as theory and practice benefited from an out-pouring of discourse concerning the theme, both by and about sup-porters of black nationalism. This discourse emanated mainly from two sources. First, during the decade of the 1960s, scholars produced a large number of articles and books on the subject of black nationalism. Schol-ars like Robert S. Browne, James Turner, and others offered analysis and commentary concerning the meaning and desirability of a nationalist agenda. Generally they sought to identify black nationalist politics and thought as a legitimate variety of nationalism that had appeared in other historical and geographical contexts. Economists, political scientists, sociologists, historians, and others tackled the difficult problem of char-acterizing the meaning and identifying the causes of black nationalism of the 1960s.

In addition to scholarship produced by members of the academy, a number of "paraintellectuals" – critics outside the academic profession like Malcolm X, Amiri Baraka, and Eldridge Cleaver – discoursed prolifically on the topic of black nationalism.[1] This discourse, which included speeches, poetry, novels, books and articles, signaled the appearance of an essentially new and increasingly important stratum of intellectuals who spoke and wrote about black politics, but who did not necessarily originate from the black middle class. For paraintellectuals involved in political organizations, identifying black nationalism as an authentic nationalism had its purposes: it allowed easy comparison to other Third World – especially African – nationalisms; it challenged the view of integration-as-assimilation; and it placed black nationalism on the cutting edge of radical politics and thought. Of the two groups, paraintellectuals figured more prominently in terms of volume. Through speeches, press conferences, plays, poetry, books and articles, and so forth, black nationalism as an idea reached a black popular audience. Black nationalists could then offer analyses that responded to black powerlessness and the apparent failure of nonviolent integration. The Nation of Islam's *Muhammad Speaks*, the Revolutionary Action Movement's *RAM Speaks*, the Black Panther Party's *The Black Panther*, and journals like the *Liberator, Black World*, the *Black Journal of Poetry*, and the *Black Scholar* served as outlets for this sort of intellectual output.

Martin Kilson argues that the development of this new stratum of black thinkers meant that "intellectual activity [was] found more and more on the street corner, among popular groups with charismatic leaders, or in community organizations." Further, and more importantly, the development of paraintellectuals "led to the pressure for nationalism or separatism" because their discourse played a greater role in disseminating and legitimating black nationalism as a paradigm.[2] Activists often had a wider audience, and they wielded greater influence over a younger, largely urban, and mostly northern constituency. In the aftermath of the riots of the 1960s, paraintellectuals came to represent an "authentic" voice of the black masses, and an alternative vision to that of the dominant middle-class civil rights leadership. In short, paraintellectuals determined what would count as black nationalism.

Taken together, the sheer volume of discourse, coupled with the repetition of key themes, legitimized the idea of black people as a kind of nation. Although different types of intellectuals produced studies and commentary concerning black nationalism, they all explored similar ideas: (1) that black nationalism rejected integration-as-assimilation; (2) that black nationalism was a tradition with "roots" in earlier times; (3) that the black population was a colony (or something like one); and (4) that, like other national communities, Afro-Americans had distinct cultural characteristics. These ideas served as criteria that helped to establish black nationalism as more than the stance of political extremists, but rather as a position rooted in U.S. history and similar to nationalisms advanced by people of color worldwide.

This discourse had another unintended effect: it obscured the fundamentally *American* epistemological premises that undergirded thinking about black life. It hid a set of assumptions about black cultural identity, and views of political power and social mobility – what I call the "ethnic paradigm" – that had academic and popular inflections. I will explore these assumptions more fully in Chapter 6.[3]

CHARACTERIZING BLACK NATIONALISM AND BLACK POWER

Generally, "black nationalism" defined a style of politics and thought that stood opposed to integration-as-assimilation. Beyond this basic position, however, definitions of black nationalism offered by advocates for and students of black nationalism from the 1960s on varied widely. Spokespersons for black nationalism crafted definitions geared toward a programmatic agenda. For instance, when Malcolm X launched his Organization for Afro-American Unity in 1964, he defined black nationalism as control over economic and political institutions; he offered no more elaborate definition than this.

RAM leader Max Stanford delineated a fairly broad notion of black nationalism. His revolutionary black nationalism reflected an ideology opposed to "white nationalism" – meaning the conspiracy of Western nations to maintain dominance over Third World nations – by creating a "consciousness of our own kind of self." Stanford suggested that black nationalism liberates and frees from exploitation and that it was "the binding force of a nation or particular group to free itself from a group or nation that is suppressing or oppressing it."[4] We know from RAM's willingness to resort to guerrilla tactics that his "revolutionary" nationalism rejected nonviolent methods.

Another writer described black nationalism as "a truthful and sincere involvement by black people with the total experience of black people in American culture. This 'soul syndrome' or black syndrome entails a commitment to the total black experience of its aspects." This writer felt that a new nationalism would emerge that could supersede the nationalism of then-existing programs like those offered by the Nation of Islam. A new black nationalist vanguard aware of the "myth of assimilation" and the impossibility of integration, and conscious of the failure of black leadership, would develop a program more in tune with the needs of a broader Afro-American population.[5]

Christian minister Albert B. Cleage, Jr., explained his use of the term "Black Christian Nationalism" as a nationalism that "demands that Black people accept Black leadership and Black institutions and delegate to them power and authority."[6] For Reverend Cleage, black nationalism meant revolutionary change regarding notions about the Christian faith.

Two scholars, James Turner and Alphonso Pinkney, offered more elaborate definitions. Turner suggested that black nationalism reflected the "desire of Afro-Americans to decide their own destiny through control of their own political organizations and the formation and preservation of their cultural, economic, and social institutions." Further, black nationalism stood opposed to white supremacy and in favor of group unity and racial pride. Lastly, black nationalism involved a "revaluation of 'self,' and relationship with the dominant group and the social system in general, and a shifting frame of reference (Africa and 'Blackism' become significant referents) and change in perspective."[7] Alphonso Pinkney concurred. Black nationalist groups, in his view, all promoted black solidarity, pride in cultural heritage, and self-determination.[8]

Of the key terms connected to the development of black nationalism during the 1960s, none was more dramatic, none struck deeper chords, than the term "Black Power." Stokely Carmichael introduced the nation to this term at a march in 1966. His militant rhetoric captured the sentiment that moved groups like SNCC and CORE toward all-black membership. Black Power became synonymous with black nationalism, and was also used by spokespersons to convey a variety of meanings. One writer claimed that each letter of "POWER" stood for something connected to empowerment. The P stood for persistence.[9] O was for the organizing necessary for gaining power. W represented Whitey, who had all the power. E stood for effort, and the R in POWER stood for results. Black Arts poet and critic Larry Neal described Black Power as "a synthesis of all of the nationalistic ideas embedded within the double consciousness of black America. But it has no one specific meaning. It is rather a kind of feeling – a kind of emotional response to one's history."[10] And Julius Lester, in his *Look Out, Whitey! Black Power's Gon' Get Your Mamma!* (1969), explained Black Power as:

the ideology for the confrontation. It is a formulation of black nationalism in the tradition of Nat Turner and Malcolm X. And it says, like the song the old folks used to sing about Samson (undoubtedly thinking of others than Samson), "If I had my way, I'd tear this building down."[11]

For Lester, Black Power also defined a politics opposed to integration and one urgently demanding autonomy and self-determination for black communities. It represented a philosophy more willing to employ militancy as a tactical weapon, inspired by often violent anticolonial efforts in Africa and other parts of the Third World.[12]

A few things stand out with regard to the definitions we considered above. First, in their breadth, these definitions allowed an enormous range of thought and behavior. Such matters as black consciousness, black control of institutions, and the symbolic meaning of Africa constituted the meaning of black nationalism for scholars and activists alike. These definitions were often not contingent to any specific historical period. Further, these notions were highly abstract and, as such, able to accommodate quite disparate content. Nevertheless, "modern" nationalists of both the "cultural" and more the "socialist" varieties shared a rejection of the goal of integration and hoped to maintain and foster cultural distinctiveness.

INTEGRATION VERSUS NATIONALISM

Black nationalist arguments rested on a revised, two-part narrative of the past. One, hardly new but nevertheless amplified by the Nation of Islam and groups like the Yoruba Temple and US, argued that slavery had robbed Africans of their identity. Slavemasters had changed Africans' names and religions, and thus severed connections with the past. In

1963 an editorial in the nationalist *Liberator* made this same basic
point:

Why should we study Negro History Week? . . . Well, for one thing, when our
ancestors were brought to this country as slaves . . . their white masters
attempted to condition them for enslavement during a period of "breaking in"
– a calculated dehumanization. An essential part of this process was the violent
uprooting of every trace of history and culture which would give a man dignity,
self-respect and a will to resist. This process continued through the years of
slavery with the result that the history and culture of the African immigrants to
America was either completely eliminated or . . . distorted out of all recognition,
thus clearing the way to establish the ideology of white supremacy.[13]

Only an analysis of this sort could reveal the lingering effects of slavery
and the real reason black people could not progress: the crisis of Afro-
American cultural and political identity.

A follow-up to this initial point observed that the crisis of political and
cultural identity manifested itself in an historical and ongoing tension
between two desires: one to integrate, one to separate. Social critic Harold
Cruse offered perhaps the most significant defense of this basic interpretation. In a number of articles published during the early to mid-1960s
Cruse laid out many of the arguments that would eventually form his
massive *Crisis of the Negro Intellectual* (1967). In this and earlier works
Cruse insisted that black politics had historically pivoted between integrationist and nationalist positions. The origins of black political developments during the 1960s were "to be found in the nationalist vs.
integrationist Frederick Douglass–Martin R. Delany–Booker T. Washington–W.E.B. DuBois conflicts through the 1920's."[14] In Cruse's view, black
leadership had not come to grips with the basic fact that all previous great
black leaders had supported black nationalism at one time or another, in
one form or another. Hence, the contemporary civil rights movement, in
Cruse's view, could not "become revolutionary until it [articulated] objectives which transcend its present aim – racial integration."[15]

Many other writers advanced similar claims about the historical
dichotomy between integrationists and nationalists. Francis L.
Broderick's "The Gnawing Dilemma: Separatism and Integration,
1865–1925" also characterized the history of people of African descent
as pivoting between the impulse to integrate and the need to separate:
"while white Americans created the conditions of the struggle, black
Americans, responding to the challenges of manhood and citizenship,
ranged the gamut from integration to separation in quest of an identity
that offered more than merely technical physical freedom."[16]

Uncovering this alleged historical dichotomy provided a firm historical basis for a nationalistic impulse in black politics. Indeed, Robert S.

Browne based his case for a separatist agenda on his understanding of the historical integrationist/nationalist dichotomy. Interestingly, Browne provided the basic ideological framework around which the RNA formulated its politics. Browne's view, carefully elaborated in an article that appeared in *The New York Times Magazine*, "The Case for Two Americas – One Black, One White," suggested that "a growing ambivalence among Negroes" that was "creating a great deal of confusion . . . within the black community . . . and within . . . segments of the white community . . . arose from the question of whether American Negroes are a cultural group significantly distinct from the majority on an ethnic rather than a socio-economic basis."[17]

For Browne, competing historical interpretations led integrationists and nationalists to answer this question differently. Integrationists believed that differences between blacks and whites were minimal and transitory. The integrationist, Browne argued, believed that black Americans wanted essentially what white Americans wanted – "that is to be 'in' in American society." This meant having access to jobs, housing, and education enjoyed by the white majority. This desire stemmed from the basic fact that blacks had been affected by a process of "Europeanization." Former Africans had been forced to abandon their traditional lifestyles and adopt the vestiges of European civilization.[18]

On the other hand, nationalists believed that the Europeanization was incomplete: "Whereas the integrationist more or less accepts the destruction of the original culture of the African slaves as a fait accompli – whether he feels it to have been morally reprehensible or not – the separatist is likely to harbor a vague resentment toward the whites for having perpetrated this cultural genocide." From their perspective, black people were and ought to remain distinct from the mainstream.[19]

Separatists felt that access to opportunity was not the central concern of the black masses. Rather, their greatest need was one of "spirit": the black man "must have an opportunity to reclaim his group individuality and have that individuality recognized as equal with other major cultural groups in the world."[20] Browne's political agenda was clear: formal partitioning of the United States into "two totally separate and independent nations, one white and one black."[21] In this manner, blacks could establish a separate polity that reflected their distinct, and historically determined, set of cultural values. Browne pointed out that the huge costs involved in such a partition could not outweigh the tragic costs of continued and intensified racial strife.

BLACK NATIONALIST TRADITIONS

If Afro-American politics had always consisted of two basic themes – integration and nationalism – it stood to reason that certain members of the black population had always understood themselves as constituting a nation. In "The Emergence of Black National Consciousness in America," Earl Ofari offered this view. Ofari claimed that the "ideological root of the Black movement has been, and still remains, black national consciousness" and that two strains of this consciousness have been ever-present in black thought: "Africa-consciousness and Black liberation in America."[22] He defended this contention by providing an historical account that explored the meaning of Africa for Afro-Americans. For some, Africa offered a symbol of ancient glory. Ofari quoted black abolitionist David Nickens, who stated in 1832:

Let those who accuse us of inferiority, as it respects our intellect and structure, look through the dark vista of past ages, and read in the history of Hannibal and others, who were Africans, the strength of intellect, the soundness of judgment, the military skill, which existed in Ancient Africa . . . From Egypt the arts of civilization were carried into Greece, and from Greece to Europe; therefore all the now civilized world is indebted to sable Africa for the arts of civilization and learning.[23]

According to Ofari, by the 1830s black organizing had already begun "to assume a national character." Black people organized conventions to formulate tactics designed to combat the problems of racism and slavery. They also debated "over the question of whites in the Black movement."[24] A more dramatic moment of national consciousness, however, occurred at a convention in 1843. At that convention what "really set off the debate . . . was a speech delivered by Garnet . . . in Buffalo . . . In the Speech, Garnet, evoking the memory of proud African and Afro-American warriors from Joseph Cinque to Nat Turner, called for the slaves of America to rise up and kill their masters . . . From his speech's content, it must rank in history as one of the most forceful examples of Black revolutionary nationalism." As evidence of national consciousness, Ofari also detailed the numerous organizations during the mid-1850s that had "Africa" and "Liberia" in their titles. The African Civilization Society, for instance, wished to "open up social and commercial ties between Africa and Afro-America." The society's constitution advanced the idea of a "principle of an African nationality" that could direct its own affairs.[25]

Another way of describing an historically recurring black national consciousness is simply to say that black nationalism represented a longstanding political tradition. Intellectuals and paraintellectuals made this claim. We saw that RAM made allusions to tradition as a rhetorical move when Sanford identified a number of historical figures as symbols of revolutionary nationalism. Black Arts activist Larry Neal claimed that Black Power sprouted from the "ideas and persons who preceded it":

The forerunners of the current movement were such nineteenth-century thinkers as David Walker, Edward Blyden, and Martin Delany. The movement takes its revolutionary zeal from Gabriel Prosser and Nat Turner. It takes its Third World outlook from W. E. B. Du Bois, Marcus Garvey, Malcolm X, and Frantz Fanon. And on its weaker side, it takes its economic and institutional philosophy from Booker T. Washington.[26]

Milton Henry drew lines connecting Henry Highland Garnet to Marcus Garvey, Elijah Muhammad, Malcolm X, and finally to the RNA. Frederick Douglass, W. E. B. Du Bois, Martin Luther King, Jr., and Bayard Rustin could be connected by an integrationist strand. The nationalist tradition, though, reflected the views of those activists "whose spirits have tingled with the very thought of self-determination and land."[27]

Many others advanced this claim as well. In his "Black Nationalism: An Integral Tradition," Rodney Carlisle argued that "Black nationalists worked within an integral tradition that has as much vitality and continuity as the liberal or the radical tradition in American life." Carlisle maintained that blacks in the United States "developed a movement that was nationalistic in the same sense that some European minority movements were nationalistic." They did this, according to Carlisle, by developing "a set of ideas, styles of involvement, doctrines, and specific plans which have been unique to Black nationalism and which repeatedly emerged in the tradition." Black nationalism during the nineteenth century proved to be a viable political force: "*political Black nationalism aiming at the creation of a Black state or nation was not a fantasy, but in fact had considerable impact in the creation of towns, migration movements, institutions, and nations.*"[28]

Carlisle then delineated a genealogy through which he attempted to demonstrate the influence of black nationalist figures and organizations on subsequent figures and organizations. The story began with Massachusetts shipbuilder Paul Cuffee and moved through Prince Saunders, who advocated Haitian emigration, and Daniel Coker, who migrated to Africa with the American Colonization Society. The first colonization leaders in Liberia as well as leaders of the Colonization Society were aware of Cuffee's work. During the mid nineteenth century, black nationalists like Henry H. Garnet, Martin Delany, James T. Holly, and others met together on several occasions. Their faction was "well aware of its Liberian and Sierra Leonean predecessors, as well as of their mutual cause." Meanwhile, in Africa, Alexander Crummell and Edward W. Blyden wove their own versions of black nationalism. After the Civil War, Henry McNeil Turner became a leading advocate of both Liberian emigration and a separate homeland in the United States. During the post–Civil War period, the search for new territory led to the development of many black communities in Kansas and Oklahoma. Booker T.

Washington "led in the movement of Blacks to Harlem in New York" and also influenced Marcus Garvey. "Garvey influenced Drew Ali, the founder of a Muslim organization," which as we know was the parent organization of the Nation of Islam.

A number of studies identified the "Founding Fathers" of black nationalism in the United States. Ronald Walters suggested that a sense of black nationhood existed and was given form during the Negro convention movements, "which essentially functioned as a Black national government, with Frederick Douglass as the President and men like James Forten, Henry Garnet and Henry Turner as assistants."[29] Floyd Miller's "The Father of Black Nationalism" identifies Martin Delany and the Reverend Henry Highland Garnet as early proponents of black nationalism. Miller claims, however, that Lewis Woodson, Delany's first teacher, was the real father of black nationalism.[30] Victor Ulman's *Martin R. Delany: The Beginnings of Black Nationalism* (1971) also identifies Delany with the origins of black nationalism in the United States.[31] And Manning Marable maintained that Booker T. Washington was an early proponent of black nationalism and economic efficiency.[32]

Traditions require canons because canons provide written evidence of allegedly timeless concerns. Sterling Stuckey's and Bracey, Meier, and Rudwick's anthologies contributed to the idea of a longstanding black nationalist political and intellectual tradition by presenting what could be described as a canon of black nationalist texts. These writings confirm the idea that black nationalism as an ideology and basis for political strategy dates back at least to the early nineteenth century.

Stuckey's anthology, *The Ideological Origins of Black Nationalism* (1969), supported the notion of a black nationalist tradition by laying out a canon of black nationalist works from the nineteenth century. Beginning with Robert Young's *The Ethiopian Manifesto* (1829) and David Walker's *Appeal to the Coloured Citizens of the World* (1829), Stuckey presented a series of texts that he argued laid the foundations for black nationalist ideology. Stuckey suggested that David Walker was the father of black nationalism, since Walker's *Appeal* "contains the most all-embracing black nationalist formulation to appear in America during the nineteenth century."[33] To Stuckey, many features of Walker's thought anticipate twentieth-century nationalists, such as:

1. a conception of the white man as the devil – which immediately brings Elijah Muhammad to mind;
2. an attitude toward white women – "I would not give a pinch of snuff to be married to any white person I ever saw in all the days of my life";
3. a concern about the possible fate for having written the Appeal – the possibility of being assassinated – which is similar to Malcolm X's remarks while writing his autobiography.[34]

Black Nationalism in America offered a still wider selection. Bracey, Meier, and Rudwick configured a canon that included a number of very diverse movements and figures: for instance, actor, writer, and activist Paul Robeson, UNIA leader Marcus Garvey, and Black Panther Party leader Huey Newton. These figures fit into the typology that we considered in the previous chapter.

This historical focus on traditions had at least two effects. First, it forced a concession: even if one could not agree with the tenets of black nationalism, at least one had to acknowledge that it reflected old and recurring sentiments. Black nationalism, after all, had its Founding Fathers and its supporting texts. This alone ought to make one pause and reconsider one's understanding and opinion of black nationalism and Black Power. Second, it contributed to the invention of a black nationalist tradition.

When I use the term *invention*, I do not mean that the authors fabricated history in order to identify black nationalism in previous centuries. However, I would suggest that making the connections between classical and modern black nationalism involved a great deal of contrivance. This, in fact, is a hallmark of all nationalisms. Traditions result when thinkers of an historical era identify thought and behavior of a recent or distant past that serves as a model for, or justification of, present behavior. Thus, "traditions" inescapably reflect the more current concerns of a group or an individual operating within a specific historical context.

This holds true for the paraintellectuals and intellectuals who identified black nationalist traditions. Armed with notions of black nationalism that were *not* contingent on any particular historical context, proponents and students of black nationalism identified innumerable examples of black nationalism of the past that looked and sounded like the 1960s versions. However, as we saw in the first chapter, ideas and movements can have profoundly different meanings across time.

Let's consider Stuckey's comparison of David Walker to twentieth-century nationalists more closely. As Wilson Moses correctly observes in his *Black Messiahs and Uncle Toms: Social and Literary Manipulations of a Religious Myth*, Malcolm X's claim that Allah would intervene and punish white America "was similar to David Walker's, 130 years earlier."[35] It is certainly true that both worked out of a jeremiadic framework. However, the similarities do not go further. Like other appeals of his time, Walker's is grounded in a Christian discourse. Moreover, Walker demands equal status for blacks in the United States.

As one-time spokesman for the Nation of Islam, and later a convert to Sunni Islam, Malcolm X embraced an entirely different religious and political perspective. As I argued in Chapter 2, Malcolm X's nationalism reflected the spirit of his times, one that sought explicitly anti-Western models, and one that responded to political developments of his day.

Stuckey's comparisons make sense in a social, political, and intellectual context where nationalism existed as the cutting edge of radical black political thought. But the apparent connections between past and present thinkers and activists reflected presentist concerns of the civil rights and Black Power eras. In 1967, Harold Cruse made a similar observation regarding radical thinkers' appropriation of the past:

> These historical episodes of force and violence in Negro history have become hallowed as prototypical examples of the revolutionary potential in the Negro presence in America. Everyone from Communist whites to nationalist blacks sees in these slave uprisings anything they want to see. Although Turner and Vesey never heard of Marx and Engels (and would not have known either one from a slavemaster), there are certain Communist historians who try to see a direct line from the slave revolts in Virginia to the projected socialist revolution . . . On the other hand, certain Black Nationalists of today see in these same revolts the beginnings of the Black Nationalist movement.[36]

Cruse failed to note that black nationalists and other radicals in the United States did what nationalists and revolutionaries generally tend to do: they read into the past instances of political resistance that justify certain types of action in the present.

Despite what we know to be the historical differences, we can understand why proponents of black nationalism would not be especially interested in them. Michael Kammen points out that "invocations of the past (as traditions) may occur as a means of resisting change *or* of achieving innovations."[37] By invoking the term "nationalism," proponents of this innovative paradigm drew legitimacy from past Afro-American figures and movements, and also invited comparisons to nationalism in a global context. To consider black people in the United States as a nation is immediately to bestow upon this population a certain culture, a certain historical past, and a certain homogeneity, and thus to legitimize demands for political sovereignty.

This makes sense for activists. Yet, we see that scholars were also enamored of the idea of black nationalism. Black nationalism not only was innovative politics, it also represented a new paradigm for understanding race and ethnic history, culture and politics in the United States. The fact that a great deal of scholarly effort was directed toward finding black nationalist roots and predecessors – a development unique to historiography of the 1960s – shows that the broader political movements defined the terms of scholarly inquiry.

INTERNAL COLONIALISM

Scholars and activists used another conceptual device to make a case for black nationhood. The analogy of a "black colony," "domestic colony," or "internal colonialism" was useful for at least two reasons. First, it defined the nation as those areas in which black people predominated: parts of the Deep South and the northern ghetto. Second, in the context of a wave of Third World nationalism, understanding the black American population as a colony provided yet another alternative to views of race relations that dominated conventional thinking. The model of internal colonialism offered an explanation of black political and economic status as well as of black cultural identity.

In the view of black nationalists, colonialism in the United States resulted from European and American imperialism. Colonialism as a system of governance grew out of the logic of European nationalism, ethnocentrism, and economic expansion. Europeans organized political units in Africa – colonies – through which they exercised direct and indirect rule over the indigenous population. Great Britain, for instance, maintained law and order by relying partly on indigenous systems of government. France regarded its African colonies as legally part of the French state. Therefore, French policy had as a basic aim assimilating the inhabitants of their colonies into French culture and civilization. Portugal and Belgium had their own assimilationist policies. Portugal had its *assimilados*, and Belgium had a class of *évolués*, who in theory could acquire the customs and language of the colonial power and thereby achieve full status.

The effects of European domination spanned the Atlantic Ocean by way of the Atlantic slave trade. During this trade, Europeans stole Africans from their homes and "established the colonial system within the Southland."[38] Like Africans on the continent, Africans in the Americas underwent a process of acculturation into European ways of life: again, as Malcolm X had explained, Africans in America were robbed of their names, their language, and their religion. Further, like colonized Africans on the continent, black people in the United States were wedded to an economic system that determined their social status and civil rights.

A number of thinkers – not all of them nationalists – suggested that a colonial analogy helped to uncover clues about the nature of Afro-American oppression *and* about black people's response to inequality. "From the beginning," Cruse wrote, "the American Negro has existed as a colonial being. His enslavement coincided with the colonial expansion of European powers and was nothing more or less than a condition of domestic colonialism."[39] Cruse's was perhaps the first of many similar formulations. A black nationalist student conference in 1964 concluded that "black people in the United States" are "a colony." Indeed, in their view the black bourgeoisie "failed to recognize the colonial nature of exploitation of the black ghettoes and were thus incapable of taking the kind of action necessary to achieve their goal."[40] Ronald Snellings suggested that black riots reflected an "historic turn from smoldering passivity toward direct action against the racist colonialism experienced at the hands of White America."[41] Sociologist Robert Blauner's *Racial Oppression in America* (1972) elaborated on the internal colonialism thesis. He argued that black protest reflected the colonized status of Afro-Americans. Blauner distinguished between "colonized" minorities and those immigrants who voluntarily came to the United States. Colonized minorities were brought to the United States by force.

One of the most comprehensive articulations of colonialism and Afro-American inequality appeared in Stokely Carmichael and Charles Hamilton's *Black Power*, written in the context of urban unrest. These authors explained that no "American Dilemma" existed at all. Black oppression did not reflect a failure of white Americans to back their "liberal creed." Rather, black inequality reflected black Americans' colonial status and the fact that it was not "in the interest of the colonial power to liberate them."[42]

The authors admitted that the analogy did not work perfectly. Colonies and metropoles were geographically separate. Under "classic colonialism, the colony is a source of cheaply produced raw materials (usually agricultural or mineral) which the 'Mother Country' then processes into finished goods and sells at high profit – sometimes back to the colony itself."[43] Nevertheless, despite some differences, race relations in the United States paralleled colonial relations abroad. First, black Americans, like other colonial subjects, were subject to indirect rule. The civil rights "establishment" represented a stratum of blacks that served as intermediaries between the white power structure and the black masses: "In the United States, as in Africa, their 'adaptation' [serves] to deprive the black community of its potential skills and brain power. All too frequently, these 'integrated' people are used to blunt the true feelings and goals of the black masses. They are picked as 'Negro leaders,' and the white power structure proceeds to talk to and deal only with them."[44] Second, blacks who experienced any social mobility in the United States did so by assimilating into "mainstream" white culture. Again, as in the case of the *assimilado* of Mozambique and Angola, who adopts "Portuguese custom, dress, language, and has achieved at least high school education," American society "indicates avenues of escape from the ghetto for those individuals who adapt to the 'mainstream'."[45] The strategy of escape involves disassociating "oneself from the black race, its culture, community and heritage and [becoming] immersed . . . in the white world."[46] Finally, the American colonizers kept the black population in a system of exploitative economic relations: "Again, as in the African colonies, the black community is sapped senseless of what economic resources it does have. Through the exploitative system of credit, people pay 'a dollar down, a dollar a week' literally for years." Further, "Out of substandard income, the black man pays exorbitant prices for cheap goods; he must then pay more for his housing than whites."[47]

Characterizing oppression in this manner gave way to a particular conception of black nationhood – that of a pre-independent colony. In turn, this formulation invited black nationalists to uncover the parallels between the political, social, and economic obstacles that obstructed Afro-American and African empowerment and thus rendered the political goals and objectives of Afro-Americans similar to those of Africans on the continent: to dislodge a Western colonial power by any means necessary. One writer offered this very understanding of black oppression and political emancipation: "Like other people who have risen to demand freedom, the Black colony in the United States constituted a nation. It is different from other emergent nations only in that it consists of forcibly transplanted colonial subjects who have acquired a cohesive identity."[48] In another account, the author argued that colonialism stripped Afro-Americans of a "frame of reference" for evaluating their place in the world, particularly with respect to the dominant majority. The dominant system of reference encouraged black people to "imitate the oppressor and thereby to deracialize" themselves. The system of colonialism especially affected the black male. In fact, "the colonized male is very much the target of the colonial system."[49]

On the basis of the colonial analogy, many nationalists and other black radicals reasoned that violent resistance might be required. Martinique-born psychiatrist Frantz Fanon's *The Wretched of the Earth* offered a defense of such efforts. Particularly important was Fanon's identification of the process whereby colonial domination results in the "native" accepting the inferiority of his culture, and his antidote: violent struggle. Fanon wrote: "The naked truth of decolonization evokes for us the searing bullets and bloodstained knives which emanate from it. For if the last shall be first, *this will only come to pass after a murderous and decisive struggle between the two protagonists.*"[50] He added that violence was a "cleansing force" for individuals: "It frees the native from his inferiority complex and from his despair and inaction; it makes him fearless and restores his self-respect." This idea appealed to a number of black nationalists fed up with the nonviolent approach, and interested in drawing parallels between struggles in Africa and Afro-America.[51]

CULTURAL REVOLUTION AND BLACK ART

Black nationalists of many varieties sought to recover, celebrate, and promote black culture. Reflecting impulses of nineteenth-century romantic racialism, many writers and activists sought to uncover the *volk* of people of African descent; the difference was that they didn't all root the unique characteristics of the race in the genes (though some did). We saw that Karenga's and Baraka's organizations urged their supporters to abandon American culture and to reclaim African culture. And, of course, the NOI and the ANPM both sought to encourage a new set of values and sense of self, rooted in a strong racial chauvinism.

In attempting to capture or locate the spirit of Afro-American culture, some writers turned to earlier forms of cultural expression. Ronald Snellings, for instance, offered an historical account of black music as the essential conduit of "African-American culture." During slavery, culture served as a medium through which black people could cultivate a sense of value. Cultural forms invented during slavery provided a form through which messages were encoded, linking networks for the Underground Railroad.[52]

Blues performers functioned as "priest-philosophers," since their art embodied the "philosophy, hopes and aspirations" of black people. Snellings claimed that this "attitude of the Black musician and poet as priest-philosopher goes back to the indigenous African civilizations, where the artist-priest had a functional role as the keeper or guardian of the spirit of the nation." Jazz artists of the fifties and sixties played a similar role but were eventually co-opted by white America. Rhythm and blues offered the latest cultural outlet of the "captive nation," with its long history of cultural production connected to an Afro-American philosophy.

For those associated with the Black Arts movement of the late 1960s and early 1970s, the idea of escaping mainstream culture was fundamental. During a tremendous proliferation of black art – poetry, plays, fiction – writers and artists organized cultural workshops which taught writing, photography, and graphic arts in every major city in the United States. New York had seven, including the Umbra Workshop and the Black Arts Repertory and School founded by Baraka. As we considered in the previous chapter, Baraka subsequently started the Spirit House Movers in Newark. The Organization of Black American Culture (OMAC) included Hoyt Fuller, editor of the *Negro Digest/Black World*, "which along with *Nommo* provided publishing outlets for OBAC writers." The Watts Writers Workshop in California included Quincy Troup, Stanley Crouch, and Jayne Cortez.[53]

The perspective of those involved in the Black Arts movement was predicated upon a Maoist conception of cultural production, where culture functioned as an arm of revolutionary struggle. Larry Neal explained that "those who thought themselves at the forefront of a black cultural revolution perceived creation as an assault weapon and an affirmation of the virtues of the common people."[54] Haki Madibuti described what functional art ought to do. It should:

1. reveal the decadence of white culture and expose the white man as the oppressor of Black people;
2. reaffirm the beauty of Black culture and history (obviously whether one meant Afro-American, African, or both cultures depended on one's definition of cultural nationalism);
3. create new and positive images; make Blackness, both the word and the concept, mean beauty;
4. make Black people conscious of the nature of their radical oppression and expose the self-defeating tendencies that have resulted from that oppression;
5. give Black people political and social direction (the proper direction varied from artist to artist).[55]

Karenga argued that "all art must reflect and support the Black Revolution, and any art that does not discuss and contribute to the revolution is invalid."[56] And James T. Steward argued that the revolutionary artist rejected "white models" and instead insisted that black "models must be consistent with a black style, our natural aesthetic styles, and our moral and spiritual styles."[57] Baraka later reflected that Black artists wanted art "to be armed with the spirit of black revolution."[58]

With these basic aims in mind, nationalist poets, playwrights, and novelists set out to rebut dominant stereotypes of blacks that were so readily apparent in many white artists' productions. If black artists could develop a range of artistic works that could counter the influence of these conceptions and promote new ones, they could strengthen efforts at nation building. Hence, in order to draw sharp distinctions between members of the races, artists crafted plays and novels that depicted white people and white values in a negative light.[59] Of all the genres that black artists produced, poetry was by far the most voluminous. In a sense, poetry provides the most clear evidence of what black artists attempted to do. Poetry could educate. It could inculcate revolutionary ideas in the black masses.

A number of points stand out with respect to these *volkish* formulations. The first point, one that Jennifer Jordan carefully articulates in her

"Cultural Nationalism in the 1960s," is that black artists of the period attempted to capture a very elusive entity: black culture. Typically, analyses of the origins and evolution of black art had little conception of the role of the market in mediating artistic expression. Further, analyses of culture were highly Manichean, assuming more than proving that black culture was fundamentally different from white.

Indeed, "black culture" increasingly worked as code for "black urban culture."[60] Larry Neal, Amiri Baraka, Hoyt Fuller, and others betrayed this bias in their remarks. Fuller wrote, for instance, that "the writers are deliberately striving to invest their work with the distinctive styles and rhythms and colors of the ghetto . . . which, for example, characterize the music of a John Coltrane or a Charlie Parker or a Ray Charles."[61] Perhaps this stemmed from the fact that, in the mind of Black Arts advocates, cosmopolitan culture – captured by avant-garde trends in jazz music – represented the militant cutting edge of black cultural nationalism. Most probably, these distinctions reflected the impossible task of disentangling black from white culture, "conservative" from "revolutionary" culture.

CONCLUSION

This chapter has attempted to explore the relation between discourse concerning black nationalism and the "nation-building" projects of the various individuals and groups considered in previous chapters. The interwoven terms – black nationalism/Black Power, black nationalist traditions, internal colony, and cultural revolution/Black Arts – worked to reinforce the idea of black nationalism as a real, historically determined nationalism. Students as well as advocates of black nationalism now had clear criteria by which they could understand and defend the importance of black nationalism as a political and intellectual persuasion. According to the historical revisions, black nationalism was an old and recurring sentiment. It reflected an unresolved tension between the desire to integrate and the wish to separate. Indeed, the black nation had Founding Fathers just as the white one did, as well as its own canonical texts. By relying on theories of colonialism and its effect on the psyche, black nationalists had a model that could explain the commitment of the black bourgeoisie to the goal of integration and, ultimately, why such a goal failed to meet the material and psychological needs of the black masses. Through the internal colonialism model, intellectuals and paraintellectuals formulated an analysis which invited easy comparison between the struggles of racial minorities in the United States and the struggles of nonwhite populations worldwide. They also brought a more Marxian analysis to bear on the question of black inequality, since colonies were, by design, exploitable territories.

Activists and commentators argued persuasively that black nationalism in the United States was composed of elements that one could identify in nationalist movements more generally – particularly in African
nationalist movements. They argued that black nationalism had deep historical roots, that black people had a separate language and culture, and
that black people, because of demographic patterns, inhabited a separate "colonized" territory. As scholars and activists elaborated such perspectives, they became part of the phenomenon they described: they
helped to legitimize black nationalism as a form of political expression.
They also tended to help obscure the fundamentally American quality of
black nationalist theory and politics. The next two chapters address this
issue.

5

Black Nationalism as Ethnic Pluralism

Although Third World nationalist politics could inspire black nationalist theory and strategy in the United States, it could not alter the fact that, from the early 1960s to the early 1970s, black nationalists confronted challenges and obstacles born on American soil. Ultimately, black nationalists had to square off against those who held power in the United States. This is not to say that certain political questions were not relevant to both Africans and blacks in the United States. It is to say, as Harold Cruse noted at the time, that nationalists here faced uniquely American – not Algerian, or Kenyan – conditions, shaped again by local political terrain.

Of course, at the time, many people failed to note this important historical truth: that black politics – even black nationalist politics – tends to draw upon intellectual and political currents in American society and build upon them to advance the cause of Afro-Americans. The reason is simple: from early in the history of the United States, Afro-Americans have been embedded in the same matrices of thought, culture, society, and politics as white Americans.

Modern black nationalism did not differ from earlier forms of black nationalism in this respect. Where classical or Anglo-African nationalism pursued emigration and commerce, modern black nationalists initiated political and economic projects homologous to those of their own period. Leaving aside revolutionary groups that sought to topple capitalism, most of what passed as black nationalism/Black Power during the 1960s (especially by the mid-1960s) looked much like black efforts to do what other "ethnic" groups had done: to pursue their interests in a pluralistic political system, subsumed by a capitalistic economic one. When the dust had finally cleared, none of the more elaborate nationalistic schemes had succeeded. No group's plans to forge a separate territory materialized. No group relocated blacks – in large numbers, anyway – to Africa. And, ultimately, few groups created lasting, alternative

"African" lifestyles. The stream of black nationalist politics, rather, flowed down more conventional channels. Activists united under a Black Power slogan demanded a greater piece of the action: (1) more say in the direction and control of government programs; (2) more access to resources that would advance and facilitate black economic development; and (3) control of, or greater influence on, city government and administration.

The notion that modern black nationalism parallels forms of political thought and behavior of its historical period may not appear immediately evident. After all, black nationalists of the 1960s formulated theories and created institutions that highlighted and attempted to challenge white supremacy in U.S. society. This being the case, black nationalists rejected mainstream or conventional ideas and practices of all sorts. The Nation of Islam, for instance, rejected Christianity – a bold position considering the black church's perceived role in Afro-American life. Other groups' efforts at reclaiming African roots and values, encouraging a black aesthetic, and even instituting a cooperative economics (*ujamaa*) reflected attempts to promote alternatives to a racist, materialistic, immoral white society. Black nationalists also tended to shun the dominant goal of the civil rights movement – integration – and its dominant strategy – nonviolent passive resistance. Groups like the Nation of Islam, the ANPM, RAM, and the RNA rejected the goal *and* the method.

Further, modern black nationalism, unlike earlier forms, profoundly influenced the radical politics of its era. In fact, black nationalism, especially by the late 1960s, set the tone for radicalism of that period. Radical feminism, the student rebellion, and the peace movement formulated their radicalism in part by drawing upon the rhetoric and militance of Black Power. Black nationalism also fueled the ethnic revival, or "ethnic fever," that swept the 1960s. As Steinberg notes, "One after another, the nation's racial and ethnic minorities sought to rediscover their waning ethnicity and reaffirm their ties to the cultural past."[1] Nevertheless, despite these clear attempts to fashion something new, and even despite its profound influence on radicalism and other trends of that period, black nationalism bore the markings of its era.

Why? Repression at the local, state, and national levels undermined militant socialistic groups and made things difficult even for militants of the nonsocialistic variety. Minus the far left of the political spectrum, what remained of black nationalist radicalism was reformist and identity-based politics.

Robert Allen, Meier, Bracey, and Rudwick, and Adolph Reed, Jr., have raised many of these points. Allen argued that particular groups like CORE and Baraka's United Brothers represented "bourgeois" nationalistic interests. By this he meant that mostly middle-class blacks benefited from black nationalist proposals and that many of these welded "black communities more firmly into the structure of American corporate capitalism."[2] Meier, Bracey, and Rudwick suggested that "[i]n the arena of *politics*, black nationalism at its mildest is *bourgeois reformism*, a view which assumes that the United States is politically pluralistic and that liberal values concerning democracy and the political process are operative."[3] And Reed pointed out that, far from radically altering existing institutions, Black Power generally meant placing *individuals* into administrative positions in city government, or promoting black control of antipoverty and development agencies.[4]

Making the case that modern black nationalism resembled the politics of its era requires expanding my analysis to include not only the more narrowly defined black nationalist projects that have been my main focus, but also the numerous other projects in which (1) black nationalists participated in significant ways, and (2) a loosely defined black nationalist/Black Power concept undergirded political and economic efforts. By exploring various facets of "community control," "black economic development," and electoral strategy and politics of the late 1960s and early 1970s, I will attempt to explain why black nationalism mainly took the form of "ethnic pluralism."

HISTORICAL CONTEXT

It appeared that a template for ethnic politics existed in urban America. The history of city politics, after all, was the history of ethnic politics. Robert Dahl's important *Who Governs?* (1961) identified ethnic politics as a sort of phase of urban political development. According to Dahl, ethnic politics provided the means by which immigrants and the children of immigrants were assimilated into U.S. society, politically and economically. For much of the twentieth century, Dahl noted, ethnic politicians had sought to win votes "by conferring divisible benefits on individuals . . . according to ethnic criteria."[5] More importantly, "ethnicity" had deep and lasting significance in politics, because it had deep and lasting significance in American society. Unlike other advanced industrial democracies, where class represented the fault line, "ethnic characteristics" often superseded those of class in the United States. This "ethnic awareness of identification" was created not by politicians but "by the whole social system." "Ethnic similarities," Dahl writes, "are a palpable reality, built into the everyday awareness of the ethnic from early childhood to old age. Nor are they always subordinate to socioeconomic ones."[6]

For Black Power activists, the Irish case was especially noteworthy. As Steven Erie notes in his study *Rainbow's End: Irish-Americans and the Dilemmas of Urban Machine Politics, 1840–1985* (1988), the Irish enjoyed great success as "urban ethnic party bosses," and "they were also the architects of the strongest and most long-lived big-city machines." And this was good for Irish Americans: "the Irish in the early twentieth century crowded into the middling ranks of the public sector – in police and fire departments, utilities, and government clerkships."[7] Control of urban machines secured access to social services and jobs.

Not surprisingly, then, "Irish power" served as a blueprint for Black Power, and by the late 1960s black people were poised to assume a more significant role in city politics across the country. The conditions were especially ripe in northern cities. By virtue of black migration and white flight, black people could rightly expect greater influence in electoral politics.

The protest and unrest of the late 1960s and early 1970s had the effect of increasing black representation in institutions of all sorts – from mayoral offices and city councils to social welfare agencies run by federal, state, and local governments. From 1970 to 1974, the number of black-led municipal regimes increased, as did the number of blacks working in housing authorities, redevelopment agencies, and welfare departments. Much of the increase in black employment "can be traced to the Great Society, either in terms of legislative initiatives (Medicare, Medicaid, public housing, manpower training) or in terms such as the massive expansion of preexisting programs, such as AFDC, due to the political climate created by the declaration of the national anti-poverty objective."[8] Indeed, when Congress created the Office of Economic Opportunity (OEO) in 1964, it transformed city politics across the country by establishing thousands of community action agencies "designed to give low-income Americans an opportunity to identify, design, plan, and initiate their own priorities and emphases in more than a thousand communities across the nation."[9] These agencies were created to provide services to low-income and minority groups; some of OEO's noteworthy programs included Headstart, Upward Bound, VISTA, Legal Services, the Job Corps, and the Neighborhood Youth Corps.[10]

The federal government's War on Poverty efforts all flowed from the notion that poor people suffered from a "culture of poverty" – an allegedly debilitating set of behaviors and attitudes thought to constrain the actions of the poor. "Citizen participation" was thought to be the cure. War on Poverty soldiers hoped to increase poor people's participation in projects that would counter their sense of helplessness and hopelessness. This interpretation is supported by the text of the *Community Action Program Guide*:

... the long range objective of every community action program is to effect a permanent increase in the capacity of individuals, groups, and communities afflicted by poverty to deal effectively with their own problems so that they need no further assistance. Poverty is a condition of need, helplessness and hopelessness.[11]

Another idea tied to the War on Poverty was the notion of economic development. True to the logic of the "pro-growth" ideology that political leaders had developed following World War II, Washington bureaucrats and business leaders were convinced that the solution to social problems lay in an expanding economy. Wolfe argues that economic growth offered a smoother and more harmonious solution to struggles "over redistributional issues." Speedy economic growth would "expand the pie sufficiently, so it would not have to be cut in a different way."[12]

Economic development of poor neighborhoods conformed to this vision. As a first step, the Economic Development Administration (EDA) was established in 1965 to "encourage economic development in certain 'lagging communities' throughout the country." EDA, a federal agency under the Department of Commerce, offered public works grants and loans, business loans, and grants for technical assistance. The average loan in fiscal 1969 was $1,004,000. For smaller amounts, EDA referred borrowers to the Small Business Administration – the first agency that would "attempt to promote minority economic development."[13]

Notions of citizen participation and economic development dovetailed. Across the political spectrum, politicians reasoned that economic development would ultimately lift people out of poverty.[14] Robert Kennedy's remarks in 1966 demonstrate how citizen participation meshed with economic development:

The measure of the success of this or any program will be the extent to which it helps the ghetto become a community – a functional unit, its people acting together on matters of mutual concern, with the power and the resources to affect the conditions of their own lives. Therefore, the heart of the program, I believe, should be the creation of community development corporations [CDCs] which would carry out the work of construction, the hiring and training of workers, the provision of service.

And Nixon's Executive Order 11458, which created the Office of Minority Business Enterprise (OMBE), expressed a related perspective: "I have often made the point," Nixon declared, "that to foster the economic status and pride of members of our minority groups, we must seek to involve them more fully in our private enterprise system." "Involvement in business," he reasoned, "has always been a major route toward participation in the mainstream of American life."[15]

Many commentators of that time noted the limitations of War on Poverty efforts, including insufficient funding and its failure to faciliate poor people's participation. Critics also challenged the idea of economic development as a solution to enduring economic inequality. Nevertheless, these national policies profoundly shaped the context of urban black politics.

CITIZEN PARTICIPATION AS COMMUNITY CONTROL

In this period of fertile, if failed, political and economic effort, black nationalism/Black Power had its comparable agenda. "Citizen participation" submerged and came up as "community control," in the language of Black Power ideology. Demands for control of institutions central to the lives of central-city residents increased during the late 1960s. Alan A. Altshuler characterizes community control in the following manner:

... (1) devolution of as much authority as possible to neighborhood communities; (2) direct representation of such communities on the city council, the board of education, the police commission, and other significant policy bodies; (3) black representation at all levels of the public service in far more than token numbers; (4) similar representation on the labor forces of government contractors; and (5) the vigorous application of public resources to facilitate the development of black-controlled businesses.[16]

Stokely Carmichael's and Charles Hamilton's *Black Power* (1967) can almost be read as a blueprint for community control. Carmichael and Hamilton theorized that the political arena in the United States was one of competing ethnic groups; they also offered suggestions for how black Americans could ensure self-determination despite their "colonial subject" status. "Black Power," they wrote, "recognizes ... the ethnic basis of American politics as well as the power-oriented nature of American politics." Therefore, before a group "can enter the open society, it must first close ranks ... By this we mean that group solidarity is necessary before a group can operate effectively from a bargaining position of strength in a pluralistic society."[17] As a necessary component of this "closed ranks" strategy, the authors pointed to the need for black people to "lead and run their own organizations. Only black people can convey the revolutionary idea – and it is a revolutionary idea – that black people are able to do things themselves." Black people, simply put, needed more control over institutions that affected their lives. Black police officers would end police brutality. A black board of revenue could "channel tax monies for the building of better road and schools serving black people." Indeed, black people had to do what other ethnic groups had done: traditionally, each new ethnic group had "found the route to social and political viability through the organization of its own institutions with which to represent its needs within the larger society."[18]

Black-Power-as-community-control informed the efforts of black people in cities across the country. Yet their demand for community control derived not from Carmichael's and Hamilton's treatise, but rather from observing the failures of school systems, social service agencies, and "urban renewal" plans, and the limitations of War on Poverty projects. In cities across the country, Black Power advocates thus worked to reorient the institutions most central to the daily lives of black people – schools, hospitals, government agencies, and city councils – in a way that would bring the goals of these crucial institutions in line with the needs of the black population.

The battles over school control provide a good example. City governments had not equalized resources between wealthier and poorer city schools. Further, from the standpoint of many Black Power advocates, schools taught black children how to be "white." That is, they failed to offer a curriculum that reflected the emerging sense of black consciousness. Commenting on the dramatic, bitter, and tumultuous battle raging in Harlem in the late 1960s, Albert Vann, principal of P.S. 271 in New York, explained that " 'The Man' is not going to give these values to us," but rather that "[t]hey have to be earned by a new kind of black man that we don't have yet. His values are going to have to be different."[19] Schools like the African Free School of Newark, Uhuru Sasa in Brooklyn, and Boston's Roxbury Community School were schools that tried to instill a certain type of black consciousness into their pupils.

BLACK CAPITALISM

Community control had an economic component. "Black capitalism" or "black economic development" submerged and came up as black nationalism. Despite the fact that the idea of black capitalism could be tied to non-nationalistic agendas, black-run businesses were central to the strategies of numerous nationalist goups. Even before the idea of creating black-run businesses gained national attention under Nixon, groups like the Nation of Islam had achieved relative success in establishing a number of businesses in cities across the country. Indeed, by the early 1960s the Nation of Islam was the most successful black business of that period.

Earlier, we briefly considered the notions of black capitalism advanced by CORE under Floyd McKissick and Roy Innis. Black capitalism was not, according to Innis, a matter of the government creating or opening jobs for black people. Nor did black capitalism mean inviting white corporations into ghettos in order to create jobs. Rather, capitalism was tied to the project of nation building:

A modern nation becomes viable through the creation of capital instruments. We can't make money through jobs. You make money through owning capital instruments: land and other properties.[20]

The first step in securing capital instruments involved controlling various institutions in inner cities – community control. Innis was part of the failed effort to pass the Community Development Act. The key institution set up by the act, the Community Development Corporation, "was to be a private profit-making corporation operating in a poor urban or rural area. Any resident of the area sixteen or over could buy a share in the corporation at par value of five dollars."[21]

Robert S. Browne had still another plan for capitalist development. With a gift of one million dollars from a benefactor, Browne launched three associated institutions: the Black Economic Research Center, the Emergency Land Fund, and the Twenty-first Century Foundation. According to Browne, these organizations shared the goal of "encouraging and supporting those efforts which will extend the area of black economic independence in the hope that some far off day there will have developed an array of financially independent black institutions which can fund the needs of the black community without reliance on sympathetic whites or on special government programs."[22]

The idea of black economic development was the main goal of an organization called NEGRO (National Economic Growth and Reconstruction Organization). NEGRO was originally established in "the early sixties as the Interfaith Health Association, a nonprofit corporation which owned and operated a 140-bed hospital in Queens." Its aim was to promote "the self-help concept among the Negro people." The president of the organization, Dr. Thomas W. Matthew, offered the group's definition of black power. He considered black power to be the "marshaling of all the resources of a particular group." Matthew reasoned that through proper training, black people could gain the skills and respect necessary to enter the industrial workforce as other ethnic groups had done. Blacks who had been chronically unemployed lacked the proper attitude and work ethic. Black Power, then, took the form of self-help capitalism. NEGRO's projects included a chemical plant, a paint factory, a metal-fabricating plant, bus companies in Watts and Harlem, a textile firm, and more than six hundred housing units, "many of which had been refurbished by its own Spartacus Construction Company." By the summer of 1968, NEGRO had over seven hundred employees.[23]

Other leaders and groups across the country turned to economic development schemes. Jesse Jackson, as one example, created Operation Breadbasket to "feed the poor and to create black business." The Rochester-based militant organization FIGHT built an electronics plant. And in Los Angeles, "a group of unemployed blacks was running a toy factory making dolls." Xerox helped the FIGHT organization, while General Electric invested a quarter-million dollars in the toy factory.[24]

POLITICS

Community control had political implications. Amiri Baraka's efforts were most notable in this regard. Baraka and the Committee for a Unitied Newark (CFUN) were instrumental in electing Newark's first black mayor, Kenneth Gibson. And, to the extent that Baraka did have a grassroots constituency during the early 1970s, he was able to exert some pressure on Mayor Gibson.[25] Baraka's vision of the politician's role was clearly informed by the idea that black-run governments could do for blacks what, for instance, Irish-run governments had once done for Irish Americans. Black mayors had to use their power to dispense patronage to benefit blacks. They should hire Afro-Americans to direct the police and fire departments. Blacks should head medical, educational, and social welfare services. For Baraka, success in Newark could serve as a model for cities across the country. During the early 1970s many black nationalists like Baraka had real grassroots political bases. It was these political bases that caught the attention of mainline black political officials.[26]

CORE was another black nationalist organization that would have a large impact on electoral politics during the late 1960s. Especially active in Harlem and Cleveland, CORE registered voters in the hope of influencing city elections. CORE's efforts helped Carl Stokes win his mayoral bid in Cleveland in 1968.

NATIONAL CONVENTIONS

Community development, economic development, and electoral strategy were themes addressed in a number of national black nationalist/Black Power conventions during the late 1960s and early 1970s. These conventions all represented efforts by nationalists and mainstream politicians to formulate broad social, political, and economic agendas. For my purposes, the conferences are also important because they demonstrate the extent to which notions of ethnic pluralism and pro-growth capitalism formed the parameters within which nationalistic agendas were generated.

The first Black Power conference was held in Washington, D.C, in 1966 with the sponsorship of Congressman Adam Clayton Powell; the second was held in 1967 in Newark.[27] The Newark conference was held under the chairmanship of Reverend Dr. Nathan Wright, Jr., who was then urban affairs director for the Newark Episcopal Diocese.[28] This conference attracted some two thousand delegates from a variety of political persuasions, and came one week after a major riot in Newark had left twenty-six dead.

The delegation was quite diverse, including members of the Nation of Islam and RAM, cultural nationalists of various sorts, younger activists from SNCC and CORE, black Greek-letter organizations, black student organizations, the SCLC, the NAACP, Pepsi-Cola, the American Medical Association, and the National Council of Negro Women. The familiar themes of Black Power were evident at the conference. Placards urged black people to "buy black," to support neighborhood credit unions, to pursue cultural autonomy, and to exercise community control of key institutions like school boards. A number of resolutions grew out of this conference. The economic resolutions included such ideas as promoting "buy black" campaigns, establishing neighborhood black credit unions, and establishing a general fund for the creation of nonprofit and co-operative ventures. The political resolutions included plans to generate a Black Power lobby in Washington, D.C.; to work toward tripling the black congressional representation; and to hold a "national grass roots political convention following the conventions of the two major political parties in the same city." Resolutions also proclaimed the right of self-defense and the desire to consider partitioning the United States into separate black and white nations. From Wright's perspective, Black Power as addressed at this conference was informed by the knowledge that "no rising ethnic group in this nation . . . has ever asked for integration." The Black Power conference dealt with the two most "pervasive problems of our society – identity and empowerment for fulfillment." According to Wright:

We had 14 parallel workshops dealing with such subjects as "the City and the Black People, Black Power and American Religion, New Roles for Black Youth, the Black Home, Black Power Through Economic Development," etc . . . The conference issued a "Black Power Manifesto" which spoke to the need of setting up regional black-power conferences, and a year hence to hold another national conference. And after that, within 18 months, an international congress of black power.[29]

Like the Black Power Conference, the Congress of African Peoples[30] attracted activists and groups committed to some idea of nationalism and/or Pan-Africanism. We should note, in both cases, that more mainstream politicians and activists were attracted to nationalist rhetoric partly because "militants" appeared to wield increasing power over informal constituencies. Not surprisingly, then, even at the Congress of African Peoples, individuals like Whitney Young, Jr., of the Urban League and Ralph Abernathy of SCLC were in attendance. Amiri Baraka presided at this meeting in Atlanta, in September of 1970. The conference drew organizations like the Republic of New Africa, proponents of black art like Haki Madhubuti (Don L. Lee), and intellectuals committed to nationalism like Robert S. Browne and John Henrik Clarke. The conference included workshops on political liberation, social organization, creativity, black technology, religion, education, community organization, law and justice, history, communications, and economics. The primary focus of the gathering was the formation of the Congress of African Peoples (CAP), which "was conceived as a party as well as a united front."[31]

Drawing on Karenga's *Kaiwada* concept, Baraka discussed four areas of political power based on (1) public office (elected or appointed), (2) community organizations, (3) alliances and coalitions, and (4) and disruption (actual or threatened).[32] An independent black political party, according to Baraka, needed to pursue all four strategies. Baraka proposed a number of measures directed toward the final goal of an independent black party, including voter registration, mobilizing black citizens to face racist policy, running candidates who supported the interests of black communities, and establishing alliances with Third World governments and movements.[33]

In statements that foreshadowed those proposed at the Gary Convention of 1972, the delegates concluded that the main objective of blacks in the political arena was the formation of a political party. This was clearly spelled out in a statement by the Philadelphia Congress of African Peoples:

A PARTY IS THE FIRST STEP TOWARD BUILDING A NATION. HISTORICAL CIRCUMSTANCES DICTATE THE NEED FOR FORMING A NATIONAL BLACK POLITICAL PARTY AT HOME.[34]

The proposed black political party would invite a new type of black politician to participate. Further, the black political party would be "involved in community control of institutions such as health, welfare, housing, land, or any struggle deemed important by Black people."[35] Among the Philadelphia CAP's proposals were registering all black people to vote, electing black men and women to every public office, and the freeing of political prisoners, to name a few. Following this convention, CAP grew. Activists eventually established chapters in Chicago, Boston, Delaware, Albany, San Diego, and many other cities.

Because of its sheer numbers, perhaps no event highlighted the black nationalist and non-nationalist attempt to formulate a common political agenda better than the Gary Convention held in Gary, Indiana, in March of 1972. This convention invited some four thousand delegates from forty-five states, though according to participants as many as eight thousand people made the trip.[36] The convention's theme was Unity without

Uniformity, and the goal of the delegates was to formulate a national black agenda. The city of Gary, Indiana, was draped in red, black, and green for the occasion.

As at other conferences of this period, black nationalists represented a substantial proportion of the total body of delegates. Amiri Baraka chaired much of the convention, and did so in part to mediate any conflicts that developed. A general if inchoate sense of nationalism was expressed in a chant that erupted on many occasions during the convention – "Nation Time!" The hope that the body of delegates would formulate a national black agenda reflected the idea that black people shared a common political destiny.

The *National Black Political Agenda* came out of the Gary Convention, and declared that no basic change for the benefit of black people could occur "unless [black people] organize to initiate that change."[37] This document represented the delegates' attempt to formulate some basic agreement on general goals, and it was quite sweeping in its demands: "*The American system does not work for the masses of our people, and it cannot be made to work without radical fundamental change.*"[38] This fundamental change was necessary given the fact that, historically, both political parties had betrayed the interests of black people whenever they had found it necessary. The failure of white liberalism, "unbridled monopoly capitalism," and "ruthless military imperialism" set the stage for the crises affecting black people. Some of the numerous agenda items included reparations for slavery, opposition to busing, proportional representation of blacks in Congress, and national health insurance.[39]

Despite the seeming convergence of nationalist and non-nationalist sentiment, the Gary Convention did reveal important tensions within the general body of delegates. Unity without Uniformity, from our historical vantage point, blurred important conflicts of interest that existed among blacks. Delegates were divided on substantive issues like busing, and the Israeli-Arab conflict in the Middle East, as well as strategic matters concerning tactics and leadership.[40]

These cleavages were even more apparent by the time of the second National Black Political Convention, held in Little Rock in 1974. This convention had the same theme, Black Unity without Uniformity, and attracted some two thousand delegates. Unlike the convention at Gary, however, notable politicians and civil rights leaders were absent; many of them had become increasingly uneasy about the nationalists' posture. Even among the members of the steering committee, there was some dissension about the agenda of the convention and the extent to which it was dominated by the nationalist cadre. Indeed, Congressman Charles Diggs vacated the presidency of the National Black Political Assembly following the Little Rock convention. Ron Daniels, an avowed nationalist, replaced Diggs.[41]

The National Black Political Assembly (NBPA) "grew from the Gary Convention, and was spearheaded by the cultural nationalist camp, headed by Baraka." This organization formed around the same Unity without Uniformity theme. The activists associated with the NBPA hoped to inject a black nationalist agenda or perspective into mainstream politics. Nationalists hoped to steer mainstream politicians toward a more nationalist agenda and consciousness. There was also great overlap in terms of membership with another organization, the African Liberation Support Committee (ALSC). Both organizations attempted to mark a place for black radicalism in the post-segregation context. ALSC hoped to organize political actions in support of African liberation movements. It arguably had a greater focus on popular mobilization and was less "oriented to building formal relationships with mainstream politicians."[42]

Before we consider the reasons why black nationalism of the 1960s looked like the politics of its day, it is worth reiterating a few points. First, the various strategies associated with black nationalism that called for black control of social, political, and economic institutions were not "nationalist" in the strict sense of the term. Second, my generalizations exclude the far-reaching goals of black revolutionary organizations. Minus the revolutionary forms, modern black nationalism looked like ethnic politics both for structural and ideological reasons. Without demands for separate territory, Black Power ideology was close in form to ethnic pluralism. After all, "community control" ultimately meant that blacks ought to have greater representation in various public and private institutions.

BRIEF CASES

Briefly consider the cases of New Haven, Newark, and Cleveland. Black nationalist agendas enjoyed different rates of success in these three cities. Nevertheless, the range of political and economic strategies shows some interesting parallels. In different ways, and for different reasons, New Haven and Cleveland's far-left nationalist groups were not significant players – mostly due to coercive efforts by law enforcement officials, but also due to the failure of these groups to fashion broad popular support. In the case of Newark, a number of far-left organizations actually seized control of certain antipoverty agencies. All three cities had Black Power organizations demanding community control. New Haven had the Hill Parents Association led by Robert Harris; Newark had Baraka's United Brothers; and Cleveland had CORE.

Each city had an umbrella organization, informed by a Black Power orientation and generally directed toward community control. New

Haven had the Black Coalition; Cleveland had the Operation of Black Unity (OBU); and Newark had the CFUN. These generalizations do not, of course, tease out the subtle differences in strategy and orientation among these various organizations, nor the differences in city politics.

The threat of urban unrest provided the catalyst for federal action. For much of 1960s the federal government directed money toward inner cities in the hope of quelling discontent. In the cases we've considered, some black nationalist/Black Power advocates received resources and "status" following these outbreaks. CORE arguably benefited most. Under a $150,000 grant from the Ford Foundation, Cleveland's chapter of CORE started the Target City Project, specifically designed to help end racial tensions on Cleveland's East Side. The Target City Project, which got under way in November 1967, included a "four point program which was to include leadership training, voter education and registration, research in economic development and conferences to focus attention on the problems of the black community."[43] CORE received a second grant from Ford in the amount of $300,000. Indeed, as early as 1961 the Ford Foundation had donated money to projects aimed at quelling urban unrest. As Allen explains:

From the Foundation's point of view, old-style moderate leaders no longer exercised any real control, while genuine black radicals were too dangerous. CORE fit the bill because its talk about black revolution was believed to appeal to discontented blacks, while its program of achieving black power through massive injections of governmental, business, and Foundation aid seemingly opened the way for continued corporate domination of black communities by means of a new black elite.[44]

Roy Innis's business schemes appeared at precisely the time when the Ford Foundation was directing money toward CORE as an appropriate or legitimate black nationalist organization. Interestingly, it was also "the Ford Foundation's underwriting of a CORE voter registration project that enabled Stokes to win the Cleveland mayoral election on his second attempt."[45]

Similar events unfolded in other cities. Following a relatively small riot in New Haven in 1967, Yale gave money to the Black Coalition ($100,000) and offered summer jobs to local youth.[46] Local firms started the Urban Alliance of Greater New Haven, a development organization. In Newark, the riot of 1967 created a sense of urgency and greater attention to the need for Black Power and political organization.

The result of these developments, combined with police repression, was that black nationalist/Black Power radicalism was contained. In New Haven, for instance, the Panthers were neutralized, and black leaders "found jobs with the city; advocacy organizations got contracts to provide social services; and the intransigent few were driven out of town, jailed or killed."[47] In Newark more moderate proposals for Black Power drew the grudging support of corporations and political leaders, as was the case in New Haven.

These developments blunted the true force of a nationalistic agenda for two related reasons. First, public and private institutions directed money toward conventional community control projects. Second, the federal government gave professionals control of most of the antipoverty and development agencies, which in turn employed neighborhood leaders to the exclusion of the more militant, and more radical, groups and individuals. Partly out of their concern to avoid blame for urban unrest, and sometimes because of public outcry, OEO bureaucrats forbade the use of community action funds in connection with militant nationalist activity. Thus, for example, Baraka's short-lived Black Arts Theater was cut off from Harlem's antipoverty agency in 1965. The OEO suspended a summer training program that had employed Ron Karenga in 1967. And Nashville's Metropolitan Action Committee in 1967 eliminated the "liberation school" that was staffed by a number of SNCC members.[48] These patterns suggest that the type of black "nationalists" who could take most advantage of the new policies and funding tended to be those already more inclined toward conventional politics, like those working with HPA and CORE.[49] As the FBI annihilated nationalists on the far left, the structure of urban policy, and the project of electoral strategies, tended to mold Black Power radicalism into ethnic pluralist patterns.

CONCLUSION

This chapter has attempted to show that modern black nationalism drew upon strategies for political and economic empowerment that had analogies in the wider political landscape. The War on Poverty transformed the character of urban politics, creating agencies that often bypassed local city government control. This was also the era following the passage of the Civil Rights and Voting Rights Acts – the era of Black Power. Finally, this period was dominated by the pro-growth framework. Political leaders and business leaders figured that the key to ending urban blight lay in economic production. As was the case during early periods of U.S. history, black nationalist political and economic schemes had white homologies.

And while the Black Power era saw important gains for a professional stratum of black Americans – in social services, administration, and increasingly in public office – these opportunities did not benefit blacks uniformly. Further, by taking community control to be the principal or organizing demand, activists of all sorts failed to appreciate fully how the problems of wages, jobs, inferior education, and insufficient housing had roots *outside* of America's ghettos. Hence, community control, though "radical" in its novelty, failed to budge the deeper structures and forces responsible for black inequality.

6

Black Nationalism and the Ethnic Paradigm

Black nationalism of the post–World War II period differed from earlier varieties as it related to the *ethnic paradigm*.[1] Where Christianity and civilization once represented the central concepts on which Anglo-Saxon and Anglo-African nationalism rested, modern black nationalism rested on a new set of assumptions: (1) that American culture is purely, or largely, Anglo-Saxon; and (2) that "culture" determines a group's social, political, and economic status in U.S. society. These ideas emerged over the course of the twentieth century to form a residual set of assumptions – a sort of social epistemology – that appeared to explain cultural identity and the processes of acculturation and economic mobility in the United States. Like all ideologies, the ethnic paradigm grew out of the need for people to make sense of social hierarchy in the United States, particularly in a land of immigrants and relatively great economic mobility. Like the civilizationist paradigm of earlier times, the ethnic paradigm rested on a view of social hierarchy according to which the "lower" groups rise and prosper to the extent that they become like those at the "higher" end. The assumptions about higher and lower cultures served as proxies for class, and also depended on Victorian, patriarchal conceptions of gender and social mores, again not unlike the civilizationist paradigm. Where Christianity and civilization once represented the central concepts on which Anglo-Saxon and Anglo-African nationalism rested, modern black nationalism rested on the ethnic paradigm.

Ethnic paradigmatic assumptions informed the enormous twentieth-century body of thought concerning the culture, assimilation, and upward mobility of the poor, immigrant populations and blacks. There have been a number of theoretical strands – "Anglo-conformity," the "melting pot," and "cultural pluralism."[2] Each represents bundles of ideas, and each has evolved during the course of the twentieth century. Anglo-conformity has been associated with the attempts, draconian in some instances, to get immigrants to conform to an Anglo-Saxon, individualistic, Protestant ethos; and it underlay important studies of assimilation in American life, beginning with the "Chicago school" of sociology. This tradition of scholarship informed policy and thinking about assimilation for much of this century. As we will consider later, the Chicago school also influenced the "culture of poverty" perspective that became central to public policy debates during the 1960s. This theory held that "cultural traits" of the poor themselves – evident in family structure – reproduced poverty independent of, or largely independent of, political and economic factors.

Melting pot and cultural pluralist theories had a more democratic core: melting pot theorists focused on cultural exchange between immigrants and the mainstream; cultural pluralists highlighted and defended the preservation of tradition, language, and customs of the Old World. Cultural pluralists have therefore historically opposed both the Anglo-conformist and melting pot perspectives. Nevertheless, these terms – Anglo-conformity, melting pot, and cultural pluralism – are not mutually exclusive. As we will see, scholars and commentators have often woven analyses beholden to more than one of these perspectives. And all were subsumed by the ethnic paradigm.

Black nationalist theory of the 1960s and early 1970s was no exception. My argument is that the ethnic paradigm was to this wave of 1960s and early 1970s black nationalism what the civilizationist paradigm was to classical black nationalism. In the same way that nineteenth-century nationalists assumed the importance of Christianity and civilization to Negro advancement, 1960s and early 1970s black nationalists, especially of the non-Marxist varieties, were often beholden to the assumptions of the ethnic paradigm, which, incidentally, collapse under close scrutiny. Since blacks have helped constitute American culture, both popular and political, a focus on black "culture" cannot satisfactorily explain black social, political, and economic status in the United States.

Ironically, despite its explicitly anti-American and anti-Western cast, modern black nationalism shared and confirmed old romantic racialist ideas that confused Afro-American "cultural" identity with a "racial" one.[3] By starting with this premise, many nationalists reproduced claims that disproportionate poverty, lack of mobility, and social problems like crime and drug abuse had to do with this distinct, and deformed, culture. Where Anglo-African nationalists argued, like Anglo-Saxon nationalists of the same period, that black people needed Christianity and civilization, modern black nationalists argued that they needed to return to their Islamic or African roots in order to jump-start their sputtering and defective cultural engine, an engine partly responsible for their

destructive behavior and powerlessness. Where Garvey sounded like
a social Darwinist, "return to African culture" nationalists sounded
like "culture of poverty" theorists. Many therefore hoped to transform
an allegedly pathological black culture characterized by violence,
drug dependency, broken homes, and self-hatred. New "Afrocentric"
interpretations of the past, dietary codes, dress codes, gender roles,
and an essentially pro-black doctrine would lead to racial
redemption.

ANGLO-CONFORMITY

When black nationalists challenged integration-as-assimilation,
they rejected the tradition of thought and practice known as
"Anglo-conformity." The basic assumption that has united Anglo-
conformist views and policy is that Americans should maintain
English institutions, speak the English language, and follow "English-
oriented patterns as dominant in American life."[4] In some senses,
Anglo-conformity predated American independence; however, although
the idea that American political institutions and values reflect inherent
Anglo-Saxon traits is an old one, the notion that people could adopt
Anglo-Saxon cultural patterns had its origins in the early part of the
twentieth century.

Since that time, Anglo-conformity has ranged from biological
notions about Aryan supremacy to arguments that immigrant populations should adopt "standard Anglo-Saxon cultural patterns."[5]
Anglo-conformity arguably reached its most fevered pitch during the
Americanization movement of the World War I period. Federal
agencies like the Bureau of Education, the Bureau of Naturalization,
and the Committee on Public Information, state and city governments,
"and a veritable host of private organizations joined the effort to
persuade the immigrant to learn English, take out naturalization
papers, buy war bonds, forget his former origins, and give himself
over to the full flush of patriotic hysteria."[6] Private groups like the
Daughters of the American Revolution, the Society of Colonial Dames,
and the Sons of the American Revolution worked to design educational
programs that would teach immigrants about American political
institutions, and about the naturalization process. The business and
industrial community also attempted to educate and indoctrinate immigrants along Anglo-conformist lines. A typical statement of Anglo-
conformist sentiment went as follows: "Broadly speaking, we mean . . .
an appreciation of the institutions of this country, absolute forgetfulness
of all obligations or connections with other countries because of descent
or birth."[7]

THE CHICAGO SCHOOL OF SOCIOLOGY

Anglo-conformity subsumed a tradition of sociological scholarship unrivaled in its impact on popular and academic thinking about ethnic group acculturation. Beginning in the second decade of this century, sociologists affiliated with the University of Chicago advanced a perspective on assimilation "that rejected the vulgar racism with which Anglo-Americanism had become tainted." In so doing, they were "among the first American scholars to point the way toward a new intellectual climate of ethnic accommodation and goodwill." Nevertheless, the sociologists at the University of Chicago understood assimilation along Anglo-conformist lines. They simply wanted a kinder, more gentle approach to this ultimate end. Draconian Americanization methods, from the Chicago school perspective, were far less efficient, and certainly less democratic.[8] They reasoned that the United States' unique challenge was to assimilate all its citizens, thus ensuring moral and political order.[9]

The Chicago school scholars advanced a general method that influenced academic thinking about assimilation for the better part of this century. The Chicago school's methodological innovations included the following: first, in contrast to earlier "biologically" oriented approaches to racial differences, the Chicago approach emphasized the significance of culture and descent.[10] " 'Culture' in this formulation included such diverse factors as religion, language, 'customs,' nationality, and political identification."[11] Second, they emphasized conflict and interaction among human groups. Beginning with W. I. Thomas, Robert E. Park, and Ernest Burgess, the Chicago school's fundamental framework emphasized social interactions as a dynamic process – a cycle of assimilation. The cycle involved a number of stages, including contact, competition, accommodation, and ultimately assimilation and amalgamation. Park and his student Louis Wirth identified ethnic enclaves as representative of one of the phases of the assimilation cycle. Assimilation and amalgamation occurred for immigrant groups of European stock; however, the phenotypical differences of blacks, "Orientals," and other racial minority groups thwarted their assimilation. Finally, this school of thought deemphasized the significance of politics and class as it affected the culture, assimilation, and socioeconomic mobility of immigrant groups.[12] And rather than understanding "culture," "race," and class as social and political constructions, they took these categories to be fairly fixed, if not natural.

A number of key concepts grew out of their general methodological approach. Imperfect assimilation created the "marginal man": such an individual straddled more than one set of cultural traditions. Jews and mulattos were the prototypes, but the term also applied to plantation blacks, Eurasians, mestizos, and the Cajuns of Louisiana. Park's student Everett V. Stonequist provided the most elaborate theory of the marginal man in his book *The Marginal Man: A Study in Personality and Culture Contact* (1937).

Another Chicago theme has special relevance to discourse about ethnicity and culture during this century – that of "disorganization" and the related notion of "demoralization." W. I. Thomas and Florian Znanieki characterized disorganization as the process whereby *"the influence of existing social rules of behavior upon indiviudal members of the group"* decreases.[13] Disorganization could lead to "demoraliza-tion," which in turn seemed to take the form of a lack of discipline, criminality, and disrespectful attitudes, especially evident among second-generation immigrants. Thomas and Znanieki identified this apparent phenomenon by comparing Old World and immigrant Poles in *The Polish Peasant* (1918). The notion of disorganization pivoted "on a premise that a hierarchy of norms of social behavior exists and is discernable." Deviance from those norms impeded assimilation and allegedly promoted dysfunction.[14]

Another legacy of the Chicago school method was the tendency to draw analogies between European peasants and rural blacks. Classify-ing rural black Americans as peasants carried a number of implications. One was that it allowed the sociologists to apply the same concepts to blacks as they did to European immigrants. Another was that compar-isons between rural blacks and immigrants minimized the particular patterns of discrimination that blacks faced. Such comparisons also obscured the formal and informal processes by which "whiteness" was extended to initially "nonwhite" European populations.

Of the black sociologists connected to the Chicago school, E. Franklin Frazier was of special significance.[15] His studies of the "Negro family" focused heavily on the themes of assimilation and "disorganization." He argued, for instance, that the rampant "disorganization" of black fami-lies in northern cities – evident in rates of illegitimacy, family desertion, juvenile delinquency, and so forth – resulted from the erosion of the folk culture of the rural community during the process of urban migration.[16]

No scholars associated with this school made assimilation their primary focus of study; and this analytical weakness would be repro-duced even by scholars not directly connected to the Chicago school. Park and Burgess, for instance, characterized assimilation as an exchange of culture between majority and minority populations.[17] They "also defined assimilation as the process by which the culture of a country was transmitted to its adopted citizens." "It was clearly implied that there was a distinctive national culture to be assimilated by newcomers, even though it might simultaneously be undergoing modification."[18] Without acknowledging any sense of inconsistency, Park and Burgess offered both Anglo-conformist and melting-pot type definitions of assimilation.[19] Another product of Chicago's Department of Sociology, Edward Bryrn Reuter, characterized assimilation as "the incorporation and conversion into the substance of the assimilating body."[20]

"Assimilation" remained broadly defined through the forties, fifties, and sixties. Brewton Berry, for instance, suggests that "[b]y assimilation we mean the *process whereby groups with different cultures come to have a common culture.*"[21] In his 1956 text *Sociology: The Study of Human Relations*, Arnold Rose defined assimilation as "the adoption by a person or group of the culture of another social group to such a complete extent that the person or group no longer has any characteristics identifying him with his former culture."[22]

Perhaps the most important study of acculturation in the 1960s, Milton Gordon's *Assimilation in American Life* (1964), noted that "[i]f there is anything in American life which can be described as an over-all American culture which serves as a reference point for immigrants and their children, it can best be described, it seems to us, as the middle-class cultural patterns of, largely, white Protestant, Anglo-Saxon origins."[23] For Gordon, assimilation has occurred when an ethnic group (1) has changed its cultural patterns to match those of the majority; (2) has taken on primary group relationships with the majority; (3) has intermarried and interbred fully with the majority; (4) has developed a sense of peoplehood, or nationality, or ethnicity, that matches that of the majority population; (5) has "reached a point where they encounter no prejudiced attitudes"; and (6) does not raise demands relating to matters of "value and power conflict with the original group."[24]

Despite the ambiguity around the concept of "assimilation," scholars typically defined blacks as cultural outsiders. In his introduction to Johnson's *In the Shadow of the Plantation*, Robert E. Park offered commentary indicative of this tendency:

It is very curious that anyone in America should still think of the Negro, even the Negro peasant of the "black belts," as in any sense an alien or stranger, since he has lived here longer than most of us, has interbred to a greater extent than the white man with the native Indian, and is more completely a product than anyone of European origin is likely to be of the local conditions under which he was born and bred . . . There is, nevertheless, a sense in which the Negro, even culturally be he a purely native product, is not assimilated, though in just what sense this is true it is difficult to say.[25]

Saying in what way, precisely, blacks remained unassimilated was not a special concern for Parks.

Edward Byron Reuter casually remarked that "[t]he assimilation of the Negroes by the European culture went on with remarkable ease and unusual rapidity. The individual Negroes were highly plastic and the external conditions were highly favorable."[26] Reuter also noted that "[t]he participation of the Negroes in the group life was always limited and their assimilation of the culture values correspondingly retarded and imperfect. *Even today there are many Negroes who are not in the European culture*"[27] (emphasis supplied).

Frazier's insistence that blacks had lost all ties to African culture and traditions suggests that he viewed black Americans as assimilated.[28] Although "distinguished from other racial or cultural minorities the Negro is not distinguished by culture from the dominant group." Slowly, he wrote, "the Negro, like the European immigrant has acquired the manners and customs of America."[29] On the other hand, Frazier also found that middle-class blacks had "no cultural roots in either the Negro or white world."[30]

Gordon argued that cultural assimilation differed within the black population according to class standing. In a footnote Gordon asserts, "Although few, if any, African cultural survivals are to be found among American Negroes, lower-class Negro life with its derivations from slavery, post–Civil War discrimination, both rural and urban poverty, and enforced isolation from the middle-class white world, is still at considerable distance from the American cultural norm. Middle and upper-class Negroes, on the other hand, are acculturated to American core culture."[31]

MODERN BLACK NATIONALIST THEORY ON ASSIMILATION

Black nationalist theory, as articulated by the likes of Malcolm X, Amiri Baraka, and Robert S. Browne, rejected assimilation both as an analytic concept and as a goal of social policy, and argued for cultural and political pluralism. As an analytic tool, the model was defective, wholly inapplicable to black people and other "racial" minorities. White society, modern black nationalists pointed out, refused to assimilate blacks into American life. The cycle short-circuited when it came to blacks because their subordination benefited the majority white population. Hence, the analogy between blacks and European immigrants was fundamentally flawed. Such an analogy belittled the intensity and duration of discrimination, racial bigotry, and disenfranchisement that black Americans had faced. Plus, the idea that groups became increasingly Anglo-American did not seem to explain black cultural uniqueness.

Moreover, during the 1960s and 1970s black nationalists argued that blacks should resist assimilation. As history demonstrated, Anglo-conformity, embodied in Protestant Christianity and U.S. political institutions, was linked to materialism, racism, and exploitation. Why should blacks care to embrace these values? Certainly the most voluminous articulations of the anti-assimilationist perspective flowed from the pens of those associated with the Black Arts movement. In different ways, but especially through drama and poetry, Black Arts practitioners identified black culture as distinct from the mainstream, and they celebrated these alleged differences.

Nevertheless, modern black nationalist theory was no less loose in its formulations of black culture and assimilation than were other theoretical perspectives. Elijah Muhammad, Carlos Cooks, Ron Karenga, Amiri Baraka, and others were undecided on the question of black assimilation. For most nationalists, blacks were assimilated enough to engage in acts of self-hatred: modifying their looks to conform to a white standard, and desiring to "integrate" into a racist society. Because slavery had stripped black people of their heritage and culture, they had no "knowledge of self." With no knowledge of self, black people did misguided things – used drugs, engaged in crime, and so on. While the specific "knowledge" differed between the NOI and other nationalist groups, the message was the same. Karenga's *Kawaida* doctrine offered a corrective to a population whose ideas and values reflected a Western socialization.

On the other hand, many nationalistic theorists suggested that black culture was already distinct, or somewhat distinct. Black Arts proponents insisted that there was a "black" way of doing things. Robert S. Browne argued that the assimilation process was incomplete, and by implication that black culture was hybrid. Carmichael and Hamilton suggested, like Frazier and Gordon, that only a certain stratum of blacks had adopted "mainstream" white culture.

CULTURAL PLURALISM

In its rejection of Anglo-conformity, modern black nationalist theory most closely resembled cultural pluralism, particularly in its later, 1960s manifestations. Jewish scholar Horace Kallen first articulated the classic cultural pluralist position in 1915 in a series of articles published in *The Nation*. In these articles, Kallen rejected the idea of Anglo-conformity both as a prescription for European immigrant assimilation and as a description of what actually happened to immigrant culture. Instead, Kallen highlighted the ways in which ethnic groups preserved their languages, religions, and customs over time. Kallen based his idea on kinship and lineage: "Men may change their clothes, their politics, their wives . . . they cannot change their grandfathers."[32]

The cultural pluralist perspective lay dormant until the 1960s, when Nathan Glazer and Daniel Patrick Moynihan offered a new account of ethnic group politics and acculturation. In *Beyond the Melting Pot*

(1963), Glazer and Moynihan noticed that ethnic groups both maintained cultural distinctiveness and assimilated American cultural patterns, especially political ones. Yet unlike Kallen's use of the term "pluralism," Glazer and Moynihan's concept was taken from political science. "Pluralism" described the workings of the American political system as one of vying and contending interest groups. "Ethnic group pluralism" wedded political pluralism to cultural pluralism. Glazer and Moynihan argued, somewhat like Kallen, that ethnic identity did not melt. Rather, *modified* ethnic identities were tied to political behavior. As they explained, "someone who is Irish or Jewish or Italian generally has other traits than the mere existence of the name that associated him [sic] with other people attached to the group. A man is connected to his group by ties of family and friendship. But he is also connected by ties of interest. The ethnic groups of New York are also *"interest groups."*[33] Still, according to Glazer and Moynihan, some assimilation had occurred:

The assimilating power of American society and culture operated on immigrant groups in different ways, to make them, it is true, something they had not been, but still something distinct and identifiable ... In the third generation, the descendants of the immigrants confronted each other, and knew they were both Americans, in the same dress, with the same language, using the same artifacts, troubled by the same things, *but they voted differently, had different ideas about education and sex, and were still, in many essential ways, as different from one another as their grandfathers had been.*[34] (emphasis supplied)

Like Glazer and Moynihan, Carmichael and Hamilton adopted a strategy that began with the premise of ethnic group pluralism: "Black Power recognizes ... the ethnic basis of American politics" and seeks "an effective share in the total power of society." Echoing Glazer and Moynihan, the authors of *Black Power* pointed out that studies of voting behavior made it clear that the pot had not melted in the political arena: "Italians vote for Rubino over O'Brian; Irish for Murphy over Goldberg, etc." While this phenomenon was hardly ideal, it nevertheless remained "a central fact of the American political system."[35]

But Glazer and Moynihan's study didn't explain only how and why ethnic identities failed to melt. These authors also attempted to explain social mobility and political power as a function of cultural traits and familial patterns. The Irish had not prospered as much as, say, the Jews, because of their propensity toward alcoholism. Catholicism explained both Irish success in the political process and Irish failure to achieve the same sort of socioeconomic mobility that Jewish Americans had acquired.[36] Moreover, the form of "individuality and ambition" characteristic of Protestant and Anglo-Saxon culture was absent among

Italian Americans. Jews prospered partly because of their thirst for education. Marital breakup was less common among Jews, and the Jewish parents' control of their children resulted in significant "neurosis" but "less psychosis."[37]

Blacks, by contrast, had been crippled by slavery. The peculiar institution weakened black family structure, and that weakness had important effects. One was that blacks lacked the clannishness that other ethnic groups had used to create and sustain separate economic markets and clientele. The relatively large number of female-headed households also increased the chance of psychological difficulties among black boys. Despite the many social problems that afflicted Afro-Americans, "the middle-class Negro contributes little, in money, organization, or involvement, to the solution" of these problems.[38]

Moynihan expanded the thesis of black familial pathology in his controversial *The Negro Family: The Case for National Action* (1965). Drawing on Frazier's studies of social disorganization among black families, Moynihan suggested that slavery, Jim Crow, continuing disparities in employment opportunities (especially for males) and income, as well as grinding poverty, forced "the Negro community" into a matriarchal family structure. This structure, Moynihan contended, "seriously retards the progress of the groups as a whole, and imposes a crushing burden on the Negro male and, in consequence, on a great many Negro women as well."[39] Thus assigning a range of statistical patterns – work and educational achievement, crime and delinquency – to one source, matriarchy, Moynihan could declare, "[T]he present tangle of pathology is capable of perpetuating itself without assistance from the white world."[40]

While focussed on the urban rebellions of the period, *The Kerner Report* (1968) also linked the lack of black mobility partly to family structure among blacks. "Cultural factors . . . made it easier for the immigrants to escape from poverty." Their "families were large, and . . . patriarchal . . . so men found satisfactions in family life that helped compensate for the bad jobs they had to take and the hard work they had to endure." Blacks, by contrast, "came to the city under quite different circumstances." Because of slavery and unemployment, "the Negro family structure had become matriarchal," thus providing fewer "cultural and psychological rewards" to the black man.[41]

In light of the reigning theories about culture, family structure, dysfunction, and mobility, it should not be entirely surprising that nationalist calls for "manhood" were linked to demands for female subordination and patriarchal family structures. The Nation of Islam was the best example of this tendency, with extreme gender segregation in school and mosque, and middle-class, nuclear standards of family life;

but cultural and revolutionary organizations operated on similar assumptions of patriarchy and gender subordination. That most black nationalist organizations saw a rehabilitated "manhood" as essential to black progress and esteem shows the extent to which their ideas fit within a broader constellation of American social and political thought.

Like Glazer and Moynihan, black nationalists of the 1960s and 1970s linked disparities in wealth, income, and social stability to weak efforts on the part of black people themselves. Carlos Cooks and Malcolm X, for instance, offer similar versions of this perspective. Cooks complained that blacks failed to prosper in a predominantly black Harlem, while Jews, Chinese, Italian, Irish, and "other minorities" had utilized all the advantages of the system and simultaneously retained "an affinity with the old sod."[42]

Malcolm X offered a similar analysis in an October 1963 speech at Berkeley. Still representing the Nation of Islam, Malcolm X took this occasion to explain the causes and meaning of rising racial tensions. He also spoke about the conditions that led to the problems poor blacks faced in the United States. For my purposes, the most interesting aspect of this talk was one response during the question-and-answer period. A member of the audience asked how descendants of immigrants had come to develop prejudicial attitudes, even though their parents and grand-parents had faced virulent xenophobia. Malcolm X responded by sug-gesting that "modern slavery" – by which he meant patterns of white exploitation of blacks – perpetuated racial prejudice. Because black people occupied the bottom tier of the socioeconomic ladder – again, as a result of white supremacy – white people could easily "blame the victim" and develop a set of ideas to justify their attitudes. Yet Malcolm X also took the opportunity to expound on the failure of black leader-ship to do what other ethnic leadership had done:

The mistake that we made differs from the mistake you didn't make. Your parents solved your problems economically, of their own volition, with their own inge-nuity. Our leaders have done nothing to teach us how to go in business. They have done nothing to teach us how to elevate the levels of our schools.[43] (empha-sis supplied)

Rather than responding in the way one might expect – "numerous discriminatory practices frustrated efforts of black entrepreneurs to create viable businesses," for example, or "white ethnic groups deliber-ately kept Afro-Americans out of their unions" – Malcolm X, like Glazer and Moynihan, identified *black leaders* as a large part of the problem. Since Afro-American leadership had not encouraged the development of black businesses and had not adequately stressed the importance of edu-cation, blacks had been unable to achieve the gains of other groups.

Hence, from Malcolm X's perspective, Afro-Americans had failed to do what other "ethnic" groups had done.

BLACKS AS CULTURAL OUTSIDERS

Through his entire public career, Ralph Ellison repeatedly insisted that the view of blacks as alien to American culture was inaccurate. In an essay published in *Time* magazine in 1971, Ellison argued that those who would rid America of its black inhabitants never stop to "imagine what the United States would have been, or not been, had there been no blacks to give it – if I may be so bold as to say – color."[44] The short answer is "nothing recognizably American." The long answer takes us through a complex and certainly underappreciated story of political, economic, and cultural history in the United States, which bears a decidedly Afro-American stamp. From the patterns and style of American colloquial speech to jazz, rock 'n' roll, and hip-hop in the contemporary period, blacks have influenced American popular culture. Without blacks, U.S. economic and political history would have been different. "No slave economy, no Civil War; no violent destruction of the Reconstruction; no K.K.K. and no Jim Crow system." Without the disenfranchisement of Afro-Americans and the "manipulation of racial fears," Southern politicians would not have enjoyed the disproportionate power they have enjoyed over domestic policy. "Indeed," Ellison wrote, "it is almost impossible to conceive of what our political system would have become without the snarl of forces – cultural, racial, religious – that make our nation what it is today."[45]

Ellison's observations contrast sharply with Anglo-conformist theory in general, and the Chicago school version in particular. Anglo-conformist theory assumes that "out-groups" assimilate into a fundamentally Anglo cultural milieu. While it is true that an Anglo tradition has profoundly influenced American culture, that same Anglo tradition evolved in response to uniquely American demographic, economic, and intellectual trends. Further, from any angle one approaches the matter of American culture, one must conclude that it is part Afro-American.

Ellison's theory contrasts in the same way with black nationalist theory of the 1960s and early 1970s. Through the black nationalist lens of this period, American culture was Anglo, Protestant, and white. By definition, blacks were cultural outsiders, and their culture was defective. But again, the ambiguous and even arbitrary constructions of black culture, consciousness, and aesthetics – from US to the Black Arts movement – suggest that cultural identity sprang not from organic sources, but was self-consciously constituted. After all, "racial," "ethnic" and "cultural" categories ultimately result from social and *political* practice. Further, while we can easily speak of, say, different linguistic patterns or dietary patterns among immigrant populations of *specific* times in *specific* places, "culture" is under constant transformation. Moreover, traditions and cultures reflect patterns of economic organization, gender, and class.

Aside from its interpretive error – that of conceiving U.S. culture in wholly inadequate "black" and "white" terms – the idea that black people are cultural outsiders has been offered as an explanation for their unequal status and relative lack of socioeconomic mobility. The style of thought Stephen Steinberg calls "New Darwinism" holds that different cultural attributes resulted in different rates of success for white ethnic groups. The required values, according to Steinberg, "are familiar to anyone who has heard Benjamin Franklin's homilies or read Horatio Alger novels – frugality, industry, foresight, perseverance, ingenuity, and the like."[46]

But culture did not and does not explain mobility and its opposite. As Steinberg persuasively argues, pre-immigration factors – skills, literacy or lack thereof – more effectively explain different rates of upward mobility among, say, Irish, Italians, and Jews, than does culture. Glazer and Moynihan completely ignored such factors. For instance, at the height of European immigration, the vast majority of Jewish immigrants were classified as skilled laborers. Conversely, Irish and Italian immigrants were overwhelmingly unskilled laborers. This fact alone would give Jewish immigrants a different kind of advantage in the U.S. labor market. Concerning blacks, Steinberg points to patterns of housing discrimination, job discrimination, and poor education to explain why blacks have not kept pace with other "ethnic" groups.[47]

Indeed, the notion that blacks' social and economic status stems from group culture may assume more homogeneity among Afro-Americans than is warranted. Their "racial" similarity – already an ideological construction – serves as proxy for a unified "cultural identity." Even if one *could* speak of an authentic black culture, not mediated by a mass-consumption oriented market economy, status in U.S. society is a function of many facets of one's identity – class, gender, sexual orientation, occupation, age. Without theories that accounted for these differences within the black population, nationalists simply flipped New Darwinist arguments, assuming too easily that "black consciousness" or pseudo-African lifestyles would have uniformly beneficial effects on all black people.

Thus, when nationalists like Nation of Islam leader Elijah Muhammad, cultural nationalist Amiri Baraka, and economist Robert Browne argued about the biological and/or cultural distinctiveness of black people, they followed an old script, modified by a new political and intellectual landscape. Cultural nationalists involved in the Black Arts movement, for instance, tried to create a revolutionary black aesthetic as an antidote to white, Western materialistic culture. Barbara Ann Teer, for example, identified black culture in "the way we talk (the rhythms of our speech which naturally fit our impulses), the way we walk, sing, dance, pray, laugh, eat, make love, and finally . . . the way we look, make up our cultural heritage."[48] More sophisticated arguments suggested that "a unique and particular way of being" was born out of "the conditioning of black people leasing time on a planet controlled by whitemen."[49] But in suggesting that the "black way" was opposed to the "white way," nationalists extended arguments first made during the antebellum period to distinguish blacks from others. The artists and poets associated with the Black Arts movement found themselves searching for a black *volk* or spirit that Harriet Beecher Stowe thought she had identified more than a century before.

CONCLUSION

The ethnic paradigm formed the template against which theories about acculturation and mobility were forged. In the nineteenth century, conceptions of romantic racialism and "civilization" and "Christianity" formed the ideology or social epistemology that seemed to explain American identity and social mobility. By the second decade of the twentieth century, the ethnic paradigm had evolved to serve this function. Given the unique social and ethnic makeup of the United States, its historical relationship to the peculiar institution, and its economic development, the ethnic paradigm answered the fundamental question about the meaning of American identity and the persistence of inequality. The ethnic paradigm's rendition of American identity obscured a more complex reality, and it shaped all theories about acculturation during the twentieth century. Hence, the Chicago school, for all its progressive tendencies, reproduced conventional thinking in a number of important respects. So did cultural pluralism; and so, too, did much black nationalism of the 1960s and early 1970s. Black nationalist theorists attempted to fashion perspectives that were not beholden to reigning theories about race and ethnicity; and, unlike the Anglo-conformists, and more thoroughly than did the cultural pluralists, they attempted to draw distinctions between the experience of blacks and the experience of white ethnics. However, all too often, 1960s and 1970s black nationalists also assumed that blacks were "cultural outsiders" and that their culture was in need of reform.

7

Black Nationalism in the Contemporary Era

This chapter brings my analysis of black nationalism in the United States to the end of the twentieth century. It investigates the two most prominent manifestations of black nationalism since the end of the black freedom struggle in the mid-1970s, the NOI under the leadership of Louis Farrakhan, and Afrocentricity as principally defined by Molefi Kete Asante. Of course, as in the past, black nationalism takes more forms than these two; and of the two, Afrocentricity as a scholarly enterprise doesn't meet my strict definition: this mostly scholar-led movement does not seek to establish a separate state. Nevertheless, Afrocentricity definitely grows out of the cultural nationalist tendency of the late 1960s and early 1970s.

Both Farrakhan's nationalism and Afrocentricity rest on assumptions that have dominated thinking about black life, culture, and mobility in the United States for more than half a century – what I referred to in the previous chapter as the "ethnic paradigm." Reflecting nineteenth-century organic assumptions about race and culture, the NOI and Afrocentrists take as given the idea that cultures, if not races, are fundamentally different. They then make the New Darwinian argument that a defective culture, or "lack of identity," hinders black progress. Both make some demands on the state; but, thus far, neither tendency firmly links its political trajectory to the efforts of labor, feminist, or other typically progressive political forces. Both offer, instead, highly idealistic proposals – one explicitly religious, the other quasi-religious – for group empowerment.

The current activities of the NOI under Farrakhan, and Afrocentricity as a scholarly enterprise, must be understood in the context of post–segregation era black politics. This is an era in which the impressive gains made by a certain portion of the Afro-American population stand in glaring contrast to economic difficulties of roughly a third of that same population. Largely because of affirmative action, the strength of antidiscrimination laws, and a growing economy, the black middle class has grown. On the other hand, according to official statistics, roughly one-third of the Afro-American population falls below the poverty line; and forty percent of black American children do so. And even in the current period of economic growth, unemployment rates for black men and women are double those of their white counterparts – 7.7 percent to 3.5 percent respectively.[1]

The trajectory of black politics since the late 1960s has shifted from protest to incorporation. However, although blacks have been elected to public office in increasing numbers – 1,468 officeholders in 1970, 8,656 in 1997[2] – these officials have been unable to deliver policies that benefit all segments, particularly poorer segments, of the black population. Nor have the numerous black regimes – black mayors with the support of black majority city councils – been able to do much to address deep-seated problems like low wages and joblessness in central cities.[3] Neither long-standing organizations like the NAACP, the Urban League, and CORE, nor newer organizations like Jesse Jackson's Operation PUSH (People United to Serve Humanity) have fashioned strategies that effectively address the problems of the black poor. Despite its strange cosmology, the NOI stands as the sole *national* black political organization that has a strategy explicitly aimed at improving the lot of the most disadvantaged.

Post–segregation era politics operates in an increasingly conservative political environment, most dramatically signaled by the Republican capture of the House and Senate in 1994, but initiated by developments growing out of the Reagan/Bush era. Reagan initiated what may be understood as a dismantling of the second Reconstruction, when programs and entitlements secured by the social movements of the 1960s have been abolished or effectively reduced. Reflecting a two-decade-long effort of Republican strategists, the business lobby, and the religious right, as well as the efforts of a number of conservative policy institutes or think tanks, conservatives have dominated the contemporary domestic policy debate, and they have encouraged the view that governmental solutions to domestic problems like poverty and racial inequality are untenable. A number of noteworthy studies explaining racial inequality have been advanced by scholars with ties to these think tanks, including Thomas Sowell's *Ethnic America* (1981), Charles Murray and Richard Hernstein's *The Bell Curve* (1995), and D'nesh D'Souza's *The End of Racism* (1997), to name three. Where Murray and Hernstein root inequality in the genes via IQ measurements, Sowell and D'Souza root inequality in defective culture.

Nor can the resurgence in political activism among evangelical Christians be underemphasized. This segment of the population has, over the last three decades, changed from being the least politically active population of Christians in the United States to the *most* active.[4] Some of their concerns – outlawing or restricting abortion, challenging gay and lesbian lifestyles, "getting tough" on crime, allowing prayer in public schools, the use of public vouchers in private schools, challenging affirmative action, and lowering taxes – have greatly affected the orientation of the GOP. Organized under the Christian Coalition and supported by influential leaders like Pat Robertson of "The 700 Club," talk show host James Dobson, and the Family Research Council's Gary Bauer, these Christian conservatives are among those who have helped discredit the idea that government can effectively solve pressing social problems. For this constituency, government is the problem.

FARRAKHAN AND THE NEW NOI

Farrakhan's increased visibility and significance to contemporary black politics traces back to Malcolm X's split with the NOI. After Malcolm X's defection, Farrakhan replaced him as minister of the Harlem temple, and as chief spokesman for Elijah Muhammad. And although Farrakhan denies any direct involvement in Malcolm X's assassination, he does admit to helping to foster the climate that led to Malcolm X's death. In the pages of *Muhammad Speaks*, Farrakhan wrote:

Only those who wish to be led to hell, or to their doom will follow Malcolm. The die is set and Malcolm shall not escape, especially after such foolish talk about his benefactor in trying to rob him of the divine glory which Allah has bestowed upon him. Such a man as Malcolm is worthy of death – and would have met with death if it had not been for Muhammad's confidence in Allah for victory over the enemies.[5]

After Elijah Muhammad's death in 1975, Muhammad's seventh son, Warith Deen Muhammad, succeeded his father and transformed the Nation of Islam. W.D. Muhammad repudiated his father's teachings and redirected the new "World Community of al-Islam in the West" toward Sunni Islam. Warith Deen replaced his top administrators, abolished the Fruit of Islam and Muslim Girls Training, and relaxed the dress code. Most dramatically, he changed the policy that excluded whites, allowing nonblacks to join his organization. The fact that "devils" were permitted to join meant that Warith Deen had abandoned the NOI's remarkable creation mythology. These doctrinal changes also meant that Warith Deen had rejected such ideas as Fard's divinity, Elijah Muhammad as prophet, and the imminent apocalypse. Warith Deen also urged his followers to participate in politics. He consistently endorsed Republican candidates "throughout the 1980s and early 1990s, including his backing of George Bush over Bill Clinton."[6]

Farrakhan made known his intention to break from the World Community of al-Islam in November of 1977. By this time, Warith Deen was struggling to settle the debts of his organization, which had resulted from poor management and the fact that E. Muhammad had died intestate. Farrakhan's movement "began subterraneanly, reproducing itself in temporary storefronts and makeshift back rooms."[7] Farrakhan's popularity increased following his first Savior's Day Convention in 1981, and, more importantly, after the presidential campaign in 1984.

Farrakhan's new Nation competed with others. Silis Muhammad and Abu Kossn established the Lost-Found Nation of Islam (LFNOI), basing it in Atlanta. Brother Solomon and former secretary Abass Rassoul created the United Nation of Islam in Camp Springs, Maryland. And, while not following Farrakhan, Elijah Muhammad's younger brother, John Muhammad, maintained the Nation of Islam name for his Detroit temple.[8] Of these rivals, Silis Muhammad's organization commands the biggest following, with more than twenty mosques, although Farrakhan's NOI dwarfs the LFNOI in terms of membership and resources.[9]

Upon establishing his Nation of Islam, Farrakhan worked over the next two decades to rebuild the old empire. He bought and moved into the mansion once occupied by Elijah Muhammad, reestablished the Fruit of Islam and Muslim Girls Training, and built a number of schools modeled on the old system. He also pursued numerous business projects. In the mid-1980s, for instance, Farrakhan unfurled his POWER (People Organized and Working for Economic Rebirth) enterprise, through which, for a fee, members purchased POWER products at a reduced rate. POWER hoped to elevate black America: "This productivity of black people will cause us to address our own unemployment concerns. It will enable us to rebuild a stable black family life. It will drastically reduce the involvement of black people in crime and drugs."[10] Other ventures included a chain of Salaam restaurants, bakeries, a line of clothing, skin and hair care products, food markets, tapes, books, and the *Final Call* newspaper. Articles in the publication appeal to a broad audience. The newspaper's range of stories – from alleged CIA collusion in the crack trade, to prison development, to discrimination in the legal system – touch on issues of broad concern to the black population. The publication is also fortified with excerpts from Elijah Muhammad's teachings, as well as often arcane and esoteric commentary by Minister Farrakhan and contributing editors. The *Final Call* is littered with ads for the NOI's products – from bottled water, to multitudes of books that explain NOI theology, to videos and cassettes featuring Farrakhan's speeches. Since the late 1980s, the NOI has also established a number of security agencies that patrol neighborhoods and housing complexes in Chicago, New York, Washington, D.C., and other cities. For these services, the NOI-affiliated agencies have received millions of dollars in public funds.[11]

In a departure from the past, Farrakhan has sought greater international visibility – particularly in the Arab world – and has incorporated more elements of conventional Islam into the NOI's practices. In 1986 Farrakhan embarked on an international tour that included stops in Ghana, Pakistan, Japan, Iran, and China. A more recent world tour included stops in Nigeria, Sudan, South Africa, Tunisia, Iraq, and Libya.[12] Furthermore, over the years the NOI has maintained ties to Libya, receiving a million-dollar loan from the Libyan government in 1972, and unsuccessfully attempting to secure a billion-dollar gift from the Libyan government in 1996. Through such exchange, Farrakhan and the leadership of the NOI have gained more fluency regarding Islamic rituals and behavior patterns, as well as greater familiarity with Islamic religious literature.[13]

Indeed, where before Farrakhan and the NOI insisted on the practice of Islam as taught by Elijah Muhammad – that W. D. Fard was the incarnation of Allah, and that Fard's successor, Elijah Muhammad, was a prophet – at the most recent annual Savior's Day convention in Chicago, Farrakhan declared, "We bear witness that there is no prophet after the prophet Mohammed."[14] Farrakhan has not, however, renounced the Yacub mythology, although he has eschewed the "white devil" rhetoric for some time.

In another departure from the past, Farrakhan has assumed a more active role in electoral politics. In fact, Farrakhan first came to national attention in connection with Jesse Jackson and his presidential bid in 1984. Farrakhan endorsed Jackson, and registered to vote on February 9, 1984.[15] The Nation of Islam provided campaign workers for Jackson, as well as Fruit of Islam guards who provided personal security for the candidate. This alliance proved to be short-lived. When the *Washington Post* reporter Milton Coleman disclosed the fact that Jackson had referred to Jews as "Hymies" and to New York City as "Hymietown," Farrakahn issued a threat: "we're going to make an example of Mr. Coleman. I'm going to stay on his case until we make him a fit example for the rest of them . . . One day soon we will punish you with death."[16] Farrakhan's insensitive pronouncement of Hitler as "great" (in the sense of significance) and other incendiary remarks about Judaism as a "gutter religion" forced Jackson to publicly disavow the statements and distance himself from the NOI leader.

Farrakhan's popularity during the early 1990s was tied to the media exposure he enjoyed after the Jackson campaign. From that point forward, mainstream media featured Farrakhan frequently, publishing stories that exposed the minister's inflamed and sometimes anti-Semitic remarks. In fact, Smith observes that since the mid-1980s Farrakhan has been the second most frequently featured black activist, the first being Jesse Jackson.[17] Farrakhan and the NOI drew intense and shrill criticism when his former spokesman, Khalid Muhammad, delivered a highly incendiary and offensive speech at Kean College on November 23, 1993. The Jewish Anti-Defamation League took out a full-page ad in the *New York Times* in January of 1994 to expose the scandalously racist, homophobic, anti-Semitic remarks. The February 28, 1994, issue of *Time* magazine featured Farrakhan with the subtitle, "Minister of Hate."

Farrakhan was propelled through other forums. He appeared on "The Phil Donahue Show" in March of 1990. He also visited "The Arsenio Hall Show" in February 1994. And, most significantly, the Million Man March on October 16, 1995, gave Farrakhan far-reaching media exposure. Not only did CNN cover the rally in its entirety, but the network also provided periodic analysis and commentary by observers, critics, and participants. Following the historic event, Farrakhan appeared on "Larry King Live" with Jesse Jackson and Harvard psychiatrist Dr. Alvin Poussaint. Robert Novak interviewed Farrakhan on CNN in February 1997, and on April 13, 1997, Farrakhan appeared on "Meet the Press." Coverage of Farrakhan in the mainstream media does not match the exposure he receives on local radio and cable stations. Farrakhan's addresses can be heard on radio and television in dozens of cities across the United States.

This notoriety fueled Farrakhan's rise in at least two ways. First, the periodic media coverage increased Farrakhan's name recognition, both here and abroad. This is not to suggest, as Singh correctly notes, that Farrakhan is simply a media creation, as some have contended.[18] Nevertheless, Farrakhan's image has been amplified by the sort of coverage he has received over the years. Conversely, over the years the minister has been effective in turning this intense scrutiny and criticism to his advantage.

Public opinion studies registered considerable support during the early to mid-1990s. According to the University of Chicago's 1993–94 black politics study, two-thirds of Afro-Americans considered Farrakhan a good leader. Only 28 percent considered him dangerous. A 1994 poll revealed that "70 percent of African-Americans felt Farrakhan 'says things the country should hear'; 67 percent saw him as an 'effective leader'; 62 percent held him to be 'good for the black community'; and . . . 63 percent believed he 'speaks the truth.'"[19]

These figures seem to be borne out by the audiences that line up to hear the minister speak. Since the mid-1980s, Farrakhan has drawn tens of thousands to hear him speak in auditoriums across the United States. He has been popular as well on the college speaking circuit.

Most dramatically, Farrakhan successfully called the Million Man March, which in terms of numbers (850,000 to upwards of one million) represented the largest gathering of blacks in United States history.

Nevertheless, it is difficult to determine what these large numbers mean in terms of support for Farrakhan's full agenda. Clearly, a few things are at work. First, black elected officials have been unable to deliver policies that would benefit the unemployed and the working black poor. Also, given the fact that black political discourse takes "race" as its principal analytic category – a legacy of the Black Power era – Farrakhan, like Garvey and Malcolm X before him, has been able to position himself as the "authentic" militant race spokesman. The range and variety of criticism of Farrakhan has, in turn, ironically affirmed the minister's role as an authentic and radical spokesman for black issues. The sensationalistic coverage of Farrakhan's unsavory remarks has fueled a sort of racial defensiveness on the part of many black Americans. As Reed notes, "Farrakhan has been attacked so vigorously and singularly *in part* because he is black. He has been invented by whites as a symbol embodying, and therefore justifying, their fears of a black peril. Blacks have come to his defense *mainly* because he is black and perceived to be a victim of racially inspired defamation." It is doubtful, Reed adds, that those "who rally to vindicate him know or have anything substantive to say about his program."[20] Third, Farrakhan's talks are immensely entertaining, combining political commentary with feel-good catharsis. Reed suggests that for younger, particularly male, supporters, "embrace of the image of Farrakhan . . . is a totemic act of the sort distinctive to mass consumption culture: highly salient but without clear meaning, easily and effortlessly accessible." His older supporters are attracted by the "cathartic, feel-good militancy and conservative substance" that Farrakhan offers.[21]

However, if conversion is the best way to measure Farrakhan's success, he has failed to attract large numbers of black Americans, on or off college campuses. He has not won in the arena of public opinion. And even after making a few efforts, the NOI has not enjoyed electoral success. Farrakhan has enjoyed *most* success as a public orator.

THE MILLION MAN MARCH

Called by Louis Farrakhan, the Million Man March was organized under the theme Atonement, Responsibility, and Reconciliation, wherein black men would acknowledge their moral failure and commit themselves to a new type of community activism. Organizers of the march encouraged participants to register to vote, if they had not. Buckets were circulated by the FOI to collect money for a black development fund, the precise accounting of which remains unclear. Finally, Farrakhan himself urged his audience to join *any* political organization.[22]

In contrast to the March on Washington in 1963, the Million Man March had no clear policy agenda. Where the marchers in 1963 assembled to pressure President John F. Kennedy and the Congress for civil rights legislation, and where the 1963 march culminated roughly a decade of sustained grassroots mobilization, the Million Man March represented neither. If anything, Farrakhan and the March reproduced conservative tendencies in black nationalism and black politics more generally. Unlike, say, the Gary Convention and its call for a number of policy proposals geared toward addressing the problems of inadequate health care, schools, jobs, and so on, the themes of the Million Man March encouraged self-help more than government policy. In fact, very few of the speeches that day referred explicitly to the effects of conservative policy on black life in America.

Further, the absence of women at the March signaled the continuing existence of a deep and enduring sexism prevalent in black uplift ideology. The marchers agreed that black men had particular responsibilities in need of address; and in this and other respects, the Million Man March articulated sentiments not unlike those of the evangelical Christian men's group the Promise Keepers, who are determined to reassert themselves as proper heads of their households and who root that alleged mandate in scripture.[23]

Despite the large turnout, analysts are divided about the March's significance. Million Man Marchers surveyed, for instance, declared that "support for the black family" was far more important to most marchers than "support for Minister Farrakhan."[24] Clearly, the marchers who assembled did so because of a shared concern about problems confronting black America. Yet, neither Farrakhan's speech nor his post-March efforts suggest that he can offer much in the way of strategy. This was evident not long after Farrakhan began to address the Million Man Marchers, when he embarked on a bizarre application of numerology, apparently aimed at fraternal and lodge organizations represented at the March:

There, in the middle of this mall is the Washington Monument, 555 feet high. But if we put a 1 in front of that 555 feet, we get 1555, the year that our first fathers landed on the shores of Jamestown, Virginia as slaves . . . Abraham Lincoln is the 16th president. Thomas Jefferson is the third president. 16 and 3 make 19 again. What is so deep about this number 19? Why we are standing on the Capital steps today? That number 19! When you have nine, you have a womb that is pregnant. And when you have a one standing by the nine, it means that there's something secret that has to be unfolded.[25]

While Farrakhan spent considerable time on numerological themes, as well as on concepts like "atonement," he spent little time discussing a policy agenda of any kind, notwithstanding his urging of his listeners to join *any* political effort. Roughly one year after the Republican Party seized control of both houses of Congress, unfurled their Contract with America, and sought to make their agenda a reality, Farrakhan was surprisingly silent about the dangerous potential the conservative agenda held for the very people to whom he ministers.

POPULIST CONSERVATISM IN BLACKFACE

Reed's observation of the conservative substance of Farrakhan's message needs to be underscored. Aside from Farrakhan's discourse on racism in America – the same discourse that has defined the NOI's posture for decades – his political and ideological viewpoints position him at the far right end of the political spectrum. In fact, since competing black nationalistic groups are largely absent from the present political context, the NOI and Farrakhan can be usefully compared to a number of far right, white nationalist proponents.

A number of scholars have shown how this is so. Singh situated Farrakhan's "conservative authoritarianism" within the broader historical tradition of paranoid politics in America.[26] And Marable characterized NOI ideology as "deeply conservative and fundamentalist."[27] Noting the organization's view of black people as biologically distinct and behaviorally pathological, and generally conservative on political and economic issues, Reed argued that Louis Farrakhan and the NOI stand on "common conceptual ground with all manner of racists."[28] Gardell likened Farrakhan's perspective to that of European "third positionists," who espouse a form of national socialism that combines anticapitalism, anticommunism, environmentalism, and racial separatism."[29]

To be sure, white separatists occupy a different place in America's racial hierarchy – they are white people, after all – and they form part of the constellation of conservative forces that work to maintain the racial status quo. As Ezekiel, Zeskind, Daniels, and others have noted, the sentiments and policy preferences of many white separatists blend with considerable ease into contemporary conservatism, particularly the pro-gun, pro-Western values, antigay, and antifeminist agendas associated with "populists" like Pat Buchanan.[30] Further, unlike some white separatists and nationalists, the NOI has not been linked to a single hate crime. Due to its longstanding function as a mutual aid, self-help organization, the NOI assumes a more defensive posture than many contemporary white supremacists.

Nevertheless, three similarities stand out with respect to the various groups and activists. First, racial separatists and nationalists articulate the real and imagined economic concerns of a largely – though not exclusively – working-class, heterosexual, male constituency. Second, the call for separatism grows out of the conviction that "racial" groups compete against others in a Darwinian struggle. Third, racial separatists argue that contemporary political developments, from NAFTA to affirmative action policies, have secret, conspiratorial causes, most of which implicate Jews.

Further, the NOI has flirted with elements of the far right over the years. The NOI, as Malcolm X disclosed, met with leaders of the Georgia Klan in 1961,[31] and Nazi leader Norman Rockwell offered an address at the annual Savior's Day convention in 1962.[32] More recently, in 1990, Farrakhan granted an interview to the far right *Spotlight* in which he suggested that blacks had to improve their condition "so that the communities of the world will not mind accepting us as an equal member among the community of family of nations."[33] During the early 1990s, the NOI also fostered exchanges with supporters of far right activist Lyndon LaRouche.[34]

POST-NATIONALISTIC POLITICS?

In light of Farrakhan's apparent aspirations for political power, and in light of his efforts to move his organization in the direction of orthodox Islamic practice, it may be that Louis Farrakhan's vision is more akin to that of the religious right, but with a left-of-center, populist inflection. Farrakhan tends to agree with leaders of the religious right on social issues like homosexuality, drug use, and the goal of strengthening marital bonds. Like Robertson and other religious right leaders he argues that the black poor need to do more by themselves to solve their problems, on the ground that poverty is largely a function of bad behavior. However, Farrakhan also thinks that government ought to address matters of racial, gender, and economic inequality.

Louis Farrakhan's *Torchlight for America* (1993) shows how this is so. In it, Farrakhan attributes declining voter turnout, and declining wages for U.S. workers, partly to the corrupting influence of money in American politics. He notes that public schools in the United States do not offer the quality that schools in other industrialized nations do, and that infant mortality and levels of obesity are embarrassing for a nation of vast wealth and resources. Farrakhan also criticizes the "greed" that has driven corporations to forsake U.S. workers and relocate overseas.

However, his prescriptions in *Torchlight* do not call for any action associated with the political movements – labor, civil rights, feminist – that arguably offer most hope for empowerment of poorer Americans generally, and of people of color specifically. His solutions ask the individual to transform himself. For instance, while he supports "a reasonable universal health-care coverage plan," Farrakhan believes that "making America healthy must become the personal responsibility of each citizen, and not the responsibility of government."[35]

Farrakhan argues that educational reform requires longer school years, higher wages for teachers, and more participation by parents. But it also means, as it does for Pat Robertson, "Recognition of God [as] the proper beginning point for understanding every discipline. If we cannot honor God, the Supreme Teacher, then how can the children honor their teachers? We have this thing all backwards. You don't pledge your allegiance to a flag, which is merely the symbol of a nation. You pledge allegiance to God, and you work for your flag and country."[36]

Farrakhan understands the problems of contemporary society to be a result of deep spiritual corruption.[37] Like Pat Robertson, he maintains that national disasters are signs of God's displeasure: "Natural disasters are God's way of indicating His displeasure and are a sign of impending doom . . . And more of these catastrophes are on the way to America with ever-increasing rapidity. This is God's way of nudging or forcing government leadership to accept real solutions to the country's problems."[38] He therefore calls for "a convening of the spiritual leadership to spearhead a moral rejuvenation among the American people."[39]

Farrakhan's strategic moves are not unlike the efforts of some nationalists during the late 1960s and early 1970s to enhance the status of Afro-Americans in a pluralistic political system. Indeed, there are signs that Farrakhan is in the process of softening his stance on racial separatism and reformulating his ideas about political strategy. Where before Farrakhan and the NOI tended to stress self-help solutions to the problems of blacks in the United States, Farrakhan is now attempting – under the aegis of the Million Family March scheduled for October 2000 – to fashion a *multiracial* coalition that can fight for public policies that support families. Farrakhan introduces *The National Agenda* (2000) by noting the decline in voter turnout in U.S. elections, the narrow range of debate about policy issues among the contending presidential candidates, and the large sums of money corporations have directed toward lobbying efforts and political campaigns.[40] Though fortified with references from the Bible and Quran, the agenda contains numerous policy prescriptions, from guaranteed family income to affordable child care and health care. Farrakhan hopes to enlighten the public in such a way that they "will make proper choices as to who will lead us and help to create a future for us and our children."[41]

AFROCENTRICITY

The term "Afrocentric" has broad meaning, and was used at least as early as the 1960s. Typically "Afrocentric" suggests an emphasis on

African history and culture. But, beginning in the late 1980s, increasing numbers of scholars have employed the term "Afrocentric" to denote a new African-centered perspective, one shorn of problematic "Eurocentric" assumptions, and one fashioned to produce more accurate and sympathetic assessments of African life. Molefi Kete Asante has written widely on the subject, and has offered the most influential defense of this new perspective, although others – most notably Marimba Ani – have offered similar "African-centered" perspectives.[42] The Georgia-born Asante (originally Arthur Lee Smith) holds a Ph.D. in communications and teaches in the African American Studies Department at Temple University. He has worked as editor of the movement's chief organ, the *Journal of Black Studies*. Maulana Ron Karenga was an important influence on Asante's views, although Asante defines the criteria for Afrocentricity (the perspective) and Africology (the discipline) in highly iconoclastic fashion. And where Karenga's US organization continues to promote a pseudo-African lifestyle (his Kwaanza celebration is now widely observed during the holiday season), Asante leads no such political group. Nevertheless, Asante's paradigm extends many arguments associated with the cultural nationalism of the 1960s.

Asante has attacked the epistemological underpinnings of Western knowledge as inappropriate to the study of African people. For Asante, Afrocentricity first places "African ideals and values at the center of inquiry."[43] These values do not reflect the beliefs of "a specific, discrete African ethnicity, which would more narrowly mean African American, Yoruba, Ibo, Fulani, Zulu, Mandinka, Kikongo, etc."; rather, by "African" Asante means the blended, "composite African."[44] Second, investigating life from the standpoint of an African involves rooting one's inquiry in an understanding of ancient Egypt, a major *black* civilization in world history and a cultural influence on the African continent.[45] Asante is not new in his contention that Egyptian civilization influenced culture across the African continent, and that African people share a basic unity of culture and values. What is new is the historiographical apparatus he unfurls in a number of writings, including *The Afrocentric Idea* (1987), *Afrocentrism* (1988), *Kemet, Afrocentricity and Knowledge* (1990), and *Malcolm X as Cultural Hero and Other Afrocentric Essays* (1993). In these books and articles, "Afrocentricity" has a fairly narrow usage. Simply writing about black people in a sympathetic manner does not suffice. Since Afrocentricity is a metatheoretical framework, "one cannot speak logically of several types of Afrocentricity."[46] "The anteriority of the classical African civilizations," he writes, "must be entertained in any Africalogical inquiry. Classical references are necessary as baseline frames for discussing the development of African cultural phenomena. Without such reference points most research would appear disconnected, without historical continuity, discrete and isolated, incidental and nonorganic."[47]

Like nationalists of the past, Asante invents a sort of Afrocentric tradition that includes familiar names like Martin Delaney, Edward Wilmot Blyden, Marcus Garvey, Ida B. Wells, Booker T. Washington, W. E. B. Du Bois, and others. Of Delaney and Blyden, Asante writes that these activists established "the intellectual bases of the Afrocentric reclamation of African history, both on the continent and in the diaspora."[48] In *Kemet*, Asante even claims that Frantz Fanon and the Guyanese Marxist scholar Walter Rodney were a few steps away from fashioning an Afrocentric approach of the sort he favors.[49] Like many before him, however, Asante is inattentive to the manner in which his alleged predecessors differed in worldview from contemporary advocates and from each other; nor does Asante explore substantive debates, and the political contexts to which antecedent activists responded. Asante's inattentiveness suggests that the race of the antecedent thinker, coupled with Asante's contemporary assessment of the thinker's commitment to black or African equality, are the criteria on which he fashions his tradition.

In a massive anthology edited with Abu S. Abarry, *African Intellectual Heritage* (1996), Asante offers something of a canon of African discourse, beginning with texts from ancient Kemet and extending to the mid-1990s. The editors group the texts into six categories, spanning roughly four millennia: "The Creation of the Universe," "Religious Ideas," "Culture and Identity," "Philosophy and Morality," "Society and Politics," "Resistance and Renewal." The Pharaoh Pepi, Kenyan political leader Jomo Kenyatta, literary critic Houston A. Baker, Jr., Marcus Garvey, writer James Baldwin, and political activist and writer Angela Davis are among the authors featured in this collection. Abarry and Asante struggle to find commonalities among the enormous array of writers they include, acknowledging the diversity of African peoples. Nevertheless, their effort is to stress similarity; so, for instance, they write concerning African religion and the diffusion of African culture that "[i]n the African world view, it was not so much that nature was god as that humans and nature were from the same source,"[50] and that "the spread of ancient myths and beliefs . . . have [sic] thrust elements of the African life style and civilization across the entire continent."[51] Of political commonality, the editors write that "the inspiration of the heroic ancestors is found in every African community."[52]

Asante and Aburry establish more of a "black" canon than an "African" one. Although canons invariably require arbitrary rules to determine which texts will be included, the works represent such a range of ideas, commentary of such breadth, and a time span of such enormous length, that racial identity seems to be the sole characteristic that unites the many perspectives. The belief in commonality ultimately derives from the belief that blacks exist as a form of organic community.

Assumptions of organicism explain why Asante settles a long-debated matter – the cultural identity of black Americans – with a simple assertion: Afro-Americans are African. By doing so, Asante demonstrates a tendency in nationalist theory to simplify a more complex historical and sociological story. He fails to consider syncretism between "black culture" and "white culture" in the United States. His Afrocentricity sits atop the assumptions of the ethnic paradigm, and so argues that blacks in the United States are cultural outsiders and that improper understanding of that unique identity thwarts group progress. But the same question that bothered the cultural nationalists of the 1960s bothers Asante: if black Americans are indeed so profoundly different, why is the sophisticated theoretical apparatus he proposes necessary to identify those distinctive cultural features?

Indeed, despite Asante's contention, black American culture is hardly analogous to any sub-Saharan black African *ethnos*. Anthony Appiah notes that neither the experience of racism nor the penetration of European culture was the same for black Africans as for Afro-Americans. Rather, according to Appiah, "the experience of the vast majority of these citizens of Europe's African colonies was one of essentially shallow penetration by the colonizer." Appiah argues that "cognitive and moral traditions" of indigenous people remained largely unaffected by a European presence. More precisely, the European metropole was "culturally marginal even though formally politically overwhelming."[53]

Even if scholars could establish the cultural unity of Africa, and its roots in ancient Egyptian society, they would still need to establish how these Egyptian-rooted African norms made their way to the Americas and manifested themselves in contemporary black life. Certainly, "African" elements permeate cultures in the Caribbean, Latin America, and North America. But given historical developments unique to each region – for instance, the ratio of blacks to whites, the average size of plantations, the number of African slaves brought to particular regions – we should expect these retentions to manifest themselves in different ways and to different degrees.[54] Yet, without hesitation, Asante claims that there is as much cultural similarity between Barbados and Zimbabwe as there is between Florence and Brisbane[55] – and further, that a study of inner city blacks in Boston or New York should "be done with the idea in the back of the mind that one is studying *African* people, not 'made-in-America Negroes' without historical depth."[56]

Not only does Asante reproduce assumptions linked to nineteenth-century romantic racialism – the idea of African people as an organic

unit and the significance of "civilization" as the measure of progress –
but he launches his critique in a startlingly poststructuralist manner,
recalling the antifoundational theories that in the mid-1980s found some
space in fields like literary criticism, communications, and philosophy.
Asante's metatheory germinates in similar academic soil. Especially ironically in his case, the fact that Asante has stressed the importance of
knowledge and epistemological premises reveals again how closely black
nationalism reflects its own contemporary intellectual context.[57]

There is a presumption lurking below Asante's analysis that sees Afrocentrism as implicitly tied to black empowerment. Asante and his disci-
ples place enormous emphasis on the potential effect that Afrocentricity
could have on African lives, as if paradigms or theoretical frameworks
were the keys to group progress. Offering a secular version of the NOI's
vision of group empowerment, Asante sees his worldview as a means
through which blacks can "move beyond the intellectual plantation that
constrains our economic, cultural and intellectual development."[58] In
Kemet, Asante argues that "[t]o reclaim a centered place in economic,
social, or political contexts, the African must first find centering in a cultural and psychological sense."[59]

Other proponents offer similar arguments. Victor O. Okafor cham-
pions Afrocentrism on the grounds that it gives black children "a correct
cultural and historical image of themselves so that they can function well
in society."[60] William Oliver suggests that Afrocentricity can correct
social problems among blacks, since currently blacks are "socialized to
be incapable of solving or helping to produce solutions to problems
posed by the environment."[61] "The failure to develop an Afrocentric cultural ideology," in Oliver's view, was "a major source of psychological,
social, political, and economic dysfunction among Black Americans."
Since America promoted "pro-White socialization," black youth needed
"Afrocentric socialization" through which they could internalize the
proper African-centered values. Linus A. Hoskins also argues that Afrocentrism facilitates "a positive, subconscious self-confidence and self-
empowerment"[62] and "represents the most potent challenge to the
European power structure (European nationalism) in the last 100 years."
Marian Ma' At-Ka-Re Monges looks to roles of ancient Egyptian female
deities and queens for help with contemporary problems between black
men and women.[63]

Sidney Lemmelle notes that Asante and many Afrocentrists, like
Hegel, favor "ideas over material reality." "They claim that by using
'ideas' and 'words' to critique a society and its ruling ideology" words
will "provide a racial assessment of a given reality" and thus "create,
among other things, another reality."[64] A strategy of empowerment
rooted in idealism tends to be naïve, ignoring the developments in poli-

tics and economics that mark its era. Indeed, in the corpus of his work, Asante has neglected to say how, precisely, group empowerment is to take place. Surely, knowledge of the past alone – whatever form that might take – is insufficient to the task. Nevertheless, other than his call for Afrocentric analysis, Asante offers little in the way of concrete strategy.

Ironically, Afrocentricity as offered by Asante and Islam as offered by Farrakhan again demonstrate the enduring significance of the "ethnic paradigm" to contemporary nationalist movements. These movements – one rooted in major metropolitan areas, the other in the academy – have reproduced some of the most conservative ideas in U.S. history on issues of race, economic disparity, and social mobility. Both tendencies emphasize an organic, elitist, and often male-centered conception of black identity that obscures differences within the black population. Both tendencies presume, incorrectly, that a crisis in "culture" – beliefs, values, sense of self – explains many if not all problems blacks face in contemporary society. And both tendencies, despite bold claims to the contrary, urge self-help by way of religious or intellectual conversion.

CONCLUSION

The organicist and often male-centered conceptions of black identity are hardly unique to black nationalism. However, within this style of black politics such tendencies appear to be most pronounced. After all, "nationalism" presumes uniform interests, at least concerning the issue of sovereignty. But interests are uniform only in the abstract; and so, invariably, once activists move from the level of theory down to the level of practice, the "texture" of their politics, their ideas, and their values respond to and often mirror those of the larger society. Moreover, on the level of practice, the heterogeneous character of the black population becomes more important.

Similarly, while political and economic conservatism has not characterized all forms of black nationalism historically, the fact that the two most successful organizations in terms of membership – the UNIA and the NOI – have also been two of the more conservative organizations strongly suggests that, in its modal form, black nationalism represents an almost willed alternative to radical politics. Garvey offered scant political strategy, conceding the United States to the white man and simply assuming that blacks would benefit uniformly under his leadership. For most of its political history, the NOI has eschewed political activity, and even with its new interest in politics since the mid-1980s the organization has not demonstrated much in the way of effective strategy. The "revolutionary" organizations – particularly the African Blood Brotherhood and the Black Panther Party – offered innovative analysis and tactics that sought to transform the social, economic, and political order of the United States. Yet, for reasons discussed earlier, revolutionary nationalists have never attracted followings comparable to their more conservative counterparts.

In a society where racial identity has affected and continues deeply to affect one's life chances, Farrakhan and Malcolm X, Marcus Garvey and others have taken that identity as the crucial one and have tried to organize on that basis. But too often, and perhaps inescapably, starting from a "race first" position assumes problematically that group oppression has nearly similar, if not identical, causes, and therefore nearly similar, if not identical, solutions. Such a stance overlooks the fact that black "interests" converge on some issues, and diverge on others.

Contemporary Afrocentrists seek to justify a "race first" approach by attempting to ground that political stance in a deeper metaphysical structure. In fact, they seek to fashion a Pan-African conception of a "race first" model by employing highly abstract theory based on an allegedly different set of epistemological principles. Yet that metatheory, even in its most sophisticated forms, simplifies complex matters. Further, although many proponents understand their ultimate objective as political power and full equality for people of African descent, advocates of Afrocentric theory confront pragmatic concerns tied to academic, not insurgent or electoral, politics. Afrocentric scholars must demonstrate the relevance of their theory by fashioning analyses that offer insight into African history, culture, and politics that "Eurocentric" analyses cannot. Given their academic habitat, actions and concrete political goals with respect to public policy are neither required nor expected of Afrocentric proponents.

By contrast, Farrakhan must lead his nationalistic, Islamic sect while at the same time fashioning a political agenda and method that has broader appeal. As result, Minister Farrakhan must test his political discourse and strategy against his political ambitions, modifying his message and tactics in order to retain or expand his following, or otherwise face decline and possible extinction. In seeking electoral power and changes in public policy, Farrakhan faces the more difficult challenge.

Neither contemporary movement inspires much confidence, because both strain against patterns of thought and practice that have hampered black nationalist strategy for decades. In every historical case, or nearly every case, black nationalists of earlier and later periods have had little basis for formulating strategies and anticipating outcomes with respect to different elements of a black population divided by age, gender, sexual orientation, class, and so forth. This explains why, in retrospect, the chief beneficiaries of Black Power radicalism were those middle-class black Americans most suited to new roles in urban municipal regimes. It also explains why black nationalists like Louis Farrakhan – and a multitude of activists before him – have to this point been unable to respond effectively to the many challenges and obstacles black men and women face in their pursuit of full equality in the United States.

Notes

INTRODUCTION

1. Wilson J. Moses, *The Golden Age of Black Nationalism: 1850–1925* (New York: Oxford University Press, 1978).

2. Joyce Hope Scott argues that black nationalism prior to the Black Power movement was relatively egalitarian regarding gender. See "From Foreground to Margin: Female Configuration and Masculine Self-Representation in Black Nationalist Fiction," in Andrew Parker, Mary Russo, Doris Summer, and Patricia Yeager (eds.), *Nationalisms and Sexualities* (New York: Routledge, 1992).

3. Benedict R. Anderson, *Imagined Communities: Reflections on the Origin and Spread of Nationalism* (London: Verso, 1983), 15.

4. Ralph Ellison, *Going to the Territory* (New York: Vintage, 1986), 105.

5. William Van Deburg makes such a distinction in his *A New Day in Babylon: The Black Power Movement and American Culture, 1965–1975* (Chicago: University of Chicago Press, 1992), 25.

6. Wilson Jeremiah Moses (ed.), *Classical Black Nationalism* (New York: New York University Press, 1996), 3.

7. John H. Bracey, Jr., August Meier, and Elliot Rudwick (eds.), *Black Nationalism in America* (Indianapolis: Bobbs-Merrill, 1970); Sterling Stuckey (ed.), *The Ideological Origins of Black Nationalism* (Boston: Beacon Press, 1972); Floyd B. Barbour (ed.), *Black Power Revolt* (Boston: Extending Horizons Books, 1968).

8. Manning Marable and Leith Mullings, "The Divided Mind of Black America: Race, Ideology and Politics in the Post–Civil Rights Era," in Manning Marable (ed.), *Beyond Black and White: Transforming African-American Politics* (New York: Verso, 1995), 210–211; emphasis in original.

9. William Van Deburg (ed.), *Modern Black Nationalism: From Marcus Garvey to Louis Farrakhan* (New York: New York University Press, 1997), 2–3.

10. Ibid., 4.

11. Moses, *Golden Age*, 7–10.

12. Judith Stein, *The World of Marcus Garvey: Race and Class in Modern Society* (Baton Rouge: Louisiana State University Press, 1986); Robert A. Hill (ed.), *The Marcus Garvey and Universal Negro Improvement Association Papers* (Berkeley: University of California Press, 1983); Marcus Garvey and Barbara Bair (eds.), *Marcus Garvey, Life and Lessons: A Centennial Companion to the Marcus Gavey and Universal Negro Improvement Association Papers* (Berkeley: University of California Press, 1987).

13. Moses, *Golden Age*, 11.

CHAPTER 1. ANGLO-AFRICAN NATIONALISM

1. See Gaile Bederman, *Manliness and Civilization: A Cultural History of Gender and Race in the United States, 1880–1917* (Chicago: University of Chicago Press, 1995).

2. Thomas Jefferson, *Notes on the State of Virginia* (Chapel Hill: University of North Carolina Press, 1955), 138.

3. Jefferson, 137–143.

4. In Andrew Delbanco (ed.), *The Portable Abraham Lincoln* (New York: Penguin, 1992), 235.

5. Eric Foner, *A Short History of Reconstruction, 1863–1877* (New York: Perennial, 1990), 11.

6. Rogers Smith, *Civic Ideals: Conflicting Visions of Citizenship in U.S. History* (New Haven, CT: Yale University Press, 1997), 255.

7. Wilson Jeremiah Moses, *The Golden Age of Black Nationalism: 1850–1925* (New York: Oxford University Press, 1978), 27.

8. In Sheldon Goldman, *Constitutional Law: Cases and Essays* (New York: Harper and Row, 1987), 206.

9. George M. Frederickson, *The Black Image in the White Mind: The Debate on Afro-American Character and Destiny* (Middletown, CT: Wesleyan University Press, 1987), 131. Frederickson borrows this term from Harmannus Hoetink, *The Two Variants in Caribbean Race Relations: A Contribution to the Sociology of Segmented Societies* (London: Oxford University Press, 1967), 106–110.

10. Barbara Fields, "Slavery, Race, and Ideology in the United States," *New Left Review* (May/June 1990): 106.

11. Alexander Saxton, *The Rise and Fall of the White Republic: Class Politics and Mass Culture in Nineteenth-Century America* (New York: Verso, 1990).

12. See, for example, David R. Roediger, *The Wages of Whiteness: Race and the Making of the American Working Class* (New York: Verso, 1991), and Noel Ignatiev, *How the Irish Became White* (New York: Routledge, 1995).

13. See Thomas F. Gossett, *Race: The History of an Idea in America* (New York: Oxford University Press, 1997); and Reginald Horsman, *Race and Manifest Destiny: The Origins of American Racial Anglo-Saxonism* (Cambridge: Harvard University Press, 1981).

14. Frederickson, 98.

15. Ibid., 102.
16. Harriet Beecher Stowe, *Uncle Tom's Cabin* (New York: Penguin, 1981), 197.
17. Ralph Waldo Emerson, *English Traits* (Cambridge: The Riverside Press, 1896), 133.
18. Ibid., 137.
19. Gould shows how Morton's methods were flawed. Not only were Morton's skulls unrepresentative of the general population in terms of "race" and gender, but even more significant, Morton began with an assumption that "race" existed as a meaningful "scientific" category in the first place. See Stephen Jay Gould, *The Mismeasure of Man* (New York: Norton, 1981), 30–112.
20. The editors concede that this categorization is arbitrary. Josiah Nott and George R. Gliddon (eds.), *Types of Mankind* (Philadelphia: Lippincott, 1857), 8th ed., 83.
21. Quoted in Horsman, 136.
22. Nott and Gliddon (eds.), *Types of Mankind*, 52–53.
23. Ibid., 69.
24. Smith, 204.
25. Bill McAdoo, *Pre-Civil War Black Nationalism* (New York: The David Walker Press, 1983).
26. David Walker, *Appeal in Four Articles* (New York: Hill and Wang, 1965), 26.
27. Ibid., 65.
28. Wilson Jeremiah Moses, *Black Messiahs and Uncle Toms: Social and Literary Manipulations of a Religious Myth* (University Park: Pennsylvania State University Press, 1993), 38.
29. Sterling Stuckey, *Slave Culture* (New York: Oxford University Press, 1987), 123.
30. E. J. Hobsbawm, *Nations and Nationalism Since 1780: Programme, Myth, Realty* (Cambridge: Cambridge University Press, 1990), 11.
31. Quoted in John H. Bracey, August Meier, and Elliot Rudwick (eds.), *Black Nationalism in America* (Indianapolis: Bobbs-Merril, 1970), 91.
32. Ibid., 93.
33. Ibid., 95.
34. In Theodore Draper, "The Father of American Black Nationalism," *The New York Review of Books*, March 12, 1970, pp. 33–41.
35. Quoted in Wilson J. Moses (ed.), *Classical Black Nationalism: From the American Revolution to Marcus Garvey* (New York: New York University Press, 1996), 120 (emphasis supplied). In a later work, his *Principia of Ethnology: The Origin of Races and Color, with an Archeological Compendium of Ethiopian and Egyptian Civilization, from Years of Careful Examination and Enquiry* (1879), Delany sets as his target those who argued in favor of polygeny and those who denied the Negro identity of the ancient Egyptians. He did this in part by attempting to establish the cultural influences of the Ethiopians on the Egyptians.

36. Victor Ulman, *Martin R. Delany: The Beginnings of Black Nationalism* (Boston: Beacon Press, 1971), 221.
37. From Moses, *Classical*, 131.
38. Ibid., 133.
39. See Henry Highland Garnet, "An Address to the Slaves of the United States of America," in Bracey, Meier, and Rudwick (eds.), 67.
40. In Howard Brotz (ed.), *African American Social and Political Thought* (New Brunswick, NJ: Transaction Publishers, 1997), 191–192.
41. Moses, *Golden Age*, 37.
42. In Brotz (ed.), *African American Social and Political Thought*, 194.
43. Moses, *Classical*, 24.
44. Alexander Crummell, "The Progress of Civilization along the West Coast of Africa," in his *The Future of Africa* (New York: Negro Universities Press, 1969 reprint edition), 122–123.
45. Alexander Crummel, "The Relations and Duties of Free Colored Men in America to Africa," in *The Future of Africa*, 221–222.
46. In Brotz (ed.), *African American Social and Political Thought*, 203.
47. "The Claims of the Negro Ethnologically Considered," in Brotz (ed.), *African American Social and Political Thought*, 228.
48. "Letter to Harriet Beecher Stowe," in Brotz (ed.), *African American Social and Political Thought*, 233.
49. *Douglass Monthly*, February 1859.
50. Quoted in Ulman, 273.
51. Rogers, 292–293.
52. Hollis Read, *The Negro Problem Solved* (New York: Negro Universities Press, 1969), v.
53. Ibid., 346.
54. J. H. Van Evrie, *White Supremacy and Negro Subordination* (New York: Van Evrie, Horton & Co., 1868), reprinted in John David Smith (ed.), *Anti-Black Thought 1863–1925* (New York: Garland, 1993), vol. 3, 52.
55. Van Evrie, 323.
56. Ibid., 326–327.
57. "Negro Colonization, An Open Letter to Hon. Wade Hampton," in Smith (ed.), *Anti-Black Thought*, vol. 10, 111.
58. Smith, *Civic Ideals*, 348.
59. See Edwin S. Redkey, *Black Exodus: Black Nationalist and Back-to-Africa Movements, 1890–1910* (New Haven, CT: Yale University Press, 1969).
60. Bracey, Meier, and Rudwick (eds.), *Black Nationalism in America*, 173.
61. Robert A. Hill (ed.), *The Marcus Garvey and Universal Negro Improvement Association Papers* (Los Angeles: University of California Press, 1983), vol. 3, xxxiii.
62. Ernest Allen argues that the "NOI has proved to be the largest and longest-lived institutionalized nationalist movement among blacks in the United States, far outstripping the widespread appeal and influence of the Marcus Garvey's Universal Negro Improvement Association which flourished during World War I and the immediate post-war years." See "Religious

Heterodoxy and Nationalist Tradition: The Continuing Evolution of the Nation of Islam," *The Black Scholar* 26, no. 3–4 (Fall–Winter 1996): 2.

63. Briggs founded the ABB in 1919.
64. Judith Stein, *The World of Marcus Garvey* (London: Louisiana State University Press, 1986), 53; Hill (ed.), *Garvey Papers*, vol. 1, lxx–lxxi.
65. Ibid., 62–63.
66. Theodore G. Vincent, *Black Power and the Garvey Movement* (Berkeley, CA: Ramparts, 1971), 166.
67. Robert A. Hill and Barbara Bair (eds.), *Marcus Garvey Life and Lessons* (Berkeley: University of California Press, 1987), lii–liii.
68. Philip S. Foner, *Organized Labor and the Black Worker: 1619–1981* (New York: International Publishers, 1981), 144.
69. Kenneth T. Jackson, *The Ku Klux Klan in the City, 1915–1930* (New York: Oxford University Press, 1967), 15; David H. Bennett, *The Party of Fear: The American Far Right from Nativism to the Militia Movement* (New York: Vintage Books, 1995), 210; David A. Horowitz, *Inside the Klavern: The Secret History of a Ku Klux Klan of the 1920s* (Carbondale, IL: Southern Illinois University Press, 1999), 3.
70. Stein, *The World of Marcus Garvey*, 155.
71. E. A. Ross taught at the University of Wisconsin and later at Stanford University. Grant was an officer of the American Eugenics Society and for twenty-five years served as vice president of the Immigration Restriction League.
72. Thomas F. Gossett, *Race: The History of an Idea in America* (New York: Oxford University Press, 1997), 168–172, 353–364.
73. Ibid., 363.
74. Lothrop Stoddard, *The Rising Tide of Color against White World-Supremacy* (New York: Scribner, 1969), 12.
75. Ibid., 308.
76. Ibid., xxx–xxxi.
77. Elton C. Fax, *Garvey: The Story of a Pioneer Black Nationallist* (New York: Dodd, Mead, 1972), 1.
78. Ibid., 2.
79. Amy Jacques-Garvey (ed.), *Philosophy and Opinions of Marcus Garvey* (New York: Antheneum, 1992), vol. 1, 138–139.
80. Judith Stein, "Uplifting the Race," in Werner Sollors (ed.), *The Invention of Ethnicity* (New York: Oxford University Press, 1989), 94–104.
81. For a full account of uplift ideology, see Kevin Gaines, *Uplifting the Race: Black Leadership, Politics, and Culture in the Twentieth Century* (Chapel Hill: University of North Carolina Press, 1996).
82. Wilson J. Moses, *The Golden Age of Black Nationalism* (New York: Oxford University Press, 1978), 265; Stein, "Uplifting the Race," 89; Robert A. Hill (ed.), *Garvey Papers*, vol. 1, li.
83. Michele Mitchell notes that Garvey's followers had the additional mandate of maintaining racial purity. See Mitchell, "Adjusting the Race: Gender, Sexuality, and the Question of African-American Destiny, 1877–1930" (unpublished Ph.D. dissertation, 1998), 307–353.

84. Marcus Garvey, "What Garvey Thinks of Du Bois," in Theodore Vincent (ed.), *Voices of Journalism in the Harlem Renaissance* (Trenton, NJ: Africa World Press, 1990), 98. This essay appeared in the January 1, 1921, issue of the *Negro World*.

85. Marcus Garvey, speech delivered in New York on September 4, 1921. Reproduced in Robert A. Hill (ed.), *Garvey Papers*, vol. 4, 25.

86. Marcus Garvey, "The Negro, Communism, Trade Unionism and His (?) Friend," in Jacques-Garvey (ed.), *Philosophy and Opinions*, vol. 2, 70.

87. Marcus Garvey, "Editorial," *Negro World*, February 1, 1919. Reprinted in Hill (ed.), *Garvey Papers*, vol. 1, 351.

88. Marcus Garvey, "Editorial," *Negro World*, July 19, 1919. Reprinted in Hill (ed.), *Garvey Papers*, vol. 1, 461.

89. Garvey, speech on September 4, 1921. Reprinted in Hill (ed.), *Garvey Papers*, vol. 4, 28.

90. Marcus Garvey, "Editorial," *Negro World*, September 17, 1921.

91. Marcus Garvey, "Editorial," *Negro World*, October 15, 1921.

92. Hill (ed.), *Garvey Papers*, vol. 3, xxxiii.

93. Marcus Garvey, "Race First!," *Negro World*, July 26, 1919. Reprinted in Hill (ed.), *Garvey Papers*, vol. 1, 469.

94. Marcus Garvey, "African Fundamentalism," reprinted in Robert A. Hill (ed.), *Marcus Garvey: Life and Lessons* (Berkeley: University of California Press, 1987), 3.

95. Nathan Huggins, "Afro-American History: Myths, Heroes, Reality," in Nathan I. Huggins, Martin Kilson, and Daniel M. Fox, *Key Issues in the Afro-American Experience* (New York: Harcourt Brace Jovanovich, 1971), 15.

96. Stein, *The World of Marcus Garvey*, 231.

97. Ibid., 242.

98. Ibid., 239.

99. Ibid., 236–238.

100. Ibid., 153.

101. See Robert Lewis and Maureen Warner-Lewis (eds.), *Garvey: Africa, Europe, the Americas* (Trenton, NJ: Africa World Press, 1994); Rupert Lewis, *Marcus Garvey: Anti-Colonial Champion* (Trenton, NJ: Africa World Press, 1998).

102. Hill (ed.), *Garvey Papers*, vol. 4, xxxii.

103. Hill (ed.), *Garvey Papers*, vol. 1, lxxxx.

104. See Garvey's reply to James Weldon Johnson, *Negro World*, October 1, 1921. From a statement, "What We Believe," that appeared in several issues of the *Negro World*. It is reproduced in Marcus Garvey, *Philosophy and Opinions* (New York: Arno Press, 1969), vol. 2, 81. This volume was originally published in 1925.

105. Tony Martin, *Race First: The Ideological and Organizational Struggles of Marcus Garvey and the Universal Negro Improvement Association* (Dover: The Majority Press, 1976), 346.

106. Quoted in Stein, *The World of Marcus Garvey*, 154.

107. *The Messenger*, July 1922, 437.

108. "William Pickens to Marcus Garvey," reprinted in Hill (ed.), *Garvey Papers*, vol. 4, 748–749.

109. *The Crisis*, May 1924.

110. Garvey offered these remarks in a speech he delivered on February 24, 1923. His speech was reproduced in the March 3, 1923, issue of the *Negro World*.

111. Jacques-Garvey (ed.), *Philosophy and Opinions*, vol. 2, 71.

112. Vincent, 124; Hill (ed.), *Garvey Papers*, vol. 4, xxxv.

113. Hill (ed.), *Garvey Papers*, vol. 4, xxxiii.

114. Edmond David Cronon, *Black Moses: The Story of Marcus Garvey* (Madison: University of Wisconsin Press, 1955), 115; Vincent, 202; Stein, *The World of Marcus Garvey*, 186–196.

115. The most plausible explanation for this turnabout was the Liberian government's concern that UNIA settlers would become potential political rivals. See Martin, 132–136; Vincent, 180–183; Stein, *The World of Marcus Garvey*, 209–215.

116. Robert A. Hill (ed.), *Garvey Papers*, vol. 6, xxxvii.

117. *Negro World*, November 1, 1924.

118. *Negro World*, vol. 17.8.1 (1924). The UNPU endorsed Calvin Coolige for president and Democrat Al Smith in the New York gubernatorial race.

119. Hill (ed.), *Garvey Papers*, vol. 7, xli.

120. Stein, *The World of Marcus Garvey*, 146–147.

CHAPTER 2. MALCOLM X AND THE NATION OF ISLAM

1. Mattias Gardell, *In the Name of Elijah Muhammad: Louis Farrakhan and the Nation of Islam* (Durham, NC: Duke University Press, 1996), 45–50.

2. Wilson J. Moses, *Black Messiahs and Uncle Toms: Social and Literary Manipulations of a Religious Myth*, rev. ed. (University Park: Pennsylvania State University Press, 1993), 183.

3. Claude Andre Clegg III offers a thorough and engaging biography of Elijah Muhammad in his *An Original Man: The Life and Times of Elijah Muhammad* (New York: St. Martin's, 1997).

4. Martha Lee, *The Nation of Islam: An American Millenarian Movement* (Syracuse, NY: Syracuse University Press, 1996).

5. Clegg, 19.

6. Quoted in Melvin L. Oliver and Thomas Shapiro, *Black Wealth / White Wealth* (New York: Routledge, 1997), 17.

7. Hugh Davis Graham, *Civil Rights and the Presidency: Race and Gender in American Politics, 1960–1972* (New York: Oxford University Press, 1992), 13.

8. Michael C. Dawson, *Behind the Mule: Race and Class in African-American Politics* (Princeton, NJ: Princeton University Press, 1994), 24–27.

9. C. Eric Lincoln, *Sounds of the Struggle: Persons and Perspectives in Civil Rights* (New York: William Morrow, 1967), 47.

10. Malcolm X, *The Autobiography of Malcolm X* (New York: Ballantine Books, 1965), 54.

11. Elijah Muhammad, *Message to the Blackman in America* (Chicago: Muhammad's Temple No. 2, 1965), 275.
12. Malcolm X, *Malcolm X on Afro-American History* (New York: Pathfinder, 1967), 25.
13. Malcolm X, *Autobiography*, 174.
14. Ibid., 165, 166.
15. Ibid., 183.
16. Eldridge Cleaver, *Post-prison Writings and Speeches* (New York: Vintage, 1969), 13.
17. Malcolm X, *Autobiography*, 200; emphasis in original.
18. Malcolm X, *Malcolm X on Afro-American History*, 63.
19. Clegg, 110.
20. C. Eric Lincoln, *The Black Muslims in America* (Trenton, NJ: Africa World Press, 1994), 264.
21. Clegg, 157.
22. Ibid., 156.
23. Sonsyrea Tate, *Little X: Growing Up in the Nation of Islam* (San Francisco: HarperSanFrancisco, 1997), 106.
24. Cynthia S'Thembile West, "Revisiting Female Activism in the 1960s: The Newark Branch Nation of Islam," *The Black Scholar* 26, no. 3–4 (1996): 41–48.
25. Muhammad, 64.
26. Malcolm X, *Autobiography*, 226.
27. Tate, 94.
28. Bruce Berry (ed.), *Malcolm X: The Last Speeches* (New York: Pathfinder, 1989), 122.
29. Robin D. G. Kelley, *Race Rebels: Culture, Politics, and the Black Working Class* (New York: The Free Press, 1994), 163.
30. Ibid., 168.
31. See Clayborne Carson, "African American Leadership and Mass/Mobilization," *The Black Scholar* 24, no. 4 (Fall 1994): 4–5.
32. See Adolph Reed, Jr., "The Allure of Malcolm X," in *Stirrings in the Jug: Black Politics in the Post-Segregation Era* (Minneapolis: University of Minnesota Press, 1999), 220–221.
33. See, for example, Peter Goldman's *The Death and Life of Malcolm X* (Chicago: University of Illinois Press, 1979), 2nd ed., 107–108; and Bruce Perry, *Malcolm: The Life of a Man Who Changed Black America* (New York: Station Hill Press, 1992), 233–237.
34. Louis A. DeCaro, Jr., *On the Side of My People: A Religious Life of Malcolm X* (New York: New York University Press, 1996), 181.
35. Clegg, 204.
36. Malcolm X, *Autobiography*, 289.
37. George Breitman (ed.), *Malcolm X Speaks: Selected Speeches and Statements Edited with Prefatory Notes by George Breitman* (New York: Groove Weidenfeld, 1965), 5.
38. Ibid., 3.
39. Quoted in DeCaro, 250.

40. Perry (ed.), *Malcolm X: The Last Speeches*, 147.
41. George Breitman (ed.), *The Last Year of Malcolm X: The Evolution of a Revolutionary* (New York: Merit Publishers, 1967), 74.
42. George Breitman (ed.), *By Any Means Necessary: Speeches, Interviews and a Letter by Malcolm X* (New York: Pathfinder, 1970).
43. Ibid., 43.
44. Malcolm X, *Autobiography*, 374.
45. Breitman (ed.), *Malcolm X Speaks*, 57.
46. Ossie Davis, "Our Own Black Shining Prince," *Liberator* 5, no. 4 (April 1965): 7.
47. William L. Van Deburg, *New Day in Babylon: The Black Power Movement and American Culture, 1965–1975* (Chicago: University of Chicago Press, 1992), 6.
48. A. B. Spellman, "The Legacy of Malcolm X," *Liberator* 5, no. 6 (June 1965): 11–13.
49. Perry (ed.), *The Last Speeches*, 78.
50. Martinique-born psychiatrist Frantz Fanon suggested that the violent struggle offered an antidote to feelings of cultural inferiority. I will briefly take up Fanon's theory of revolution and violence in Chapter 4.
51. Imamu Amiri Baraka, *Raise Race Rays Raze* (New York: Random House, 1969), 29.
52. Larry Neal, *Visions of a Liberated Future: Black Arts Movement Writing by Larry Neal* (New York: Thunder's Mouth Press, 1989), 125.
53. Ibid., 128–129.

CHAPTER 3. BLACK NATIONALIST ORGANIZATIONS IN THE CIVIL RIGHTS ERA

1. Clayborne Carson, "African-American Leadership and Mass Mobilization," *The Black Scholar*, 24, no. 4 (1994): 2.
2. See *The Kerner Report: The 1968 Report of the National Advisory Commission on Civil Disorders* (New York: Pantheon, 1988).
3. June Jordan, "Cultural Nationalism in the 1960s," in Adolph Reed, Jr. (ed.), *Race, Politics, and Culture: Critical Essays on the Radicalism of the 1960s* (New York: Greenwood Press, 1986), 30.
4. See Kenneth O'Reilly, *Racial Matters* (New York: The Free Press, 1989).
5. E. U. Essien-Udom placed the number of black nationalist organizations in Harlem in 1963 at around "two dozen and a combined membership of about 5,000." See his "Nationalistic Movements," *Freedomways* 3, no. 3 (Summer 1963): 335.
6. Mattias Gardell, *In the Name of Elijah Muhammad: Louis Farrakhan and the Nation of Islam* (Durham, NC: Duke University Press, 1996), 224.
7. Father Allah was assassinated in June 1969, but his organization continues.
8. John Henrik Clarke, "The New Afro-American Nationalism," *Freedomways* 1, no. 3 (Fall 1961): 287. Cooks eventually split with the Universal African Nationalist Movement over tactics. He thought it inappropriate to draw support from nonblacks for any resettlement effort.

9. Peaker succeeded Carlos Cooks, who founded the African Nationalist Pioneer Movement. Cooks was born June 23, 1913, in Santo Domingo in the Dominican Republic. Cooks's father had been a longtime follower of Marcus Garvey.

10. Charles Peaker, *Black Nationalism* (New York: Africa-America Publications, 1967), 13–15.

11. Robert Harris, Nyota Harris, and Grandassa Harris (eds.), *Carlos Cooks and Black Nationalism: From Garvey to Malcolm* (Dover, MA: The Majority Press, 1992), xii.

12. Cooks used the term "caste" to refer to those blacks not committed to black nationalism.

13. Peaker, 15.

14. Quoted in ibid., 55.

15. Ibid., 17.

16. Ibid., 88.

17. Ibid., 63.

18. Harris, Harris, and Harris (eds.), *Carlos Cooks,* 21.

19. Quoted in the *Liberator* 5, no. 5 (1965): 25.

20. Quoted in Clarke, 290–291.

21. Ibid., 293.

22. In Thomas Lucien Vincent Blair, *Retreat to the Ghetto: The End of a Dream?* (New York: Hill and Wang, 1977), 150.

23. Maulana Karenga, *Introduction to Black Studies* (Los Angeles: University of Sankore Press, 1993), 173.

24. Imamu Amiri Baraka, "7 Principles of US Maulana Karenga and the Need for a Black Value System," in his *Raise Race Rays Raze* (New York: Random House, 1969), 133–159.

25. Another disciple, Mahidi Ken Msenaji, ran the NIA Cultural Organization in San Diego: see Blair, 150.

26. Imamu Amiri Baraka, *The Antobiography of LeRoi Jones* (Chicago: Lawrence Hill Books, 1997), 351–361.

27. Ibid., 385.

28. Bobby Seale, *Seize the Time: The Story of the Black Panther Party and Huey P. Newton* (New York: Random House, 1968), 162.

29. After serving several convictions for possession and use of marijuana, Cleaver was sentenced in 1958 on a conviction for assault with intent to rape and kill. During his prison term Cleaver joined the Nation of Islam, then broke from that organization following Malcolm X's assassination.

30. Huey P. Newton, *To Die for the People* (New York: Writers and Readers Publishing, 1973), 14.

31. Newton, 14–16.

32. G. Louis Heath (ed.), *The Black Panther Leaders Speak: Huey P. Newton, Bobby Seale, Eldridge Cleaver, and Company Speak Out through the Black Panther Party's Official Newspaper* (Metuchen, NJ: Scarecrow Press, 1976), 23.

33. Ibid., 1.

34. Elaine Brown, *A Taste of Power* (New York: Pantheon Books, 1992), 181–184.
35. Ibid., 356–450.
36. John H. Bracey, August Meier, and Elliot M. Rudwick (eds.), *Black Nationalism in America* (Indianapolis: Bobbs-Merrill, 1970), 509.
37. Max Stanford, "Black Guerrilla Warfare: Strategy and Tactics," in Robert Chrisman and Nathan Hare (eds.), *Contemporary Black Thought: The Best From The Black Scholar* (New York: Bobbs-Merrill, 1973), 200.
38. Bracey, Meier, and Rudwick (eds.), *Black Nationalism in America*, 514–515.
39. Robert F. Williams, *Negroes with Guns* (New York: Marzani and Munsell, 1962), 39–41, 120–24, reprinted in *Black Protest: History, Documents, and Analyses 1619 to the Present*, 340–344.
40. Bracey, Meier, and Rudwick (eds.), *Black Nationalism in America*, 509.
41. Milton Henry had accompanied Malcolm X during his final trip to Africa.
42. Milton Henry, "An Independent Black Republic in North America," in Raymond Hall (ed.), *Black Separatism and Social Realty: Rhetoric and Reason* (New York: Pergamon, 1977), 34.
43. Julius Nyerere, "African Socialism: Ujamaa in Practice," in Chrisman and Hare (eds.), *Contemporary Black Thought*, 211–219.
44. Hall, 200–223.
45. In a letter to the consulate general, Iranian Consulate, from Larry L. Edwards, consul captain, December 1979, from the Shomburg Archives.
46. See Cheryl Lynn Greenberg, *A Circle of Trust: Remembering SNCC* (New Brunswick, NJ: Rutgers University Press, 1998), 152–176.
47. Carson, 194.
48. CORE was founded in 1942.
49. Hall, 118.
50. See August Meier and Elliot Rudwick, *CORE: A Study in the Civil Rights Movement, 1942–1968* (New York: Oxford University Press, 1973), 374–431.
51. Robert L. Allen, *Black Awakening in Capitalist America* (Garden City, NY: Doubleday, 1969), 153–155.
52. Hall, 155.
53. Ibid., 146–147.
54. Baraka, *Autobiography*, 386.
55. Allen, 221.
56. Newton, 97
57. In Pinkney, 123.
58. Ibid., 123–124.
59. Ibid., 148.

CHAPTER 4. BLACK NATIONALIST DISCOURSE

1. I borrow the term "paraintellectuals" from Martin Kilson, "The New Black Intellectuals," *Dissent*, July–August 1969.
2. Kilson, 304. Harold Cruse also identifies the period of the 1950s and 1960s as an "era of black ideological transformation, especially among the newest

wave of intellectuals." Harold Cruse, *The Crisis of the Negro Intellectual* (New York: William Morrow, 1967), 356.

3. The reader should note a few important points about my method. First, because many authors wrote for a variety of audiences, I do not always identify the academic affiliation of the author. For instance, Robert S. Browne, then a professor at Fairleigh Dickinson University, published articles endorsing black separatism, and inadvertently provided the ideological base for the Republic of New Africa. Stokely Carmichael of SNCC teamed up with political scientist Charles Hamilton to write the most comprehensive, and most widely read, defense of Black Power. Second, thinkers generally did not disentangle the themes I will consider. In most cases – especially in the case of discourse produced by paraintellectuals – we find these themes thickly interwoven. Finally, I do not always follow strict chronology when I introduce the various writings. The ideas I explore appeared from the early 1960s to the early 1970s.

4. John H. Bracey, August Meier, and Elliot M. Rudwick (eds.), *Black Nationalism in America* (Indianapolis: Bobbs-Merrill, 1970), 512.

5. Clebert Ford, "Black Nationalism and the Arts," *Liberator* 3, no. 11 (November 1963): 14.

6. Albert B. Cleage, Jr., *Black Christian Nationalism: New Directions for the Black Church* (New York: William Morrow, 1972), 20.

7. James Turner, "Black Nationalism: The Inevitable Response," *Black World* (1971): 26.

8. Alphonso Pinkney, "Contemporary Black Nationalism," in Rhoda L. Goldstein (ed.), *Black Life and Culture in the United States* (New York: Thomas Y. Crowell, 1971), 243–262.

9. Arthur L. Smith (ed.), *The Rhetoric of Black Revolution* (Boston: Allyn and Bacon, 1969), 164.

10. Larry Neal, "And Shine Swam On," *Visions of a Liberated Future: Black Arts Movement Writing* (New York: Thunder's Mouth Press, 1989), 14.

11. Julius Lester, *Look Out, Whitey! Black Power's Gon' Get Your Mamma* (New York: Grove Press, 1969), 140.

12. Lester, 138.

13. *Liberator* 3, no. 2 (February 1963), 2.

14. Cruse, 344.

15. Ibid., 351.

16. Francis L. Broderick, "The Gnawing Dilemma: Separatism and Integration, 1865–1925," in Nathan I. Huggins, Martin Kilson, and Daniel M. Fox (eds.), *Key Issues in the Afro-American Experience* (New York: Harcourt Brace Jovanovich, 1971), vol. 1, 94.

17. Robert S. Browne, "The Case for Two Americas – One Black, One White," *The New York Times Magazine*, August 11, 1968, p. 48.

18. Ibid., p. 48.

19. Ibid., 12–13.

20. Ibid., 12.

21. Ibid., 56.

22. Earl Ofari, "The Emergence of Black National Consciousness in America," *Black World* 20, no. 4 (February 1971): 76.
23. Ibid., 77.
24. Ibid., 78.
25. Ibid., 79.
26. Larry Neal, "Any Day Now: Black Art and Black Liberation," in Woodie King and Earl Anthony (eds.), *Black Poets and Prophets: The Theory, Practice, and Esthetics of Pan-Africanist Revolution* (New York: New American Library, 1972), 14.
27. Milton R. Henry, "An Independent Black Republic in North America," in Raymond Hall (ed.), *Black Separatism and Social Reality: Rhetoric and Reason* (New York: Peragamon, 1977), 35.
28. Rodney Carlisle, "Black Nationalism: An Integral Tradition," *Black World* 22, no. 4 (February 1973): 5.
29. Ibid., 4–10.
30. Floyd J. Miller, "The Father of Black Nationalism," *Civil War History* 27, no. 4 (December 1971): 310–319.
31. Victor Ulman, *Martin R. Delaney: The Beginnings of Black Nationalism* (Boston: Beacon Press, 1971).
32. Manning W. Marable, "Booker T. Washington and African Nationalism," *Phylon: The Atlanta University Review of Race and Culture* 35, no. 4 (1974): 398–406.
33. Sterling Stuckey, *The Ideological Origins of Black Nationalism* (Boston: Beacon Press, 1972), 8.
34. Stuckey, 12–13.
35. Wilson J. Moses, *Black Messiahs and Uncle Toms* (University Park: Pennsylvania State University, 1993), 214.
36. Cruse, 350.
37. Michael Kammen, *The Mystic Chords of Memory: The Transformation of Tradition in American Culture* (New York: Knopf, 1991), 10.
38. Ronald Snellings, "Afro-American Youth and the Bandung World," *Liberator* 5, no. 2 (February 1965): 4–7.
39. Harold Cruse, "Revolutionary Nationalism and the Afro-American," in Leroi Jones and Larry Neal (eds.), *Black Fire: An Anthology of Afro-American Writing* (New York: William Morrow, 1968), 41.
40. Don Freeman, "Nationalist Student Conference," *Liberator* 5, no. 7 (July 1964): 18.
41. Snellings, 4.
42. Stokely Carmichael and Charles Hamilton, *Black Power* (New York: Vintage Books, 1967), 5.
43. Ibid., 6.
44. Ibid., 31.
45. Ibid., 30.
46. Ibid.
47. Ibid., 20–21.
48. James Turner, quoting Dr. C. T. Munford in "Black Nationalism: The Inevitable Revolution," 7.

49. Joseph Hannibal Howard III, "How to End Colonial Domination of Black America," *Black World* 19, no. 3 (January 1970): 9–10.

50. Frantz Fanon, *The Wretched of the Earth* (New York: Grove Press, 1963), 37.

51. See, for instance, Donald W. Jackson's "Violence is Necessary," *Liberator* 6, no. 3 (March 1966): 6–7.

52. Ronald Snellings, "We Are on the Move and Our Music Is Moving With Us," in Bracey, Meier, and Rudwick (eds.), *Black Nationalism in America*, 446.

53. Jennifer Jordan, "Cultural Nationalism in the 1960s: Politics and Poetry," in Adolph Reed, Jr. (ed.), *Race, Politics, and Culture* (New York: Greenwood Press, 1986), 39.

54. Neal, 3.

55. Quoted in Jordan, 40–41.

56. Ron Karenga, "Black Cultural Nationalism," in Addison Gayle, Jr. (ed.), *The Black Aesthetic* (New York: Anchor, 1971), 31.

57. James T. Steward, "The Development of the Black Revolutionary Artist," in LeRoi Jones and Larry Neal (eds.), *Black Fire: An Anthology of Afro-American Writing* (New York: Morrow, 1968), 3.

58. Imamu Amiri Baraka, *The Autobiography of Leroi Jones* (Chicago: Lawrence Hill Books, 1997), 337.

59. William L. Van Deburg, *New Day in Babylon: The Black Power Movement and American Culture, 1965–1975* (Chicago: University of Chicago Press, 1992), 260.

60. Jennifer Jordan, "Black Cultural Nationalism in the 1960s: Politics and Poetry," in Adolph Reed, Jr. (ed.), *Race, Politics, and Culture: Critical Essays on the Radicalism of the 1960s* (New York: Greenwood Press, 1986), 40.

61. Hoyt W. Fuller, "Towards a Black Aesthetic," in Jones and Neal (eds.), *Black Fire,* 9.

CHAPTER 5. BLACK NATIONALISM AS ETHNIC PLURALISM

1. Stephen Steinberg, *The Ethnic Myth* (Boston: Beacon Press, 1981), 3.

2. Robert L. Allen, *Black Awakening in Capitalist America* (Trenton, NJ: Africa World Press, 1992), 191.

3. John H. Bracey, August Meier, and Elliot Rudwick (eds.), *Black Nationalism in America* (Indianapolis: Bobbs-Merrill, 1970), xxvii.

4. See Adolph Reed, Jr., "The Black Revolution and the Reconstitution of Domination," in Adolph Reed, Jr., *Race, Politics, and Culture* (Westport, CT: Greenwood Press, 1986), 61–95.

5. Robert Dahl, *Who Governs? Democracy and Power in an American City* (New Haven, CT: Yale University Press, 1961), 53.

6. Ibid., 54.

7. Ibid., 90.

8. Michael K. Brown and Steven P. Erie, "Blacks and the Legacy of the Great Society: The Economic and Political Impact of Federal Social Policy," *Public Policy* 29, no.3 (1981): 317–318.

9. Arthur I. Blaustein and Geoffrey Faux, *The Star-Spangled Hustle* (Garden City, NY: Doubleday, 1972), 114–115.
10. This was also the period of Model Cities.
11. In Barbara Cruikshank, "The Will to Empower: Technologies of Citizenship and the War on Poverty," *Socialist Review* 23, no. 4 (Spring 1994): 36.
12. Alan Wolfe, *America's Impasse: The Rise and Fall of the Politics of Growth* (Boston: South End Press, 1981), 10.
13. Blaustein and Faux, 117–118.
14. Ibid., 34.
15. Quoted in ibid., 130.
16. Alan A. Altshuler, *Community Control: The Black Demand for Participation in Large American Cities* (New York: Pegasus, 1970), 14.
17. Stokely Carmichael and Charles V. Hamilton, *Black Power: The Politics of Liberation in America* (New York: Random House, 1967), 47.
18. Ibid., 44.
19. In Alex Poinsett, "Battle over Control of Ghetto Schools," *Ebony* (May 1969): 44.
20. Quoted in Allen, 186.
21. Blaustein and Faux, 47.
22. Quoted in Thomas L. Blair, *Retreat to the Ghetto: The End of a Dream* (New York: Hill & Wang, 1977), 167.
23. William L. Van Deburg, *New Day in Babylon: The Black Power Movement and American Culture, 1965–1975* (Chicago: University of Chicago Press, 1992), 116–117.
24. Blaustein and Faux, 42–43.
25. Blair, 207. Baraka enjoyed the most political success, but other coalitions sprouted in cities across the United States. "There was the Black United Front of Washington, D.C., the North City Congress in Philadelphia, the United Front in Boston, the Black United Conference in Denver, and the Black Congress in Los Angeles, to mention a few. All of these sought to use their influence in order to seize control of local political and economic institutions." (From Allen, 142.) See also Komozi Woodard, *A Nation within a Nation: Amiri Baraka (LeRoi Jones) and Black Power Politics* (Chapel Hill: University of North Carolina Press, 1999), 114–155.
26. Adolph L. Reed, Jr., *Stirrings in the Jug: Black Politics in the Post-Segregation Era* (Minneapolis: University of Minnesota Press, 1999), 133.
27. There were also conventions in Philadelphia, August 31–September 1, 1968, and in Bermuda in July 1969.
28. Blair, 202.
29. Interview with Dr. Nathan Wright, Jr., in the *Christian Science Monitor*, September 18, 1967.
30. The Congress of African Peoples was to function as a "federation of nationalists." See Woodard, 162–173.
31. Imamu Amiri Baraka, *The Autobiography of LeRoi Jones* (Chicago: Lawrence Hill Books, 1997), 403.
32. Imamu Amiri Baraka (ed.), *African Congress* (New York: William Morrow, 1972), 115.

33. Ibid., 168.
34. Ibid., 139; emphasis in original.
35. Ibid., 140.
36. Sam Pollard et al., *Eyes on the Prize II: Ain't Gonna Shuffle No More* (Alexandria, VA: PBS Video, 1989).
37. "The Gary Declaration" (unpublished document), 138.
38. Ibid., 140; emphasis in original.
39. Ibid., 6–30.
40. Robert Smith, *We Have No Leaders: African Americans in the Post–Civil Rights Era* (Albany: State University of New York Press, 1996), 49–56.
41. Ibid., 56–64.
42. Reed, *Stirrings in the Jug*, 136–137. The ALSC's concern was to support African liberation movements.
43. Pranab Chatterjee, *Local Leadership in Black Communities* (Cleveland: School of Applied Science, Case Western Reserve University, 1975), 77.
44. Allen, 147.
45. Adolph Reed, Jr., "The Black Urban Regime: Structural Origins and Constraints," in Michael P. Smith (ed.), *Power, Community and the City: Comparative and Community Research* (New Brunswick, NJ: Transaction, 1988), vol. 1, 147.
46. Fred Powledge, *Model City: A Test of American Liberalism: One Town's Efforts to Rebuild Itself* (New York: Simon and Schuster, 1970), 225.
47. Susan S. Fainstein and Norman I Fainstein, *Restructuring the City: The Political Economy of Urban Development* (New York: Longman, 1983), 53.
48. U.S. Office of Economic Opportunity Archives, RG 381.
49. Adolph Reed, Jr., "The Black Urban Regime: Structural Origins and Constraints," in Smith (ed.), *Power, Community and the City*, vol. 1, 145–147. See also Ralph M. Kramer, *Participation of the Poor* (Englewood Cliffs, NJ: Prentice Hall, 1969); Allen, 143.

CHAPTER 6. BLACK NATIONALISM AND THE ETHNIC PARADIGM

1. I am using the term differently from the way Omi and Winant do in their *Racial Formation in the United States* (New York: Routledge, 1994). They use the term "ethnic paradigm" to identify the "mainstream of the modern sociology of race," 14.
2. Milton Gordon, *Assimilation in American Life* (New York: Oxford University Press, 1964).
3. Ralph Ellison, *Going to the Territory* (New York: Vintage, 1986), 105.
4. Gordon, 88.
5. Ibid., 89–90.
6. Ibid., 11.
7. Quoted in ibid., 100–101.
8. Stow Persons, *Ethnic Studies at Chicago, 1905–1945* (Chicago: University of Illinois Press, 1987), 53–54.
9. Ibid., 62.

10. Michael Omi and Howard Winant, *Racial Formation in the United States* (New York: Routledge, 1994), 15.
11. Ibid.
12. Persons, 31.
13. William I. Thomas and Florian Znaniecki, *The Polish Peasant in Europe and America* (New York: Dover, 1918), vol. 2, 1128; emphasis in original.
14. Adolph Reed, Jr., *Stirrings in the Jug: Black Politics in the Post-Segregation Era* (Minneapolis: University of Minnesota Press, 1969), 29.
15. Persons, 131–132.
16. E. Franklin Frazier, *The Negro in the United States* (New York: Macmillan, 1951), 623–639.
17. Robert E. Park and Ernest W. Burgess, *Introduction to the Science of Sociology* (Chicago: University of Chicago Press, 1921), 735.
18. Persons, 84.
19. Park and Burgess, 735.
20. E. B. Reuter and C. W. Hart, *Introduction to Sociology* (New York: McGraw-Hill, 1933), 349.
21. Gordon, 64–66; Brewton Berry, *Race and Ethnic Relations* (Boston: Houghton Mifflin, 1958), 2nd ed., 210.
22. Arnold M. Rose, *Sociology: The Study of Human Relations* (New York: Knopf, 1956), 557.
23. Gordon, 72.
24. Ibid., 70.
25. Robert E. Park, *Race and Culture* (Glencoe, IL: The Free Press, 1950), 70–71.
26. Edward Byron Reuter, *The American Race Problem* (New York: Thomas Y. Crowell, 1966).
27. Ibid., 121
28. E. Franklin Frazier, "The Changing Status of the Negro Family," *Social Forces* 9 (March 1931): 386–393.
29. E. Franklin Frazier, *The Negro in the United States*, 680, 689.
30. E. Franklin Frazier, *Black Bourgeoisie* (New York: The Free Press, 1957), 112.
31. Gordon, 76.
32. Ibid., 144–145.
33. Nathan Glazer and Daniel Patrick Moynihan, *Beyond the Melting Pot* (Cambridge, MA: MIT Press, 1963), 14–16.
34. Ibid., 13–14.
35. Ibid., 44.
36. Ibid., 230–231.
37. Ibid., 165.
38. Ibid., 53.
39. Daniel P. Moynihan, "The Negro Family," in Peter Rose (ed.), *Slavery and Its Aftermath* (New York: Atherton Press, 1970), 389.
40. Ibid., 412.
41. *The Kerner Report: The 1968 Report of the National Advisory Commission on Civil Disorders* (New York: Pantheon, 1988), 280.

42. Robert Harris, Nyota Harris, and Grandassa Harris (eds.), *Carlos Cooks and Black Nationalism: From Garvey to Malcolm* (Dover, MA: The Majority Press, 1992), 38.
43. Bruce Perry (ed.), *Malcolm X: The Last Speeches* (New York: Pathfinder, 1989), 78.
44. Ellison, *Going to the Territory*, 108.
45. Ibid., 111.
46. Stephen Steinberg, *The Ethnic Myth: Race, Ethnicity, and Class in America* (Boston: Beacon Press, 1989), 79.
47. Steinberg, *The Ethnic Myth*.
48. Barbara Ann Teer, "Needed: A New Image," in Floyd B. Barbour (ed.), *The Black Power Revolt* (Boston: Extending Horizons Books, 1968), 222.
49. Ronald Milner, "Black Theater – Go Home," in Addison Gayle, Jr. (ed.), *The Black Aesthetic* (New York: Anchor Books, 1971), 288. This formulation of culture is similar to one offered by negritude proponent Leopold Sedar Senghor. See his "The Problematics of Negritude," *Black World* 20, no. 10 (1971): 6.

CHAPTER 7. BLACK NATIONALISM IN THE CONTEMPORARY ERA

1. United States Bureau of Labor Statistics, http://www.stats.bls.gov/news.release/emsit.to2.htm.
2. David A. Bositis, *Black Elected Officials: A Statistical Summary, 1993–1997* (Washington, DC: Joint Center for Political and Economic Studies, 1997), 8.
3. Adolph Reed, Jr., "The Black Urban Regime: Structural Origins and Constraints," in Michael P. Smith (ed.), *Power, Community and the City: Comparative and Community Research* (New Brunswick, NJ: Transaction, 1988), vol. 1.
4. Jerome Himmelstein, *To the Right: The Transformation of American Conservativism* (Berkeley: University of California Press, 1990), 117.
5. *Muhammad Speaks*, December 4, 1964.
6. Ernest Allen, Jr., "Minister Louis Farrakhan and the Continuing Evolution of the Nation of Islam," in Amy Alexander (ed.), *The Farrakhan Factor: African-American Writers on Leadership, Nationhood, and Minister Louis Farrakhan* (New York: Grove Press, 1998), 74–75.
7. Ernest Allen, Jr., "Religious Heterodoxy and Nationalist Tradition: The Continuing Evolution of the Nation of Islam," *The Black Scholar* 26, no. 3–4 (Fall–Winter 1996): 18.
8. Allen, "Religious Heterodoxy," 3.
9. Mattias Gardell, *In the Name of Elijah Muhammad: Louis Farrakhan and the Nation of Islam* (Durham, NC: Duke University Press, 1996), 215–223.
10. Louis Farrakhan, "P.O.W.E.R at Last and Forever," in William Van Deburg (ed.), *Modern Black Nationalism: From Garvey to Louis Farrakhan* (New York: New York University Press, 1997), 323.
11. *Security Contracts between HUD or HUD Affiliated Entities and Companies Affiliated with the Nation of Islam* (Washington, DC: U.S. Government Printing Office, 1995).

12. Maize Woodford, "A Chronology: Farrakhan's 'World Friendship Tour' to Africa and the Middle East: January–February 1996," *The Black Scholar* 26, no. 3–4 (Fall–Winter 1996): 35–37.

13. Gardell, 190.

14. *New York Times*, February 20, 2000.

15. Robert Singh, *The Farrakhan Phenomenon: Race, Reaction, and the Paranoid Style in American Politics* (Washington, DC: Georgetown University Press), 43.

16. Quoted in Singh, 45–46.

17. Erna Smith, "Who's Afraid of Louis Farrakhan: The Media and Race Relations Coverage," in Amy Alexander (ed.), *The Farrakhan Factor: African American Writers on Leadership, Nationhood, and Minister Louis Farrakhan* (New York: Grove Press, 1997), 103.

18. Singh, 210–223.

19. Singh, 204–205. A more recent 1998 poll for *Time* found blacks almost equally divided over whether or not they had a generally favorable impression of Louis Farrakhan, 38 percent to 37 percent. The survey is available on the Roper Center's website.

20. Adolph Reed, Jr., "False Prophet–II," *The Nation*, January 28, 1991.

21. Reed, "False Prophet–II," 87.

22. Louis Farrakhan, "Day of Atonement," in Haki R. Madhubuti and Maulana Karenga (eds.), *Million Man March / Day of Absence: A Commemorative Anthology* (Chicago: Third World Press, 1996), 23–24.

23. On the Promise Keepers see William Martin's *With God on Our Side: The Rise of the Religious Right in America* (New York: Broadway Books, 1996), 350–353. See also Sara Diamond, *Not by Politics Alone* (New York: Guilford Press, 1998), 224–227.

24. *Washington Post*, October 17, 1995.

25. Madhubuti and Karenga (eds.), *Million Man March / Day of Absence*, 16.

26. Singh, 156–189.

27. Manning Marable, "Black Fundamentalism: Louis Farrakhan and the Politics of Conservative Black Nationalism," in *Black Leadership* (New York: Columbia, 1998), 171.

28. Reed, "False Prophet–II," 91.

29. Gardell, 275–276.

30. Raphael S. Ezekiel, *The Racist Mind* (New York: Viking, 1995), xix; Jesse Daniels, *White Lies: Race, Class, Gender, and Sexuality in White Supremacist Discourse* (New York: Routledge, 1997), 134–135; Leonard Zeskind, "White Nationalism in the U.S.," *Searchlight*, no. 287 (May 1999): 20–23.

31. See also Claude Andrew Clegg III, *An Original Man: The Life and Times of Elijah Muhammad* (New York: St. Martin's, 1997), 152–153.

32. Singh, 169.

33. *Spotlight*, July 23, 1990.

34. Marable, 177–182.

35. Gardell, 123.

36. Ibid., 48.

37. Ibid., 96.

38. Ibid., 32–33.
39. Ibid., 96. Robertson and Farrakhan also share a vision of a vast Jewish con-
    spiracy. Robertson's *The New World Order* (1993) regurgitates old con-
    spiracy theories about vast and secretive Jewish control through financial
    institutions. In a speech in February 1995, Farrakhan noted that "[f]our
    things were set up in the year 1913 . . . the Federal Reserve Bank, the IRS,
    the FBI and the Anti-Defamation League of B'nai B'rith." Quoted in Singh,
    111.
40. *The National Agenda: Public Policy Issues, Analyses, and Programmatic
    Plan of Action, 2000–2008* (Washington, DC: Million Family March, 2000),
    ix.
41. Ibid., xi.
42. Marimba Ani, *Yurugu: An African-centered Critique of European Cultural
    Thought and Behavior* (Trenton, NJ: Africa World Press, 1994).
43. Molefi Kete Asante, *Kemet, Afrocentricity and Knowledge* (Trenton, NJ:
    Africa World Press, 1990), 5.
44. Molefi Kete Asante, *Malcolm X as Cultural Hero and Other Afrocentric
    Essays* (Trenton, NJ: Africa World Press, 1993), 106.
45. See, for instance, Molefi Kete Asante and Abu S. Abarry (eds.), *African Intel-
    lectual Heritage: A Book of Sources* (Philadelphia: Temple University Press,
    1996), 4.
46. Asante, *Malcolm X*, 100.
47. Asante and Abarry (eds.), *African Intellectual Heritage*, 259.
48. Asante, *Kemet*, 112.
49. Ibid., 174–175.
50. Asante and Abarry (eds.), *African Intellectual Heritage*, 61.
51. Ibid., 111.
52. Ibid., 598.
53. Kwame Anthony Appiah, *In My Father's House: Africa in the Philosophy
    of Culture* (New York: Oxford University Press, 1992), 9.
54. See Stephen Howe, *Afrocentrism: Mythical Pasts and Imagined Homes*
    (New York: Verso, 1998), 233.
55. Molefi Kete Asante, *The Afrocentric Idea* (Philadelphia: Temple University
    Press, 1987), 10.
56. Asante and Abarry (eds.), *African Intellectual Heritage*, 260; emphasis
    supplied.
57. Moses identifies Asante's indebtedness to a number of influential theorists,
    including Michel Foucault, Claude Lévi-Strauss, Thomus Kuhn, and
    others. See Wilson Jeremiah Moses, *Afrotopia: The Roots of African Amer-
    ican Popular History* (New York: Cambridge University Press, 1998), 2.
58. Asante, "Afrocentricity, Race, and Reason," *Race and Reason* 1, no. 1
    (Autumn 1994): 21.
59. Asante, *Kemet*, 173.
60. Victor O. Okafor, "An Afrocentric Critique of Appiah's *In My Father's
    House*," *Journal of Black Studies* 24, no. 2 (December 1993): 201.
61. William Oliver, "Black Males and Social Problems," *Journal of Black
    Studies* 20, no. 1 (September 1989): 21.

62. Linus Hoskins, "Eurocentrism v. Afrocentrism," *Journal of Black Studies* 23, no. 2 (December 1992): 254.
63. Marian Ma' At-Ka Re Monges, "Reflections on the Role of Female Deities and Queens of Ancient Kemet," *Journal of Black Studies* 23, no. 4 (June 1993): 561–570.
64. Sidney J. Lemelle, "The Politics of Cultural Existence: Pan-Africanism, Historical Materialism and Afrocentricity," in Sidney J. Lemelle and Robin D. G. Kelley (eds.), *Imagining Home: Class, Culture and Nationalism in the African Diaspora* (New York: Verso, 1994), 334.

Selected Bibliography

Alexander, Amy (ed.). *The Farrakhan Factor: African American Writers on Leadership, Nationhood, and Minister Louis Farrakhan*. New York: Grove Press, 1997.

Allen, Earnest, Jr. "Religious Heterodoxy and Nationalist Tradition: The Continuing Evolution of the Nation of Islam." *The Black Scholar* 26, no. 3–4 (Fall–Winter 1996): 18.

Allen, Robert L. *Black Awakening in Capitalist America: An Analytic History*. Garden City, NY: Doubleday, 1969.

Anderson, Benedict R. O. G. *Imagined Communities: Reflections on the Origin and Spread of Nationalism*. London: Verso, 1983.

Asante, Molefi K. *The Afrocentric Idea*. Philadelphia: Temple University Press, 1987.

Asante, Molefi K. "Afrocentricity, Race, and Reason." *Race and Reason* 1, no. 1 (1994): 21.

Asante, Molefi K. *Malcolm X as Cultural Hero and Other Afrocentric Essays*. Trenton, NJ: Africa World Press, 1993.

Asante, Molefi K. *Rhetoric of Black Revolution*. Boston: Allyn and Bacon, 1969.

Asante, Molefi K., and Abu Shardow Abarry (eds.). *African Intellectual Heritage: A Book of Sources*. Philadelphia: Temple University Press, 1996.

Baraka, Imamu Amiri. *African Congress: A Documentary of the First Modern Pan-African Congress*. New York: Morrow, 1972.

Baraka, Imamu Amiri. *The Autobiography of LeRoi Jones/Amiri Baraka*. New York: Freundlich Books, 1984.

Baraka, Imamu Amiri. *Raise, Race, Rays, Raze: Essays since 1965*. New York: Random House, 1971.

Baraka, Imamu Amiri, and Larry Neal (eds.). *Black Fire: An Anthology of Afro-American Writing*. New York: Morrow, 1968.

Barbour, Floyd B. *The Black Power Revolt: A Collection of Essays*. Boston: P. Sargent, 1968.

Bederman, Gail. *Manliness and Civilization: A Cultural History of Gender and Race in the United States, 1880–1917*. Chicago: University of Chicago Press, 1995.

Berry, Brewton. *Race and Ethnic Relations*, 2nd ed. Boston: Houghton Mifflin, 1958.

Blaustein, Arthur I., and Geoffrey P. Faux. *The Star-Spangled Hustle*. Garden City, NY: Doubleday, 1972.

Bracey, John H., August Meier, and Elliott M. Rudwick (eds.). *Black Nationalism in America*. Indianapolis: Bobbs-Merrill, 1970.

Breitman, George (ed.). *By Any Means Necessary*. New York: Pathfinder Press, 1970.

Breitman, George (ed.). *Malcolm X Speaks*. New York: Merit Publishers, 1965.

Brotz, Howard (ed.). *Negro Social and Political Thought, 1850–1920: Representative Texts*. New York: Basic Books, 1966.

Brown, Elaine. *A Taste of Power: A Black Woman's Story*. New York: Pantheon Books, 1992.

Carmichael, Stokely, and Charles V. Hamilton. *Black Power: The Politics of Liberation in America*. New York: Random House, 1967.

Chatterjee, Pranab, and Louise Wolford. *Local Leadership in Black Communities: Organizational and Electoral Developments in Cleveland in the Nineteen Sixties*. Cleveland: School of Applied Social Sciences, Case Western Reserve University, 1975.

Chrisman, Robert, and Nathan Hare (eds.). *Contemporary Black Thought: The Best from the Black Scholar*. Indianapolis: Bobbs-Merrill, 1973.

Cleage, Albert B. *Black Christian Nationalism: New Directions for the Black Church*. New York: Morrow, 1972.

Clegg, Claude Andrew. *An Original Man: The Life and Times of Elijah Muhammad*. New York: St. Martin's Press, 1997.

Coleman, Trevor M. "A Million Marches." *Emerge*, February 1999.

Cruikshank, Barbara. "The Will to Empower: Technologies of Citizenship and the War on Poverty." *Socialist Review* 23, no. 4.

Crummell, Alexander. *The Future of Africa*. New York: Negro Universities Press, 1969.

Cruse, Harold. *The Crisis of the Negro Intellectual*. New York: Quill, 1984.

Dahl, Robert Alan. *Who Governs? Democracy and Power in an American City*. New Haven, CT: Yale University Press, 1961.

Dawson, Michael C. *Behind the Mule: Race and Class in African-American Politics*. Princeton, NJ: Princeton University Press, 1994.

DeCaro, Louis A. *On the Side of My People: A Religious Life of Malcolm X*. New York: New York University Press, 1996.

Delbanco, Andrew. *The Portable Abraham Lincoln*. New York: Viking, 1992.

Elijah Muhammad. *Message to the Blackman in America*. Chicago: Muhammad Mosque of Islam No. 2, 1965.

Ellison, Ralph. *Going to the Territory*. New York: Random House, 1986.

Fainstein, Susan S. *Restructuring the City: The Political Economy of Urban Redevelopment*. New York: Longman, 1983.

Fanon, Frantz. *The Wretched of the Earth*. New York: Grove Press, 1963.

Farrakhan, Louis. *A Torchlight for America*. Chicago: FCN Publishing, 1993.

Ferris, William Henry. *The African Abroad, or, His Evolution in Western Civilization Tracing His Development under Caucasian Milieu.* New Haven, CT: Tuttle Morehouse and Taylor Press, 1913.

Foner, Eric. *A Short History of Reconstruction, 1863–1877.* New York: Harper and Row, 1990.

Frazier, E. Franklin. "The Changing Status of the Negro Family." *Social Forces* 9 (March 1931): 386–393.

Fredrickson, George M. *The Black Image in the White Mind: The Debate on Afro-American Character and Destiny, 1817–1914.* New York: Harper and Row, 1971.

Gayle, Addison. *The Black Aesthetic.* Garden City, NY: Doubleday, 1971.

Glazer, Nathan, and Daniel P. Moynihan. *Beyond the Melting Pot: The Negroes, Puerto Ricans, Jews, Italians, and Irish of New York City.* Cambridge, MA: MIT Press, 1963.

Goldman, Peter Louis. *The Death and Life of Malcolm X.* Urbana: University of Illinois Press, 1979.

Goldman, Sheldon. *Constitutional Law: Cases and Essays.* New York: HarperCollins, 1991.

Gordon, Milton Myron. *Assimilation in American Life: The Role of Race, Religion, and National Origins.* New York: Oxford University Press, 1964.

Gossett, Thomas F. *Race: The History of an Idea in America.* Dallas: Southern Methodist University Press, 1963.

Graham, Hugh Davis. *Civil Rights and the Presidency: Race and Gender in American Politics, 1960–1972.* New York: Oxford University Press, 1992.

Grant, Joanne. *Black Protest: History, Documents, and Analyses, 1619 to the Present.* New York: Fawcett World Library, 1968.

Hall, Raymond L. *Black Separatism and Social Reality: Rhetoric and Reason.* New York: Pergamon, 1977.

Harris, Robert, Nyota Harris, and Grandassa Harris. *Carlos Cooks and Black Nationalism from Garvey to Malcolm.* Dover, MA: Majority Press, 1992.

Heath, G. Louis (ed.). *The Black Panther Leaders Speak: Huey P. Newton, Bobby Seale, Eldridge Cleaver and Company Speak Out through the Black Panther Party's Official Newspaper.* Metuchen, NJ: Scarecrow Press, 1976.

Himmelstein, Jerome L. *To the Right: The Transformation of American Conservatism.* Berkeley: University of California Press, 1990.

Hobsbawm, E. J. *Nations and Nationalism since 1780: Programme, Myth, Reality.* Cambridge: Cambridge University Press, 1990.

Horsman, Reginald. *Race and Manifest Destiny: The Origins of American Racial Anglo-Saxonism.* Cambridge, MA: Harvard University Press, 1981.

Hoskins, Linus. "Eurocentrism v. Afrocentrism." *Journal of Black Studies* 23, no. 2 (December 1992): 254.

Howard, Joseph Hannibal III. "How to End Colonial Domination of Black America." *Black World*, January 1970.

Howe, Stephen. *Afrocentrism: Mythical Pasts and Imagined Homes.* London: Verso, 1998.

Huggins, Nathan Irvin, Martin Kilson, and Daniel M. Fox. *Key Issues in the Afro-American Experience*. New York: Harcourt Brace Jovanovich, 1971.

Ignatiev, Noel. *How the Irish Became White*. New York: Routledge, 1995.

Jefferson, Thomas. *Notes on the State of Virginia*. Chapel Hill: University of North Carolina Press, 1955.

Kammen, Michael G. *Mystic Chords of Memory: The Transformation of Tradition in American Culture*. New York: Knopf, 1991.

Karenga, Manlana. *Introduction to Black Studies*, 2nd ed. Los Angeles: University of Sankore Press, 1993.

Kelley, Robin D. G. *Race Rebels: Culture, Politics, and the Black Working Class*. New York: The Free Press, 1994.

King, Woodie, and Earl Anthony (eds.). *Black Poets and Prophets: The Theory, Practice, and Esthetics of the Pan-Africanist Revolution*. New York: New American Library, 1972.

Kornweibel, Theodore. *Seeing Red: Federal Campaigns against Black Militancy, 1919–1925*. Bloomington: Indiana University Press, 1998.

Kramer, Ralph M. *Participation of the Poor: Comparative Community Case Studies in the War on Poverty*. Englewood Cliffs, NJ: Prentice-Hall, 1969.

Lee, Martha F. *The Nation of Islam: An American Millenarian Movement*. Syracuse, NY: Syracuse University Press, 1996.

Lemelle, Sidney J., and Robin D. G. Kelley. *Imagining Home: Class, Culture, and Nationalism in the African Diaspora*. New York: Verso, 1994.

Lester, Julius. *Look Out, Whitey! Black Power's Gon' Get Your Mama!* New York: Grove Press, 1969.

Lincoln, C. Eric. *The Black Muslims in America*. Trenton, NJ: Africa World Press, 1994.

Lincoln, C. Eric. *Sounds of the Struggle: Persons and Perspectives in Civil Rights*. New York: Morrow, 1967.

Madhubuti, Haki R., and Maulana Karenga (eds.). *Million Man March / Day of Absence: A Commemorative Anthology: Speeches, Commentary, Photography, Poetry, Illustrations, Documents*. Los Angeles: University of Sankore Press, 1996.

Meier, August, John H. Bracey, and Elliott M. Rudwick (eds.). *Black Protest in the Sixties*. New York: M. Wiener, 1991.

Miller, Floyd John. *The Search for a Black Nationality: Black Emigration and Colonization, 1787–1863*. Urbana: University of Illinois Press, 1975.

Monges, Marian Ma'At-Ka-Re. "Reflections on the Role of Female Deities and Queens of Ancient Kemet." *Journal of Black Studies* 23, no. 4 (June 1993): 561–570.

Moses, Wilson Jeremiah. *Black Messiahs and Uncle Toms: Social and Literary Manipulations of a Religious Myth*, rev. ed. University Park: Pennsylvania State University Press, 1993.

Moses, Wilson Jeremiah (ed.). *Classical Black Nationalism: From the American Revolution to Marcus Garvey*. New York: New York University Press, 1996.

Moses, Wilson Jeremiah. *The Golden Age of Black Nationalism, 1850–1925*. Hamden, CT: Archon Books, 1978.

Neal, Larry, and Imamu Amiri Baraka (eds.). *Visions of a Liberated Future: Black Arts Movement Writings*. New York: Thunder's Mouth Press, 1989.

Newton, Huey P. *To Die for the People: The Writings of Huey P. Newton*. New York: Random House, 1972.

Nott, Josiah Clark, and George R. Gliddon. *Types of Mankind*, 6th ed. Philadelphia: Lippincott Grambo, 1854.

Okafor, Victor O. "An Afrocentric Critique of Appiah's *In My Father's House*." *Journal of Black Studies* 24, no. 2 (December 1993): 201.

Oliver, Melvin L., and Thomas M. Shapiro. *Black Wealth White Wealth: A New Perspective on Racial Inequality*. New York: Routledge, 1995.

Oliver, William. "Black Males and Social Problems." *Journal of Black Studies* 20, no. 1 (September 1989): 21.

Omi, Michael, and Howard Winant. *Racial Formation in the United States: From the 1960s to the 1990s*, 2nd ed. New York: Routledge, 1994.

Park, Robert Ezra. *Race and Culture*. Glencoe, IL: The Free Press, 1950.

Park, Robert Ezra, and Ernest Watson Burgess. *Introduction to the Science of Sociology*. Chicago: University of Chicago Press, 1921.

Parker, Andrew. *Nationalisms and Sexualities*. New York: Routledge, 1992.

Perry, Bruce. *Malcolm: The Life of a Man who Changed Black America*. Barrytown, NY: Station Hill, 1992.

Persons, Stow. *Ethnic Studies at Chicago, 1905–45*. Urbana: University of Illinois Press, 1987.

Polland, Sam, Sheila C. Bernard, Julian Bond, Henry Hampton, Blackside, Inc., and PBS Video. *Eyes on the Prize II: Ain't Gonna Shuffle No More*. Alexandria, VA: PBS Video, 1989. 1 videocassette (60 min.).

Reed, Aldolph, Jr. "False Prophet – I: The Rise of Louis Farrakhan." *The Nation*, January 21, 1991, p. 57.

Reed, Adolph L. *Race, Politics, and Culture: Critical Essays on the Radicalism of the 1960's*. Westport, CT: Greenwood Press, 1986.

Reuter, Edward Byron, and Clyde William Hart. *Introduction to Sociology*. New York: McGraw-Hill, 1933.

Reuter, Edward Byron, and Jitsuichi Masuoka. *The American Race Problem*, 3rd rev. ed. New York: Crowell, 1966.

Robertson, Pat. *The New World Order*. Dallas: Word, 1991.

Roediger, David R. *The Wages of Whiteness: Race and the Making of the American Working Class*. New York: Verso, 1991.

Rose, Arnold Marshall. *Sociology: The Study of Human Relations*. New York: Knopf, 1956.

Saxton, Alexander. *The Rise and Fall of the White Republic: Class Politics and Mass Culture in Nineteenth-Century America*. New York: Verso, 1990.

Seale, Bobby. *Seize the Time: The Story of the Black Panther Party and Huey P. Newton*. New York: Random House, 1968.

Singh, Robert. *The Farrakhan Phenomenon: Race, Reaction, and the Paranoid Style in American Politics*. Washington, DC: Georgetown University Press, 1997.

Smith, John David (ed.). *The American Colonization Society and Emigration*. New York: Garland, 1993.

Smith, Michael P. *Power, Community and the City*. New Brunswick, NJ: Transaction Books, 1988.

Smith, Michael P., and Joe R. Feagin. *The Bubbling Cauldron: Race, Ethnicity, and the Urban Crisis*. Minneapolis: University of Minnesota Press, 1995.

Smith, Rogers M. *Civic Ideals: Conflicting Visions of Citizenship in U.S. History*. New Haven, CT: Yale University Press, 1997.

Steinberg, Stephen. *The Ethnic Myth: Race, Ethnicity, and Class in America*. New York: Atheneum, 1981.

Stoddard, Lothrop. *The Rising Tide of Color against White World-Supremacy*. New York: Scribner, 1929.

Stowe, Harriet Beecher. *Uncle Tom's Cabin*. London: J. Cassell, 1852.

Stuckey, Sterling. *Slave Culture: Nationalist Theory and the Foundations of Black America*. New York: Oxford University Press, 1987.

Tate, Sonsyrea. *Little X: Growing Up in the Nation of Islam*. San Francisco: HarperSanFrancisco, 1997.

Thomas, William Isaac, and Florian Znaniecki. *The Polish Peasant in Europe and America: Monograph of an Immigrant Group*. Boston: R. G. Badger, 1918.

Ullman, Victor. *Martin R. Delany: The Beginnings of Black Nationalism*. Boston: Beacon Press, 1971.

United States. Kerner Commission. *The Kerner Report: The 1968 Report of the National Advisory Commission on Civil Disorders*. New York: Pantheon, 1988.

Valentine, Charles A. *Culture and Poverty: Critique and Counter-Proposals*. Chicago: University of Chicago Press, 1968.

Van Deburg, William L (ed.). *Modern Black Nationalism: From Marcus Garvey to Louis Farrakhan*. New York: New York University Press, 1997.

Van Deburg, William L. *New Day in Babylon: The Black Power Movement and American Culture, 1965–1975*. Chicago: University of Chicago Press, 1992.

Walker, David, and Henry Highland Garnet. *Walker's Appeal in Four Articles*. New York: Arno Press, 1969.

Williams, Robert Franklin. *Negroes with Guns*. New York: Marzani and Munsell, 1962.

Wolfe, Alan. *America's Impasse: The Rise and Fall of the Politics of Growth*. New York: Pantheon Books, 1981.

X, Malcolm, and Alex Haley. *The Autobiography of Malcolm X*. New York: Grove Press, 1965.

X, Malcolm, and Bruce Perry. *Malcolm X: The Last Speeches*. New York: Pathfinder, 1989.

Index

DATE DUE

NOV 3 0 2002			
NOV 1 9 2003			
MAY 2 5 2004			
GAYLORD			PRINTED IN U.S.A.